'Women's reproductive health is one of the most important factors in determining their quality of life and that of their children. Aminata's extraordinary efforts in her country of origin will make a life-changing difference to the mothers and children of Sierra Leone.'
PROFESSOR KERRYN PHELPS AM

'An incredible story of hope and transformation, one that we can all learn from.'
EMMA ISAACS, FOUNDER AND GLOBAL CEO, BUSINESS CHICKS

'Aminata not only gives an important voice to her own intensely personal story but also to the many forgotten women and girls caught up in war and conflict today. She is a compelling advocate for the rights of these women and also for the work of the UN Refugee Agency who supports them.'
NAOMI STEER, NATIONAL DIRECTOR, AUSTRALIA FOR UNHCR

'A powerful read that will make you cry at the injustice and brutality of our world — but then shed tears of admiration and hope. Aminata reminds us of the power of an individual to make a difference. She is an inspirational woman who has brought about extraordinary change. What a beautiful Australian story.'
NATASHA STOTT DESPOJA AO

'Aminata's courage is breathtaking and demonstrates the resilience and power of the human spirit. Simply an extraordinary woman.'
PROFESSOR FIONA WOOD FRACS AM

Aminata Conteh-Biger is an author, inspirational speaker, performer, mother and wife, and former refugee turned Founder and CEO of the Aminata Maternal Foundation. Born in Sierra Leone, she now lives in Sydney with her husband and two children.

Juliet Rieden has been a journalist for more than 30 years, working between the UK and Australia for a variety of magazines and newspapers as a writer and editor. She is currently Editor-at-Large at *The Australian Women's Weekly* where she also works as the Royal Correspondent and the Books Editor.

Juliet is also a non-fiction author with Pan Macmillan Australia. Her previous books are *The Writing on the Wall*, a personal memoir and investigation into what happened to her father and his family during the Holocaust, and *The Royals in Australia*, an illustrated investigation behind the scenes of almost 150 years of royal visits.

Rising Heart

Aminata Conteh-Biger

with Juliet Rieden

MACMILLAN
Pan Macmillan Australia

First published 2020 in Macmillan by Pan Macmillan Australia Pty Ltd
1 Market Street, Sydney, New South Wales, Australia, 2000

A catalogue record for this
book is available from the
National Library of Australia

Typeset in 12.5/17 pt Bembo by Post Pre-press Group, Brisbane
Printed by IVE

MIX
Paper from
responsible sources
FSC® C018183

To Papa Yayah Kelfala Conteh and Mama Eleas Diané

To my precious family: Antoine, Sarafina and Matisse

*And to those affected by the civil war in Sierra Leone,
especially the young girls and women*

Contents

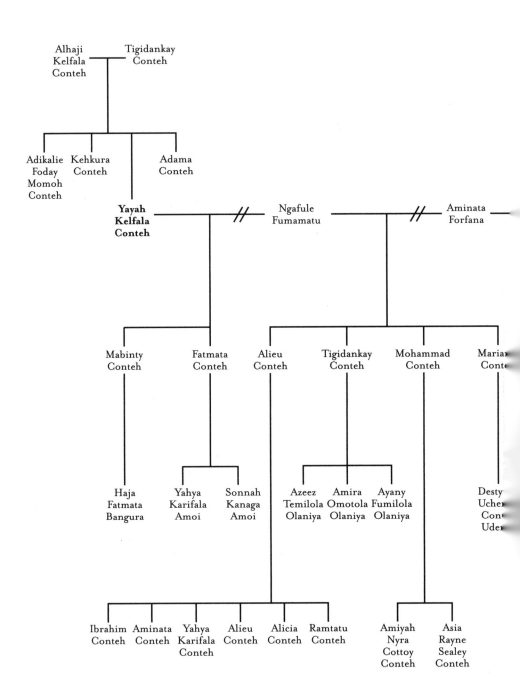

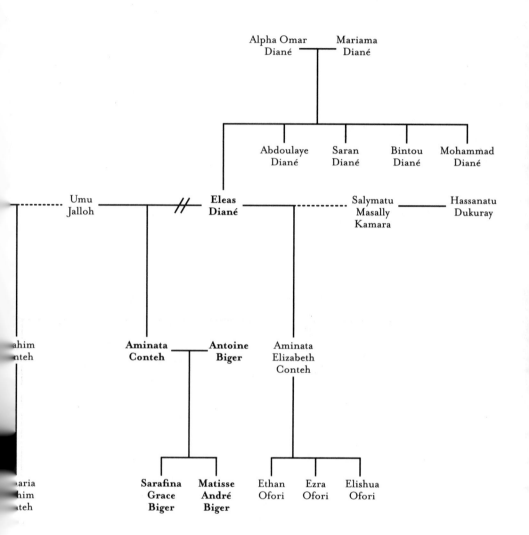

Prologue

My name is Aminata Conteh-Biger and I was born in Freetown, Sierra Leone, on the coast of West Africa. From 1991 until 2002 my country endured a vicious civil war that claimed more than 50,000 lives. The Revolutionary United Front, supported by rebels from neighbouring Liberia, launched a campaign to oust the president and seize control of the country. In the ensuing conflict thousands of civilians had their limbs hacked off by the rebels in what became their signature act of brutality and thousands of girls and women were raped. Virgins were specifically targeted, and many were abducted by the rebels and used as human shields. I was eighteen years old when the rebels kidnapped me.

★

I want to tell my story, the whole story, to help other women who are going through what I went through, to help those who committed these atrocities understand what they did to us. The shame is what isolates; the fear that people will think less of you because somebody has done that to you. You think your worth is gone.

Sometimes I think people are shocked that I am speaking about what I went through, breaking taboos – it is not something Sierra Leoneans do. It's not part of our culture to talk openly about such things. I think people from my country feel that I have lived outside my community for so long that I have become somehow different from them. In the West, people share their anguish, but it's not the African way. We keep things to ourselves. Personal burdens shouldn't be heaped on others, especially family. Most members of my own family still don't know what happened to me in any detail. We have never discussed it and I don't think we ever will.

It took me a long time even to consider talking about my experience. Above all, I didn't want anyone to think I was saying that my pain was worse than theirs. My story is in no way unique: there are so many girls who suffered as I did, and everyone is trying to deal with the trauma in their own way. I never expected this would be my way, but I'm pleased it is because I have seen how it helps others come to terms with what happened to them. Helping them gives me strength. My father, Pa Conteh, who raised me, taught me the value of helping others. It was the core of who he was. My sisters say, 'Pa Conteh is watching over you – he would be so proud of what you're doing in your life,' and I love that.

When I first came to Australia as a refugee in 2000, as one of two million Sierra Leoneans who were displaced by the war, I just dived into establishing a new life. I wanted to make a fresh start in a country that didn't know my story. I didn't want to be thought of as a victim. What I hadn't anticipated was how hard it would be to settle in a place with a culture very different from my own, nor how hard it would be for my new country to accept me. For many years it was tough and I felt very alone. Eventually, though, I started to build a life here, making good friends, doing work that I enjoyed, and meeting and marrying a wonderful man and starting a family.

But I wanted to find a meaning to my life – my calling, if you will. I know there's a meaning there and, although I am still finding my way, I felt a sense of that calling in 2012, when I nearly died while giving birth to my daughter Sarafina. Here in Australia, I was fortunate to be surrounded by seven highly trained doctors, all dedicated to saving the lives of me and my child – but if I had found myself in a similar situation in Sierra Leone, my daughter and I would have died. That realisation was an epiphany for me. It made me wonder how it is that we have such easy access to medical care, while in places like Africa women and children are dying. In Sierra Leone, as many as one in eight mothers dies during pregnancy or in childbirth, and 11,000 newborns die each year. So many of these deaths are preventable. So why are we not doing something about it?

I'm grateful for the blessed life that I have here. But why should Sarafina – and my son Matisse, who came afterwards – be more important than somebody else's child? We all feel the same love for our children.

As I considered this, something clicked for me, a switch in my head. I felt a great sense of responsibility, and I knew what I had to do: I had to help women in my country.

So, after many consultations and lots of research, and with the help of some wonderful people I had been working with when I was volunteering at the office of Australia for the United Nations High Commissioner for Refugees (UNHCR), in 2014 I founded the Aminata Maternal Foundation in Australia, to support and provide medical care to pregnant women in Sierra Leone.

I have big dreams and my heart is bursting with joy for the future. I can see it, feel it and touch it. The word 'impossible' doesn't exist for me. Life is always full of possibility and this is what I was meant to do. I hope that my story will help Sierra Leone to heal and that my work will lift up the girls of tomorrow.

And for my own children, Sarafina and Matisse, I want you to know what happened. The time for secrets is over.

CHAPTER ONE

Pa Conteh, father to all

My father's full name was Yayah Kelfala Conteh, but he was known to everyone as Pa Conteh. He didn't talk much about his childhood in Freetown, which I think is often the way with proud fathers. He wasn't interested in the past; he was focused on today and tomorrow, providing for his family and looking to the future. I do know that his parents separated early on and he grew up with his mother and her sister. His father, my grandfather (in Susu – my father's tribal language – we say Baimba), went to live in Liberia, which borders Sierra Leone to the south.

When Papa was growing up Sierra Leone was still a British colony, and while it was incredibly rich in natural resources – particularly diamonds – the wealth did not filter down through society nor did it significantly contribute to building my country's infrastructure. Poverty levels weren't addressed in any meaningful way; the elite simply got richer.

Nevertheless, smart entrepreneurs did find a way to thrive and this was the case with my father, Pa Conteh.

As a child Papa lived in a village in Kambia, a poor district in the north of the country, in a very small basic home made from cement, with a roof of corrugated iron. He was educated to secondary school level and apparently his entrepreneurial nous was evident early on. He told my sister Fatmata that he used to sell sweets to the other kids in school and also set up as a barber, cutting his friends' hair for money. So it's not surprising that when he left school Papa went straight out to work. Like many boys in his situation, Papa started by selling things. He would have sold fruit, like mangoes, before progressing to larger items, like bolts of cotton. According to my sister Mabinty, Papa developed a good line in selling pharmaceutical products including tablets and medicine. He would buy them in bulk and then sell the individual pills at a profit. He joked that people used to think he was a doctor. He began travelling between villages, but very soon he was venturing further afield – to Guinea-Conakry, which borders Sierra Leone to the north, and Liberia, where he would buy umbrellas to sell back in Sierra Leone. Eventually he wound up in Senegal. There he worked for a businessman who really liked and trusted him, and it was this man who gave Papa the money to do something for himself.

He started doing much bigger things – construction, import and export . . . I only have a vague idea of my dad's business. Traditional fathers like Pa Conteh just didn't discuss their work outside the home with their kids, so for me it remains shrouded in mystery. What I do know is that he would export goods like palm oil or peanut butter from

Sierra Leone to London. With the proceeds, he would buy stationery and bring it back to Sierra Leone. He imported huge container loads of stationery, mainly paper, and sometimes I would go with him when customers came to pick up their orders from Papa's storage sites.

When I look back on it today with adult eyes, I realise my dad must have been selling more than paper and peanut butter in order to finance his building projects and our comfortable lifestyle. I suspect he was also selling diamonds – perhaps hidden in the jars of peanut butter. This was before the war of course and they weren't blood diamonds, sold to fund the rebel army; I know for a fact my dad didn't buy guns or support the rebels in any way. But at that time many Sierra Leonean businessmen were buying diamonds from dealers and selling them at a profit in Europe, and it seems likely that Papa was doing the same. By the time I came along, he was reasonably well off and my family never wanted for anything.

★

I was born on 8 October 1980 in hospital. My father already had five children, and he would go on to have another three. As a Muslim, he was allowed to have more than one wife, and for ambitious African men like my dad, polygamy was a beautiful thing. You have to be relatively affluent to have multiple wives, as you need to be able to support a large family, so polygamy is an outward sign that you are prosperous and doing well. My father had four wives, and he also had children by two other women out of wedlock. While he was divorced from three of his wives, including my mother, he did keep the children to raise himself. This was really important to him and unusual for an African man.

My dad's first wife was Ngafule Fumamatu and my eldest half-sisters, Mabinty and Fatmata, who now live in London, are Ngafule's twin daughters. They were born on 2 May 1965, so are fifteen years older than me, and they left Sierra Leone to be educated in Britain a few months before I was born. Even though I wasn't brought up with them, I am now really close to the twins.

Ngafule separated from our dad when the twins were about five years old. Fatmata reckons their mum's divorce was inevitable because she was a very stubborn and independent woman. Such break-ups weren't unusual in our community and Mabinty says their mum and our dad were never actually in love. The families enforced the marriage. I can't and won't judge my dad – of course he wasn't perfect, but this was the culture he was living in. That said, there's no question that Papa's broken relationships with the mothers of his children hurt everyone. The twins didn't really know their mother until they were adults and were reunited in London for the last ten years of Ngafule's life. My own relationship with my mother Eleas was shattered by my parents' divorce when I was very young. I barely knew my mum growing up and that has created a chasm in our adult relationship. I am her only child, and whenever I see her I can sense the deep sadness in Eleas's heart as I struggle to connect with her. While I love my mother dearly, having been raised by my father meant the bond I had with him was much stronger. However, the more I talk to my family, the more I understand how hard it must have been for her to lose her daughter. It wasn't her fault – something she tells me all the time – and she could do nothing about it. But we just don't connect as a mother and daughter, and now I have my own children I realise how painful that must be.

My mum, Eleas Diané, was my father's third wife. When they married, and she came to live in my dad's house, his second wife Aminata was also living there with her five-year-old son (my half-brother Alieu) and her baby daughter (my half-sister Tigidankay, who we called Tkay) as well as Mabinty and Fatmata (my half-sisters) from Papa's first marriage. (Two years after I was born, Aminata had her third child, Mohammad, and she took him to London with her to live in a house Papa owned there. The twins lived here, too, when they weren't at boarding school in Scotland. Shortly after she arrived in London, Aminata's fourth child, Mariama, was born.) For Mum this was totally normal; her own father had three wives, so it didn't bother her at all to have to share her husband and home with another wife. As part of the Muslim ceremony, before a man marries another woman he must seek permission from his existing wife. When I was born, my parents even named me Aminata to show their respect for Papa's second wife, though my mum would have liked to name me Mariama, after her own mother.

As babies, Mabinty and Fatmata lived in a house my father owned in Freetown city, before moving with Papa to Monrovia, the capital of neighbouring Liberia, where he was doing business, and where his father – Alhaji Kelfala Conteh (Baimba to us) – was living at the time. When the whole family returned home to Sierra Leone, bringing Baimba with them, they lived in a house in Wellington, a suburb of Freetown, while Papa built a new house on Macauley Street in Kissy painted mustard yellow. This would be the house where I was raised.

The Kissy house was a huge project for my dad; he shipped in all the building materials from Europe. When the house was finished it was easily the biggest in the neighbourhood and was admired by all. Baimba had his own apartment in a second building in the complex behind our house, while Papa's wives and their children each had their own floors, which were self-contained units. Each unit had a kitchen, two bathrooms, three bedrooms, a living room and a verandah. My father lived on the ground floor, my mum's floor was above, Aminata's floor was above that, and on top was the partially covered roof terrace we all used and where Pa Conteh held his business meetings. When the wives left, the upper floors were divided between us children, with the girls on the first floor and the boys on the second floor.

On his ground-floor verandah, Pa Conteh had a big brown leather chair. This was his place to relax and he would sit there quietly, thinking, even sleeping occasionally. Sometimes I would sit at his feet. It was comforting to know that he was there, watching out for us.

I was raised in the yellow house in Kissy with my half-brother Alieu and my half-sister Tigidankay. Later, another half-brother – Ibrahim – joined us. His mother Umu, like my mum, was from Guinea-Conakry, where Papa used to do a lot of business, and Papa was in a relationship with her before he met Eleas. When Umu fell pregnant, my dad wanted to marry her, but Umu's father was adamant that she should finish her education and go to university. She ended up being sent to France to give birth because her father wanted the baby to have French nationality. As the story goes, Ibrahim was born on a plane, but since the plane was in French airspace his grandfather's wish came true, and he is a French citizen.

I always thought that it was Umu's father who insisted that her baby be sent to Sierra Leone to be raised by Papa, so that his daughter's education wasn't interrupted, but Mabinty thinks it is more likely that our dad wanted his son with him, and that does seem probable, given that Papa managed to bring up all his children by himself with only minimal involvement from their mothers.

My dad was unusual in Muslim African society, not just because he was essentially a single parent, but because of the way he raised us. To begin with, he didn't hand us over to a nanny; he was very hands-on and overly protective. But what was most unusual was that he wanted his daughters to feel equal to his sons. In a lot of cultures, the boys are brought up from a young age to know they are leaders. It wasn't like that in our house, though. If anything, Papa paid us girls more attention so as to break that barrier. He believed that education was crucial, so that we could choose what we did with our lives and wouldn't have to rely on a husband or anyone else.

★

At home, Pa Conteh was very particular. Even though he employed people to help us in the house, they weren't treated like servants. They each had an important job to do and we were taught to respect that. We had cooks, and a housekeeper, and a chauffeur to drive us to school, but Papa didn't think that other people should have to clean up after you, so he would always make his own bed and keep his own room neat and tidy, with everything just so. He would often cook his own food and wash his own clothes, too.

Papa washing his clothes is a lovely memory for me, because it used to be our time together, when I would sit with him on my own and we would talk. Papa would be dressed in shorts, and we'd sit on a wooden bench or on chairs near his kitchen. He would put some soap and water in a bucket and then put his clothes in to soak. Then he would wash them, but he didn't scrub the clothes hard. He was very gentle with everything. He said unless the clothes were really dirty you simply needed to soak out the sweat. He would then rinse the clothes in fresh water. And finally, he squeezed the water out in such a wonderful way. He would say that you were spoiling the material when you wring the clothes, so he would press each item softly between his two palms, pushing the water out of every fibre. When he hung the clothes out to dry, he would never hang them in direct sunlight, because that would fade the colour. All you needed was a breeze, and since we were high up, we always had the breeze from the sea. It would take longer this way, but his clothes always looked immaculate and lasted for years. When I came to Australia, I didn't have a washing machine until after my daughter Sarafina was born. I would wash all my clothes by hand, just like Papa, including my bedsheets and towels.

★

12

From the outside, our house on Macauley Street looked pretty fearsome, because the verandahs on every floor were enclosed by iron bars. Our windows were fitted with one-way bulletproof glass, so that we could see out but those on the outside couldn't see in. Papa had the glass shipped from Europe and we were the only house in Kissy with windows like these.

We also had a guard dog called Jeff, who would growl if anyone walked too close and bark if they approached. Because Papa was away travelling a great deal for his business, the security was necessary so he could be sure that his children and his possessions were safe. Theft was common in Freetown, as it is in many cities around the world.

I have no memory of visiting anyone else's house when I was growing up. Not ever. Papa said if people wanted to see us, they should come and visit us in our house. He wanted to teach us to choose our friends wisely. He always said, 'Your children can have boyfriends and they will break up with their boyfriends, but if your children have bad friends it will influence them for the rest of their lives.' So he was very strict about the kind of friends we could have. He had to know their parents, and they weren't allowed to just drop by; any visit would have to be arranged between the parents in advance. As a result, I hardly ever had friends around to my home. Those friends who did come were the children of the teachers.

We weren't allowed to walk anywhere, either; the chauffeur would always drive us, even to school. Looking back, I can see it was quite extreme, but at the time I didn't know any different. I appreciate now that my father had seen a lot in the streets of Sierra Leone that he didn't want his children, and especially his daughters, to be exposed to. He was simply looking after us in the best way he knew.

He was also keen to teach us discipline. He didn't ever raise his voice and he taught us to do the same. We weren't to speak rudely to any single person. We were to study constantly. (He was especially strict about that: study was our future, he insisted.) And there was a certain way we had to carry ourselves, standing straight and dignified. If we had visitors, we'd dress to welcome them. His lessons were all about old-fashioned manners, and they have definitely stayed with me.

★

It was not only in our household that my father was revered. Yayah Kelfala Conteh, or Pa Conteh, was much loved in our local community. He was a leading figure in Kissy, like a mini president. There was a good deal of poverty in Kissy at the time, and Papa was always helping others. He would pay the school fees for the children of other families, be they relatives or just the children of people he knew. 'He would even pay to educate them abroad – in Italy or England,' Fatmata recalls. 'He always used to say: "What's the point of having money if you cannot share it? For people in need, the best thing you can give them is education, so they can then help their own families."'

He would also distribute food to the poor. During Eid, to celebrate the end of Ramadan, for example, Papa would kill a lot of cows and goats and organise for a truckload of rice and palm oil to be divided into plastic bags to give away. People would line up outside our house and he would give them food. They knew they could count on him to make this generous gesture every year.

People from the neighbourhood would come to Pa Conteh with their problems. He would sit down with them and see how he could help. It might be paying for a funeral or a month's rent, sharing our food with the neighbours or finding their children a place in a good school. Nothing was too much trouble and everyone knew my father could be relied on in times of need.

When I was young, I thought my dad's job was to make money so he could help other people, and I thought that when I grew up that would be my job too, that this was what I was meant to do. I always liked doing things for others. When my dad was away travelling, I would bring home the poor kids from the street, bathe them and give them clean clothes – my own clothes, that Papa had bought for me in Europe. I think it concerned my dad a bit; he thought I put everyone else before myself and he worried I might be taken advantage of, but that is happiness to me and it is what gives my life meaning. From a young age I really believed that my destiny was to be of service to others. I don't know if it was because my dad protected me in our big yellow house on the hill and provided everything we needed, but money never came into my dreams, nor did status or power or any of those things that some people seek.

Although Pa Conteh was clearly a man of conse-quence – he was always very well dressed with beautifully crisp ironed shirts and trousers; to look at him you would think he had all the degrees in the world, which he didn't – he was exceptionally well-mannered and respected every single person, from the people he did business with to the people who worked for him, the people who cooked for us, and the poor people in the streets. He taught us all the importance of respect for others, and I still live by that credo.

My father had a mantra: The world is a circle. He said, 'You have to be careful how you treat people. When you treat people unkindly, you have to remember that you're going to come back and bump into them. So are you going to look them in the eyes or are you going to bend your head down?'

That was a big lesson for us, his children, and more than anything he wanted us to have that principle to guide us through life. Looking back, it feels as if he knew that we would never grow up with him; that in the future we would all live in different parts of the world. If you're not kind to people – Papa was really kind to a fault – it will hurt *you* the most. That was what he taught us and I believe that with all my heart. He was my ultimate role model.

CHAPTER TWO

My mother's story

My mother, Eleas Diané, was born and raised in Guinea-Conakry, which is on the northern border of Sierra Leone and used to be part of French West Africa. It's a beautiful country with rainforests, plunging waterfalls, lots of farm-land and markets filled with hundreds of bolts of colourful African cotton fabric.

Eleas's father is from the Mandingo tribe and her mother is Fula. This means that my mum speaks lots of languages: French, Mandingo, Fula, Susu and, more recently, English. When she first arrived in Sierra Leone she didn't speak Krio – the language most people speak in Sierra Leone – but she learned it well enough to converse.

Eleas was the eldest of her mother Mariama's five children. My grandfather in Guinea-Conakry, Alpha Omar Diané, owned a big farm and had two other wives besides Mariama. Altogether he fathered fourteen or fifteen kids. I remember my mum telling me that he was a tough man and a strict parent, and I think she was scared of him. He died just before Mum met Papa, so I never knew him.

I didn't know much about my parents' relationship when I was growing up. Because I was raised by my dad in Sierra Leone and my mum lived in Guinea-Conakry, I have no memory of my mum from when I was a baby and toddler, though she would visit from time to time. I didn't understand why my parents weren't together and it wasn't something that was talked about. They weren't estranged – in fact, they seemed to love each other very much. They spoke on the phone all the time and much later, when my dad was ill in London, my mum went to see him every day and helped to care for him. My dad always said beautiful things to me about my mum, and Mum still says Yayah was 'the best man she knew and the best husband a woman could have', so I've never understood why they divorced when I was barely three. It has only been now, as I've been writing this book, that I've been able to fill in the gaps by talking to Eleas, and what I have learned has been quite a shock. I grew up seeing things only from my father's perspective, but now I have a fuller picture.

One thing I always understood was that it took a long time for my father to win my mother over. Eleas was a very beautiful young woman: statuesque with a fine figure, a serene face and eyes that look right into your soul. I think Papa must have been totally infatuated from the moment he set eyes on her. When they met, he was doing a lot of business in Guinea and had rented a place to work near where my mum was living at the time. Eleas's father had recently died and her mother was still in mourning, so my mum, who was seventeen, lived with her brother while she continued her education.

Eleas was an exceptionally smart student and intended to go to university. She wasn't interested in boys at all and she was well aware of the dangers of getting involved with a man; this was drilled into all young girls by their parents. But Eleas was also naive and unaccustomed to advances from the opposite sex. Her upbringing was sheltered and she was fiercely protected by the men of her family. As a result she was quiet and shy with strangers and very much out of her depth when my dad started showering her with attention.

Pa Conteh was regularly driving around Conakry (the nation's capital), and he would see Eleas lining up for the bus to school. Later, when he saw her walking by on her way to play basketball – which she was really good at – he would stop and try to talk to her. Eleas says she would keep her head down and not answer. She was terrified that her brother would find out she'd been talking to a strange man and tell the family. Even though she wasn't doing anything to encourage him, that sort of gossip was very bad for young girls in their communities.

Finally, after several encounters, a friend of my mum's started chatting to Pa Conteh and the people he was with. My dad pointed to Eleas and asked jokingly, 'This lady – can she talk? All the time she passes here and she never says hello.' This provoked my mum, who replied, 'I don't know you, that's why I don't say hello, and I have to pass by here because I am going to my basketball practice.'

She refused to be taken in by Papa's charms and with good reason. She was very focused on her education and knew that flirtations only led to one thing. However, my dad was very engaging and handsome; in his smart European clothes, he looked stylish and sophisticated. He was also determined, and the more my mum turned him down, the more he wanted to win her over. Once they had finally spoken, the ice was broken, and now my father really was totally smitten. Papa pursued her relentlessly, she recalls, though she's smiling as she tells me this so I think by this time she was enjoying the attention. He would give her a lift to and from school and take her to basketball and wouldn't take no for an answer.

He used to visit Conakry every few weeks in the course of his business, and the people he was working for were very high up and important, according to Eleas, like ministers and leaders. His business had expanded considerably and Papa was now importing all sorts of goods from Europe. He would go there with a long list from his clients and source and ship anything they wanted, from Italian furniture to beautiful floor tiles and carpets – even cars. His reputation as a solid and powerful businessman was growing.

As he began to grow more serious about Eleas, he visited her father's family, taking with him a suitcase full of gifts to try to win them over. Initially they were having none of it; they wanted to protect Eleas. Their biggest fear was that she would fall pregnant, something that happened to young girls a great deal. Also, a match had already been arranged for Eleas. The man in question was in Cuba at the time, studying; he was an intellectual, Eleas says. She was happy that the marriage wasn't imminent, though, because she had big dreams for herself: she wanted to go to college and study before marrying and starting a family.

I think my grandmother must have realised that something was going on, though, because she and Mum's aunty moved Eleas out of her brother's home and brought her to live with them. But my dad was canny. He visited the house and spoke to the aunty's husband, telling him of his desire to marry Eleas. When he was told no, that Eleas needed to stay at school, Papa said he wanted to take all the family to Mecca. For Muslims, this is a big, big deal. All Muslims who are able must make a pilgrimage to Mecca in their lifetime, but it's a costly business. The fact that Papa was willing to take my mum's family to the holy site showed that he was serious about Eleas, that he would look after the whole family and that he was devout. These were all big ticks in the eyes of the family.

Now all that was needed was to win around Eleas herself. Papa took my mum and her aunty on a holiday to Sierra Leone to show her the yellow house on Macauley Street, which was newly built then. The house was impressive – significantly nicer and bigger than the rented place she had been living in in Conakry, Mum says. When she saw the house in Kissy she knew she would be comfortable and could have a good life living there.

Nevertheless, the family still had niggling doubts. In Guinea, there were stories of girls who were married to Sierra Leonean men and taken away from their families to live with their new husbands only to be sold as part of a trafficking scam. My mum's family needed to be sure Eleas would be safe. On their visit to Freetown, my dad talked all about his plans to build a hotel in the suburb of Wellington. He said his idea was to send Eleas to Paris to be educated in hotel management, and she would then help run the hotel as a French speaker for guests. Meantime, he would send his second wife, Aminata, to London for training so she could take care of the English-speaking guests. Papa's two wives would be running the hotel while he carried on with his business concerns and raised his children.

My dad had it all worked out and he was very persuasive, but he wasn't just spinning a story; he was telling the truth. In the years that followed, the construction of the hotel filled my father's every waking hour. He spent tens of thousands of leone on it, shipping over all the supplies from Europe and constantly updating its structure as it was built. He wanted it to be the best quality.

Following Eleas and her aunt's visit to Sierra Leone, Pa Conteh took Mum's mother and uncle to Mecca, as he'd promised, and afterwards a wedding date was set. By this time my mum was happy to be marrying Pa Conteh. He had won her heart.

Eleas and Yayah married on 28 September 1979 in Guinea-Conakry. She was just nineteen. It was a big Muslim wedding, attended by all the family, and afterwards there was a ceremony in which the newlyweds signed the civil register. I have a gorgeous photo of Papa, dressed in an immaculate white robe and wearing the traditional white kufi cap, gazing at my mum while he feeds her with a silver fork. She looks so beautiful, her hair sculpted into the white tulle of her veil. Her long white dress is simple and edged with lace and she's wearing white gloves. It's a shame that only a few years later they were no longer together.

★

When she moved to the yellow house in Sierra Leone, Eleas had her own floor with her own kitchen and set of rooms. My dad's second wife, Aminata, and her son Alieu and daughter Tigidankay, who would only just have been born when my mum arrived, were on the top floor and Papa had the ground floor. Mum says there were no issues between the wives and Yayah was scrupulously fair. 'I've never seen a man more honest,' she tells me, adding, 'I will never have another husband like that man. Never.'

She says that my father was always buying things for them, and when he came back from his travels he would make sure both wives were treated equally. He would buy ten towels in different colours so they could both choose their favourites and not feel hard done by. And every month he would give them the same amount of money to buy food and anything else they needed. They didn't need much, though, because my dad filled the storerooms in the house with huge bags of rice and drums of oil and everything else needed for the household. Eleas had never seen anything like it.

The following year, my mum fell sick. She had no idea she was pregnant. Girls were not given any sex education – sex was another of those things that wasn't talked about – and so she didn't understand why her periods had stopped. But when she started vomiting the other women in the house recognised it as morning sickness and told her she was going to have a baby. Mum suffered terrible nausea – any whiff of food would set her off – and because Papa was travelling a lot she went back to Guinea where her family could care for her.

I think my mum must have been very lonely when she first moved to Sierra Leone. One minute she was at school and playing in the basketball team, and the next she was living in another country away from her family and community. Apart from one cousin already living there, who had a wife who spoke Mandingo, she didn't know anyone, and she didn't speak the language. I feel sad when I think of my mum back then. She must have felt very isolated. Having your first baby is a huge and sometimes scary thing, as I later discovered when I had my daughter Sarafina. Mama had no family or community around her, which would have been incredibly tough.

When her morning sickness stopped, Papa brought her back home from Guinea and I was born. I was a big baby and it wasn't an easy birth. In the end, Eleas had to have a caesarean. Then, once she got home, the stitches came open and she had to go back to the hospital for treatment.

She says that my dad tried not to show any preference between his children but that he loved me 'too much'. I know what she means; I think he felt I was special and he wanted to wrap me up in cotton wool. Part of this may have been because I was a very sickly child, so needed more care. Dad would always be cuddling and kissing me. I was very skinny and didn't eat well, and it probably looked as if I could be broken into pieces, I was so fragile. But there wasn't anything specific wrong with me, and looking back through a mother's eyes I think my vulnerability as a young girl may have come from missing my mum. That made me even closer to my dad; I would follow him around like a puppy.

I always thought that it was my father who divorced my mother. He would never explain why or what happened, only saying that it wasn't my mum's fault and that he still loved her. But now I have spoken to Eleas, I see there was a lot more going on and I am starting to realise how much she suffered.

My mum had to go to hospital for an operation to remove an ovarian cyst. This makes me gasp, because I have had a lot of problems with cysts also. She was given a local anaesthetic and when they opened up her abdomen she was shouting in pain because the anaesthetic didn't work. The doctor panicked and, in the confusion, took out Eleas's ovary instead of the cyst and then put clips on her stomach.

Afterwards, my mum was in a bad way. The wound wouldn't heal and became infected. Papa was busy in Wellington, working on the hotel, but eventually they had to send for him. When he saw Eleas, he realised something had to be done. He took her home and had nurses treat her at the house. Slowly she started to get better but she was still very weak. Finally, my dad decided he had to take Eleas back to her family in Guinea.

I have no memory of any of this at all.

He left Eleas there, saying he would come back to fetch her, but he never did. My mum says Papa abandoned her because she was sick. She didn't know if the botched operation meant she couldn't have any more children, but it certainly would have been dangerous for her to try to conceive at that time. So now I am wondering if this was why my dad abandoned my mum. Children were everything to him.

Whatever the reason, Papa didn't return for Eleas. He told his father, my grandfather, that it was Eleas's family who had taken her from him, but my mum says there's no truth to this. She was crying daily and her family was really angry.

Papa had taken Eleas out of school to marry her. She had given him a baby girl and then, because she fell ill, he didn't want her anymore. At least, that's what it looked like.

Eventually, Eleas decided she had to divorce Papa, to save her honour and in order to support herself financially. She set herself up in business, buying and selling – at first it was eggs, but later she would gauge what was needed and trade. It was a similar line of work to my dad but on a much smaller scale. She travelled between Freetown and Conakry every year. When she was in Freetown, Eleas would come to see me, but I don't remember these visits. She says that she tried to sue for custody for me in the courts but my father won. He had money, a big house, a good business. Eleas was powerless, and I don't think she has ever recovered from losing me. She missed me terribly and still does.

It was a challenge when I first went to live with her after the war because I just didn't know how to give affection to her. She thought it was because of what I had been through, but I just didn't know how to express my emotions. She wanted me to accept her right away. I knew that she was kind and caring. She gives so much and, in many ways, my mum is exactly the same as Papa, with the same kind of personality, but I just didn't have the sense that we belonged together. Our relationship is so much better now, our love much deeper.

The strange thing is she continued to love Pa Conteh and he continued to love her. I think Papa regretted the whole thing afterwards but it was too late. Today my mum just looks sad and defeated and says, 'It was all very hard.' I sense her torment whenever I look at her and now I understand it more.

About ten years after the divorce my mum remarried. Her husband Anfah (his real name is Ibrahim, but that's what I call him) was a soldier with the Guinean army and this was his first marriage. He is a very kind man who really loves Eleas. I visited my mum in Guinea twice before the war and was able to meet him. We got on well and we became very fond of each other. They never had children, but she became a surrogate mum to all the kids in her community in Guinea and, later, in London, where she moved in 2002. Now I see why.

CHAPTER THREE

Growing up in the yellow house

Fatmata and Mabinty were the first of my siblings to live in the yellow house. They remember it being built and how Papa wanted to have the best of everything for his family. People used to come and just stare at the house. 'They were in awe,' says Fatmata. 'It was one of the biggest houses in the area.'

Like me, the twins remember the house being massive, although when I went back recently it felt a lot smaller. I guess through a child's eyes it seemed like a palace. But it's true that, compared to the other houses in the neighbourhood – which were mostly small concrete buildings in their own compound, with tin or flat concrete roofs – our beautiful home definitely stood out.

Today Sierra Leone's population is 7.8 million; back when I was growing up it was 4.3 million. We are a small African nation with a proud heart and a strong sense of identity. Sometimes people ask me why Sierra Leone is so poor. Having left Sierra Leone many years ago and having had some of my education disrupted by the war, I cannot say I know all the answers. But I know the reasons are complex. Some are rooted in our colonial history. Under British rule from 1808, the main British interest in Sierra Leone was our resources, and how to extract and export them as efficiently as possible. The British built infrastructure to connect resources to ports, rather than to build communities and connect people to each other. Since independence in 1961, with much of its mineral wealth lost to British industrialisation, Sierra Leone has struggled to build the health, education, transport, energy and other infrastructure that society needs to blossom. Instead, it has been beset by political unrest, corruption, war, the Ebola outbreak and other natural disasters.

In the first half of the 1900s Freetown was the only major city in the country and most people were raised in villages. Today those villages have grown into towns and bigger suburbs. Up until the civil war we had a sparse but good network of roads, but many of these were destroyed during the fighting and today there is still a lot of work to be done to rebuild them.

Away from the coast, much of Sierra Leone is rural, with rice, cassava and vegetable crops. The soil is rich and the climate is tropical and hot all year round, with a dry season in winter and the monsoon season from May to November. This is the time I loved best. The sun would stay out as the heavens opened, and it was hot and humid so we longed for the rain. And when it came it poured down, hitting the red earth and creating steam and dust and the most special smell. I've never known anything like it anywhere else. Even though the rain was explosive it felt so calming, washing everything clean and leaving a rich sensual perfume in its wake.

Kissy, the suburb of Freetown where I grew up, is on the eastern side of Freetown and it's in quite a picturesque part of the country. Looking one way from our rooftop there were stunning views of the Atlantic, which brought refreshing sea breezes; in the other direction were the mountains, covered in rich tropical vegetation. Sierra Leonean forests have teak and mahogany trees and palms, which also line the beaches. Kissy was quite poor when the yellow house was first built, but by the time I came along it was a thriving community. Our neighbours were from all walks of life, some wealthy like my family, others poor and others in the middle. It was mainly residential, the houses punctuated with mosques and churches. There was also a big central food market – Kissy market – which was always very noisy and busy, with traders shouting, 'Chillies!' 'Come buy my fish!' 'No, mine is better, come over here!' Sometimes I would sneak out of the house with my close friend Safie and go to the market; all the shouting used to make me laugh.

Before sunrise Kissy woke to the melodious call to prayer from the mosques. Next came the 'cocorico' of roosters crowing in people's backyards, and slowly dawn broke. Muslims wearing their white prayer robes and holding torches – including my dad – would shuffle along the laneways, answering the muezzins' calls. Kissy people were very house proud and another early morning sound was the swish of brooms on front doorsteps, and in backyards and compounds.

For me, though, the time to rise was when I could smell the bread baking in the big bakery down the road. Shops opened around 7 am and my dad would have sent a cook to buy our breakfast food. I would shower and get myself dressed and ready for school in my uniform and then go downstairs to my dad's floor. He was very particular about how we looked for school. We had to be neat, tidy and impeccably turned out, with our clothes ironed, our white socks spotless and our shoes shiny. Then we would have breakfast with Papa. He prepared the breakfast for us himself, standing in an apron in his kitchen as he prepared our eggs, sliced the fresh bread and brewed the tea.

The house was fully wired and plumbed with hot and cold running water and, as I have said, arranged over three floors with an open-air rooftop level above. The floors were connected by an external staircase, and at the back of the house were facilities for washing clothes and preparing food, as well as the house where my grandfather lived. There was also a garage that housed some of my father's cars. It had big metal doors with my dad's initials on the outside which are still there today. The walls of the house were thick and very solid and painted a mustard colour, which is why everyone called it 'the yellow house'.

When I ask my sisters why Papa installed bulletproof windows and one-way glass, they both laugh. 'He always liked to go to the extreme,' says Fatmata. 'Pa Conteh wanted to build a fortress around his children, to protect us,' she tells me. But looking back, I think there was more to it than just paternal paranoia. I think my dad sensed that there might be some problems ahead in Sierra Leone and that he was aware of growing unrest. His doubt about the safety of our country may also explain his investment in property in London – he bought several houses – and his plans to send us all away at some point, so we all had an escape route, a back-up.

Despite the stringent security, some people were allowed into the yellow house. The house had its own water pump, which was rare, and the twins recall Papa inviting people to come and fetch water. He even let some of the neighbours do their washing at the back.

Growing up, I was the youngest of four children living in the house: me, Ibrahim, Tigidankay and Alieu, the eldest, who was four years older than me. Alieu really loved me and he did everything he could to watch over me. I think he felt he had to be the man of the house when our dad went away on business, which was often.

By this time Pa Conteh was overseas for months at a time. Because of this, we had a lot of help in the house especially from two family members who also spoke Susu, which he wanted us to learn because it was his family's tribal language. We had a cook who made our meals and cleaned the house, and we had a chauffeur who took us to school and drove us anywhere else we needed to go. Shebborah was our chauffeur for a long time and he lived in the house on the ground floor. He knew all my dad's business, every single thing, and Papa really trusted him.

Cimamie, who prepared most of our meals as well as looking after us, was the most terrible cook. She was really beautiful and joyful, but you could give her the best meat and fish and she just could not make it edible. We weren't allowed to complain, though, as our dad had taught us to be appreciative and not talk back – but I don't know how we ate the food! Cimamie lived just opposite us with her own family in a house my dad rented for her.

Fortunately, she wasn't the only one in the kitchen. There was also an older lady, Nga Kadiatu (who was a distant relative of Papa's and one of those who spoke Susu), and she would also cook as well as washing and ironing our clothes. Her food was wonderful, so tasty. My favourite was a dish we called 'potato leaves'. The leaves are actually from the sweet potato plant, the part closest to the soil. They are chopped, then cooked in palm oil with locally caught fresh fish, onions and spices. We eat it with steamed rice, using our hands. You take a small handful of rice, mould it in your hand and then scoop up the potato leaf mixture into the rice. It's delicious. Another favourite of mine is fried plantain. In fact, I am salivating as I write this! Plantain are like bananas but starchier and not as sweet. When you fry them, though, they taste like honey.

We called Kadiatu 'Nga', which is like 'Mama' in our language, as a sign of respect. We would never call an older person by their first name alone. When I came to Australia, I used to feel uncomfortable calling people by their first name. I remember someone saying to me, 'Don't call me Mrs or Miss,' and I couldn't understand why. Then I realised it was because people thought I was saying they were old and that this was considered a bad thing. I still don't get it; to me, saying you are old is saying you are wise and I look up to you. Even in the workplace in Australia I found people called by their first names directly whereas still today, in Sierra Leone, we would use Madame or Mrs. It is merely about respect.

Another person I respected was my grandfather. I loved him so much. He was really loud, the opposite of Papa. If my grandfather was speaking, you could hear him far, far away – I kid you not! Baimba spoke the Monrovian language, which is similar to Krio, but because Liberia was colonised by the US it has a lot of slang in it. He also spoke Mandingo, Susu, Fula and many other languages.

He was so beautiful. His skin was like honey, so soft and so gentle, and he smoked a pipe. As soon as he was finished with his pipe he would brush his teeth – every time, without fail. My dad did not like smoke, and he wouldn't allow it in our house, but Baimba was his own master in his apartment behind our house.

As I understand it, part of my grandfather's role when he was in Monrovia was to predict the future, which he did for the president. I don't know much about it, but I gather he was like a fortune teller. He was also very devout and would read the Koran every single day and knew it inside out. He dressed in Muslim robes and was always very nice and neat with a keffiyeh headdress like the ones they wear in Saudi Arabia.

My dad dressed very differently, more like an Englishman, and we kids also wore Western clothes. In some ways, it was almost as if we were living a British life. We drank English breakfast tea and ate digestive biscuits which my dad would ship over from London. This was because Papa spent a lot of time in London and he picked up British habits that he admired and wanted to share with us. He was also preparing us to be educated in Britain later on, which was always his plan.

He made a cinema room in the house where we all spent time together and watched movies and music videos that he brought over from London. I remember seeing Michael Jackson, Bruce Willis, Chuck Norris and many others.

★

When I was about three years old I started nursery school. I can't really remember my time there, but I know that it was a Christian school just outside Kissy. Then I went to St Michael's, a Catholic primary school. Even though my family was Muslim, my father had no problem sending me to Christian schools, as they were the best in our neighbourhood at the time. In Sierra Leone, Christians and Muslims all live happily together. We have mosques and churches and the two religions even share the same graveyards. We celebrate all the special days together – Christmas and Ramadan plus some traditional African holidays. I like to think we get the best of all worlds this way.

Faith matters a great deal to Sierra Leoneans. We are spiritual people and, although there are many different religions, we fully respect each other's beliefs. Two-thirds of the population is Muslim, a quarter Christian and 10 per cent follow traditional tribal beliefs. As well as this there's Hindu, Baha'i and Judaism.

At St Michael's the priests would give communion. I remember I wanted to take communion so badly. I was really curious about the sermons: that you could build a mansion or a mountain if you had a little faith. I had no idea what faith was, but I was all for it. I think that was the beginning of something for me. When many years later I told my dad I was a Christian, it really wasn't a big deal; for him life was all about respecting others and helping people, and religion – any religion – is part of that. My favourite biblical story was the one about the prodigal son. I was mesmerised by the father's love; how even though this child had left him and destroyed everything, the father's love and longing for his child never stopped. I didn't see the injustice in the story, as some people do. I think it was the reaction of the brother who stayed, his ego and sense of entitlement, that was most unjust. Because he stayed and worked hard, he demanded acknowledgement for that. In a way, he was the child who was really taking everything. And when his brother came home, he was so unhappy about the attention his brother received. Why, when you have everything, can't you be pleased when you see your brother coming back? I thought that was interesting. I think the story of the prodigal son is about acceptance of ourselves and each other as human beings. We are none of us perfect, and knowing that can make things so much easier and more joyful. It's a story that I'm still learning things from and I suspect I always will. The Christian spirit that I first encountered back then in St Michael's has led me to a place where today I can find peace and where I can forgive.

Although the school was near our home, my siblings and I – unlike the other local children – were chauffeured to and from school. We used to have two beautiful cars, one navy and the other cream coloured. I remember them being very classy and long, and looking a bit like limousines. We just took it for granted that we went everywhere by car, but it was unusual in Kissy.

From the car window I could see all of Kissy life. People selling things in makeshift stalls on the side of the road, kids in their uniforms walking to school in groups, mamas carrying trays on their heads laden with fruit, eggs, all sorts of things, which they would be taking to market to sell. Most people dressed in colourful local clothes or Western jeans and t-shirts. There were hardly any women in abayas. Some had headscarves on but not that many, even though they would have been Muslim. That was the Arab way of dressing, not our way.

Throughout my whole childhood Papa never let us walk to school. He was really strict about it, and the twins say it was the same for them. It was all to do with this protective bubble he kept us in. When we reached a certain age, my dad knew men were going to be watching us, and he was not going to be around that much because he was working overseas, so he sent us to boarding school a long way from the city. I think he was more concerned about my older sister Tigidankay than me. I had quite a boyish figure and I didn't have any breasts for a long time, but my sister matured very quickly. She was so tall, and she walked like a warrior. She would carry herself really well, and even I could sense that men were looking at her from afar. My dad was very aware of that too. He must have figured that in a girls' school in the countryside, we would be safe.

I was about eight or nine when I was sent to the private Christian boarding school. Tigidankay was in the secondary school and I was in the primary school. It was called Harford School for Girls and was in Moyamba, in the Southern Province, about a three-hour drive away. Papa would drive us there himself and then he would take Alieu and Ibrahim on to their school in Bo. Shebborah would drive a second car with our suitcases and boxes of food. Each term we each arrived at school with a suitcase of clothes and a wooden box which we called a chop box. It contained dry food, provisions for the three months spent away. Mine always had some of Papa's English biscuits in it. Papa would spend term time overseas doing his business and then come back to pick us up when the term ended.

I loved that drive to and from school. My dad would pack food for the journey and it was like an adventure. Once you were out of Freetown it was all green and lush with the mountains in the background. Outside of the villages there were no people, just beautiful Sierra Leone. We would pass through villages with locals selling fruit on the roadside and after an hour or so we would stop for lunch, pulling up in a picturesque spot. I remember one time there was a huge accident on the road ahead of us. Papa pulled in and wouldn't let us get out of the car, but he went to see if he could help. A big truck had overturned and there were bodies everywhere. When I looked out of the window I saw my dad on his knees praying with tears in his eyes.

We loved boarding school. We missed home, of course, but it felt like freedom. We were so happy! For the first time I started to feel independent. At last I could do things for myself. And for me, boarding school was really fun; I was already used to strict rules, so the school rules didn't bother me at all – I got into it right away. I liked the routine there and the campus and loved being with other kids. We slept in bunk beds in dormitories with one class per dormitory. This meant there were usually about twenty girls sleeping in a single room. First in chose the best bed.

Our day was determined by bells. The first one at 6 am would wake us up for our morning devotion. Straight out of bed we would line up in the hallway – the whole school was gathered there, about 150 girls or more. We would sing a hymn, pray, and then the matron would call out the name of a girl who would have to recite a Bible verse just like that. (We would learn the verses by rote, so it wasn't as terrifying as it sounds.) Morning devotion would take about fifteen minutes. Afterwards we had to make our beds and tidy our stations before going to wash. There was a roster for laying the table in the dining room, sweeping the compound and cleaning the dormitory, the toilets and the bathrooms, and if your name was on the list, this too had to be done before showering.

Once in our uniforms we would have breakfast around 8 am and school lessons would start at 8.30 am sharp. Any tardiness or bad behaviour was punished with caning or extra chores. I hated the cane. I rarely got it, but if I did it would have been for talking in class. Just the idea of it was usually enough to keep me in line, though.

I found the lessons hard. My siblings were all very smart, and even though I liked school, I struggled. I just couldn't get some of the ideas into my head. I was very creative in different ways. I loved drama and was always in the school productions. I liked the arts, music and style. But in those days, and in my dad's world, there was no place for creativity. 'What is that?' he said. 'You should be studying to become a lawyer.' I wanted to study because I thought that's why he put us in boarding school and I wanted to please him. I really tried and even though my grades were average and didn't reflect the amount of work I put in I really enjoyed learning.

I had some great times at Harford. I was a Brownie and a Scout, and I joined the band. In Sierra Leone, most schools have a band. I used to play the trumpet and the side drums and had a cute uniform which made me look like a cross between a drum majorette and a cheerleader. I have always loved clothes, fashion and dressing up.

Boarding school was also where I first started making friends of my own rather than friends my dad had chosen for me. But I think he was fine with that because this was a very prestigious school and the other students were all girls like me with strict wealthy parents who really cared about their education. We wouldn't be hanging out with someone who was smoking marijuana, or playing with boys, so he didn't need to worry. Little did he know I had my first kiss in boarding school with a girlfriend! It was all very innocent, though. She lives in America now and we're still friends. All in all, though we had our moments of naughtiness, we were pretty well behaved. In the senior years, I was even made a prefect.

At home I didn't go to church very often because my family was Muslim, but at boarding school we went every Sunday. The church was in the adjacent secondary school, where my sister Tigidankay was studying and which I later moved on to. It was Methodist, in the English style, and made from local stone with a spire. Inside were wooden pews with hymnbooks hanging on the back of each seat. There was a pulpit for the preacher, who was always a man, and an organ and a piano, and often students would perform songs. I liked the singing and the preaching; the services always left me feeling joyful and uplifted. The church was a special place, one that brought everyone in the school community together. I was really happy there, and it didn't matter that this wasn't my family's religion. I believe that all of us who are searching for faith, whether Muslim or Christian or something else, are actually all praying to the same god – we just have different routes to take. We are all individual, and that's a wonderful thing.

When I was kidnapped, it was the stories I learned from the Bible and those experiences going to church at boarding school that helped me through. It didn't come to me directly – 'Oh, God is here' – because I was surrounded by so much evil, but I definitely felt there was something, someone, protecting me. It still doesn't make sense to me, how I survived it, but I know that my faith in something higher was crucial.

CHAPTER FOUR

The war is coming

I was ten and at boarding school in Moyamba when the war started in 1991. Even though we were nowhere near the fighting, we were aware that something was going on. We'd hear stories and everybody listened to the radio – the BBC World Service, mostly, as well as the local radio station. It was through the radio and word of mouth that we heard about most things during the war. For a long time, it didn't feel as if we were in danger. The war was something that was happening to other people, and for many years my life went on much as it always had.

We were told that there was a war going on in Liberia and it had come across the border into Sierra Leone. At the time, I didn't really understand what that meant. I was too young and my world was all about school, which I loved. It was only much later that the full picture came into focus and I saw how my country was tearing itself apart.

Joseph Momoh, the leader of the All People's Congress

(APC), had become president in 1985 under a one-party state system. He was the second president since Sierra Leone became a republic in 1971. From 1808 to 1961, Sierra Leone was a British Crown Colony. In 1961, the country gained independence, and in the ten year transition to a republic, Queen Elizabeth II remained Head of State. A republic was declared in 1971.

On 23 March 1991, the Revolutionary United Front (RUF) – essentially a growing bunch of anti-government rebels led by former student activist turned army corporal turned warlord Foday Sankoh, with support from Liberian guerrilla leader Charles Taylor's National Patriotic Front of Liberia (NPFL) – attempted to overthrow the Momoh government in Sierra Leone. These were vicious people prepared to turn on their own people in the most unthinkable ways in their pursuit of power.

The boys and men (and later girls, too) who joined the RUF idolised Sankoh, calling him 'Papa', but in order to achieve the level of brutality he demanded RUF soldiers were often forced to take drugs like cocaine or 'brown-brown', which is a mixture of cocaine and gunpowder, before they went into battle. Certainly, the rebels I came into contact with later were out of their heads on a cocktail of drugs which made them angry, irrational and totally out of control. This was also why they were so terrifying: it was as if the very essence of what made them human had been taken away.

At first the RUF captured towns on the Liberian border, and from here they recruited more fighters – including thousands of child soldiers, boys and girls as young as seven. (Children were also recruited by the government forces in the war, and the government soldiers could be just as brutal towards civilians, so it was hard to know who to trust.) The rebels bought guns with diamonds – which became known as 'blood' or 'conflict' diamonds in the global debate over the trading practice – and slowly, slowly their gangs started to move through our country.

Despite instigating a new, more equitable constitution, allowing for a multi-party system, in 1992 Momoh was overthrown in a military coup led by Captain Valentine Strasser, who was frustrated by the rise of the rebels and the collapse of the economy. Sierra Leone is incredibly rich in natural resources, but the corruption – still a problem today – meant that the wealth didn't make it to the people who needed it most. In addition to the widespread poverty, there were fuel shortages and regular electricity blackouts. Meanwhile, the civil war seemed to be unstoppable.

In the beginning, people from Liberia would flee to Sierra Leone, seeking refuge in villages, including some near to our boarding school. We heard about girls being raped and how the rebels would chop off people's hands. They would ask a pregnant woman if she was expecting her baby to be a boy or a girl, and then they would cut open her belly just to see. Stories, rumours, have you heard this, have you heard that? This was all part of the constant noise about the war at school. But we didn't see it for ourselves.

Papa continued to take us to and from school as usual, though sometimes he would travel by a more circuitous route to avoid trouble spots. When we were at home between terms we just stayed inside. The rebels were nowhere near Freetown, so life carried on. It scared me a little, but it felt like it was far away from us. I don't know if that was just my age and lack of understanding, or if it was because of the secure blanket of Papa's protection. In any case, the war seemed to come to us really slowly. It's hard to believe, because Sierra Leone is such a small country, but Tigidankay and I carried on going to boarding school until 1995.

I was on school holiday back home in Freetown when the rebels arrived in Moyamba. The school had to shut down and we never went back. Papa stopped travelling overseas and stayed home with us in the yellow house. By this time, I was fifteen, and even though I knew we were at war, and it was now directly affecting us because our school was closed, we were sheltered from the bad things that were happening. We had food, clothes, all the supplies that we needed in our house, and my dad didn't talk about the war at all. Consequently, I never once felt unsafe in our house nor did I think we needed to worry. The war had been going on in the background for so long it felt almost normal. And even when the rebels moved closer, when we really could see things were happening because people were flooding into Freetown and all of them had stories to tell, our house still felt like the safest place in the world. Because of the windows my dad had installed, we could see out, but nobody could see in, and that made us feel impregnable.

Papa decided to open up his hotel in Wellington to refugees fleeing the fighting. It was still under construction, but the walls were all in place, there were doors on the rooms, and my father had the windows boarded over because glass hadn't been installed yet. The whole place was soon filled with families who stayed there all through the war. He didn't charge them any rent; he just wanted to help. And, in the end, it was this act of generosity that saved his life.

The war went on for so long before it came to Freetown that most people didn't believe it would ever get to us. My dad found me a new school to go to in the city and the chauffeur drove me there. I left after only one term, though, because my Moyamba boarding school had secured a building in Freetown from where they could continue to operate, not as a boarding school but as a day school. This was great news for me. The teachers had all come to Freetown and my friends were there too. Everything was back to normal – except it wasn't.

We knew that there were some rebels who were acting as spies inside Freetown. We had to be really cautious about who we spoke to because you couldn't tell the rebels from the civilians or the government soldiers. We were safe inside the school but there was strict security on the gate, which was all new to us.

Things were also changing at home. To begin with, we had a new stepmother. In 1997 my dad married his fourth wife, Hassanatu, with whom he would stay for the rest of his life. She was much younger than my dad, in her thirties. This was a huge shock. They didn't have children together, which is surprising looking back, but I think my dad was contemplating his own mortality and he didn't want to die alone. Hassanatu and I got on well, but it did feel rather strange having her around.

At the same time, my dad was growing more religious. Growing up we weren't particularly devout, aside from Baimba, who was always quoting the Koran. We used to have such a fun life. My sister and I used to wear short pants and sneakers. We used to go to the beach with our dad and kick a ball around, and my sister and I would play skipping games outside in the compound. We never went to the mosque to pray. But when Papa became a full-on Muslim all that changed. I guess he must have fallen under the influence of an imam. There were a lot of new rules and our house was no longer fun at all. More than ever our lives became all about studying and books. Also, we had to change the way we dressed, wearing our pants and skirts longer. In Sierra Leone people don't usually cover their heads unless they are going to pray, so I didn't have to wear a veil, thank goodness, but we did start going to the mosque. I considered myself Christian, so it was really hard. We also had to fast for Ramadan, which was new for us.

Although my dad was incredibly strict, I managed to get out of the house sometimes. I started doing this from about the age of sixteen, and at first it was to play in my band. I would put on my band uniform and tell my dad that the band was playing at a funeral, though in fact we were practising for more frivolous events, one of which was a big street carnival. One time my dad caught me coming back in and I think he realised I hadn't been to a funeral. Fortunately, he just smiled.

Then, when I was seventeen, I would sneak out to see my boyfriend. Derek lived just up the hill from our house in Kissy, only a couple of blocks away. He came from a really good family – his dad was my father's doctor and his mum worked in a bank. They were Christian, which you could tell from their British-sounding names; most likely they were

Creoles, descendants of the African slaves who were freed to return to live in the colony of Sierra Leone as part of the abolition of slavery in England.

Derek was a year or so older than me and he was a soccer player, a very good one. Sometimes he played with my brother Alieu, but Derek was in a different league altogether; he also played with the national team. He was probably the most popular soccer player in Freetown, though I didn't know that when we met because I had been away at boarding school. He was sort of like a celebrity, but he wasn't really on my radar.

Derek tells me today that he had been trying to meet me and talk to me for some time. He had seen me around after I moved back home from boarding school, but because of my dad he found it really hard to get close enough to introduce himself. Eventually he met me along the road through a mutual friend.

As Derek tells it, he was walking home from football practice when we met. He was all muddy and when his friend, who I knew, said to me, 'This is the guy who wants to talk to you,' I said, 'Who, this dirty little guy? No way would I talk to him.' But he must have made a positive impression, because apparently after we talked for a bit I said, 'Oh, you're actually not as bad as I thought you were!' It's funny to hear this, because I really was very shy. But after that first encounter Derek and I became friends, and then we started dating.

It was an innocent childlike love, but we cared deeply for each other. While my dad knew nothing about it – he would never have allowed it – Derek's parents knew about me and well aware how protective Pa Conteh was of his daughters. Derek told me that his mum used to tease him, saying, 'You have to be very serious if you want somebody like Aminata.'

They were actually very happy when we got together, because they thought if he went out with me, a girl from a strict home, he would learn some discipline. Derek was very smart at school, but he liked soccer and he liked girls. They thought I would be a good influence on him, and I was. He changed after we started dating, and his parents liked the changes. I always found him very gentle, very sweet.

I could only see Derek in the evenings because that was when my dad went to the mosque. Papa would go off to pray in the men's section and I would go off to the women's prayer room with my stepmum, only I would sneak off. Hassanatu was really devout, but she was also young enough to understand what it was like to be a teenager, and she never blew my cover. She was cool.

I would take off the prayer dress I wore over my street clothes and hide it in the bushes near the mosque, and Derek would come and get me. We would only have half an hour or so together. It felt like both the longest and the shortest time. It was so precious and beautiful. We would walk around the streets and talk. We weren't all that physical with each other, but we had our first kiss, and he would hold my hand. I think he was a bit scared of what my dad might do if he discovered us together. Today Derek laughs when I talk to him about Pa Conteh, and he recalls how he used to try to get into the house to see me. 'It was like trying to break into the White House. No males were allowed in there.'

My dad even stopped my brother from bringing girl-friends home. One time he caught two of Alieu's girlfriends at our house, and he took them to the police station. True story! They ended up spending the night there before their parents could come to get them. My father told their parents: 'Look after your kids. My son isn't ready to be a parent, yet, and neither are your daughters. And if you catch my son in your house, you should do the same as I have done.' My dad sounds pretty harsh here, and he was intimidating for sure, but it came from a good place. His message was clear: don't mess with my children, and protect your own.

There was never any question of Derek and I having sex. First, I was sure that if I had sex my dad would know. He was very quiet but very observant. I was convinced he would be able to tell straight away just by looking at me.

Second, when my girlfriends talked about it – which wasn't very often, because my friends weren't really into sex – they talked about how much it hurt. I was really scared of anything that hurts. (I still am. If my kids are given needles, I'm the one who screams.) I remember this girl saying, 'Oh, there's three veins before you have sex, and when those veins are cut, that's when you have the blood.' Sex meant cutting a vein? That was not going to happen!

Derek and I did think about the future in an abstract way and we grew quite serious about each other. Derek would always be saying things like, 'I'm going to marry you,' and he meant it. I would get excited, but I also thought that it would be far in the future, because I didn't want to leave my home. It was my happy, safe place and I couldn't imagine not living there.

Derek lives in America now. That first love is still special to both of us. But it was torn apart when the rebels came.

★

In the early hours of 6 January 1999, our worst fears were realised when the RUF finally captured Freetown from government troops and the soldiers of the Nigerian-led peacekeeping force ECOMOG, a military observer group acting under the auspices of the Economic Community of West African States. For the next three weeks, the rebels occupied the city. These three weeks represented the most concentrated period of vicious bloodshed in Sierra Leone's whole civil war, and it was civilians who suffered most.

As the rebels took control of street after street, they dragged entire families out of their homes and murdered them in broad daylight. From babies to old men, they didn't care. They used machetes to hack off the limbs of their victims. They would ask, 'Do you want short sleeves or long sleeves?' If you answered long, they would chop off your hand; if short, they would cut above your elbow. And it wasn't just arms: they cut off people's feet and legs, fingers and toes.

They burned people alive in their houses and rounded up hundreds of young women to take with them. Some people were beaten with hammers and many had petrol poured on them as they lay in their beds, then were set alight, their bodies engulfed in flames. Women were raped and slaughtered in front of their families, elders left bleeding to death. Several thousand civilians were killed in a violent spree that no one in our country will ever forget. As the ECOMOG forces counterattacked and the rebels were forced to retreat, they would set fire to entire blocks of houses, whole neighbourhoods razed to the ground.

The ECOMOG forces were totally overwhelmed. Their role was to protect civilians, but not all the ECOMOG troops acted as peacekeepers. After the war, the brutal acts carried out by some of these soldiers – including maiming, rape and murder – were uncovered. Soon my countrymen realised not all the ECOMOG forces were there to help, and it became impossible to know who you could trust as the city was subjected to a reign of terror.

CHAPTER FIVE

Kidnapped

We were sleeping when the rebels came to Macauley Street. It was a school day, but I knew early on that something was happening. Derek told me afterwards that he had his final exams on the day the rebels came. It was his last year of high school and he had been studying for weeks. He was so focused on getting to school on time that he took a shower and got ready to leave even though the streets had erupted: there were bombs and shells and grenades (RPGs) and machine-guns, all seemingly exploding and firing at once. Finally his mum said, 'What are you doing? There will be no exams today – they're killing people!'

From my room in the yellow house I could hear the noise creeping closer, a distant murmur in the background at first, and then a messy, ugly roar. It felt like I was dreaming and I was trying to wake myself up out of the dream but my eyes wouldn't open. Suddenly the noise seemed to be almost in my bedroom, echoing around my head, bouncing off the walls, shaking me awake. I could hear the rebel boys shouting and bombs and rapid pops of gunfire going off. It was getting louder and louder and louder. Eventually I forced my eyes open. It was early, very early, maybe 4 am when I stumbled to look out of the window.

At first all I could see was smoke, and then I realised houses were burning in our street – and not just houses. Over the next few days the air was filled with a smell I will never forget. I smelled it first on that morning. It was the stench of burning meat with something else, something strong and acrid, like bad eggs. As I peeked out of the window I saw people running, their bodies on fire, their flesh literally in flames, and then I heard the crying and the screams as the rebels locked people in their houses and threw in their fire bombs. These people, our neighbours, were burned alive inside.

All of a sudden, my eyes began to sting and tears streamed from them as tear gas seeped under the door from outside. The government soldiers, supported by ECOMOG, were trying to dislodge the rebels with tear gas, but it obviously wasn't working. I couldn't see clearly, but I knew that the day we had most feared was here: the rebels had come to Freetown.

Papa had already climbed the stairs from the ground floor to be with Tigidankay, Alieu and me. He said that none of us was to stand on the verandah overlooking our street. Just as we were starting to take in what was happening, we heard a loud banging. There were people pounding on the door.

We were really scared, rooted to the spot, but then my father saw that these were the people he had given refuge to in the half-built hotel in Wellington. They had fled the hotel, which had been overrun by the rebels, and joined with others who were trying to find shelter anywhere they could. They were petrified.

My dad asked Shebborah, our chauffeur, to open the door and let them in. In no time at all, our big house, which had always been so private and pristine, was filled with hundreds of people – there were men, women and children, but mostly it was women with their little ones. Many had probably seen their families being killed in front of their eyes. There was no talk, no need to explain; we could see what had happened in their faces and my father wasn't going to turn anyone away. These people were all total strangers to me – I didn't recognise one person – but they needed our help. Later, Derek told me that he and his family had also stayed in their house, which was big like ours, and their neighbours also came in to find refuge. The rebels tried to burn down his house, but Derek, his dad and brother, along with some other guys from the neighbourhood, managed to put out the flames with buckets of water. From the outside it looked like it was totally burned out, but Derek and his family managed to stay hidden up on the top floor.

Meanwhile, in our house, we pushed all the furniture in the living room to the side to make room for everyone to sleep. I stayed on the second floor with my sister. Downstairs, people were cooking in the kitchen using food from our storerooms, which were well stocked. Nobody dared go outside, and we moved around inside really cautiously. We didn't want the rebels to see even one shadow of a person; we wanted them to think the house was empty. We would crawl down the stairs between the floors, which are on the outside of the house, so we couldn't be seen. We would only talk in hushed whispers; we were so, so quiet. My grandfather's apartment behind our house was also full of neighbours on the run. Baimba was the loudest person on the planet and we were scared that he would shout over to us, but even he was super quiet. I saw mothers almost suffocating their babies to stop them from crying out.

We didn't have time to think about how frightened we were. We were just trying to get through each day without being discovered by the rebels. Outside, houses were burning and dogs were eating the dead bodies. If a body had been there for a few days, you could see it just burst open, all decaying flesh and pus.

I can still see, feel and smell every minute of those weeks in which we desperately tried to hide. I witnessed everything through my senses, which were on alert all the time. The stench, the overwhelming odour of the rotting bodies, was too much, and I lost my sense of smell – a sort of defence mechanism, I suppose – and to this day I have never regained it. This went on for a couple of weeks, all of us hiding together . . . and then it happened.

★

It was around eleven in the morning and I remember it was a very calm day, almost serene outside, eerily quiet. But we knew things were becoming very intense for the rebels; the government had been pushing and pushing, trying to force them out of Freetown, and as the pressure on them increased they were getting more and more violent.

At first there was just one rebel. We heard him say, 'Why is this house standing here? Who is in this house?' Most of the houses around us had been burned to the ground but our house hadn't been touched, not even with bullets. I always wondered why our house hadn't been targeted before. In my childish mind, it was as if my dad's creation was invincible somehow, as if it had a magic force field around it, protecting us. Now I like to think God was watching over us.

And then other people – other rebels – started talking in Krio, saying, 'What is going on in there?' They were getting more and more agitated, louder and more heated. Then they started hitting the door, trying to break it down. We were all lying flat on the floor at this point. My father always told us to stay down in case stray bullets somehow came through; it was just basic survival skills. So we all stayed flat, trying not to breathe, hoping the rebels would think the place was empty. But then we heard a rebel say, 'Okay, if nobody comes out, we're going to throw fire in. We'll burn the house down.'

We had no choice but to do what they said. I think the rebels were really shocked by the sheer number of people streaming out through the front door. Everyone instinctively ran off in different directions. Some were trying to jump the fence, but when the rebels saw that, they just shot them and soon the ground was littered with dead bodies.

I remember a few of us ran to the back of the house, thinking we could jump over the back wall. I was with my dad, holding onto his hand, which was shaking because he had Parkinson's disease, something he had suffered from for a while. We squeezed around the side of the house and made it to the back wall, and then some big strong guys reached out to help Papa, saying, 'We've got him.' They were going to lift him over the wall. The wall was high, maybe seven feet or more, but there was a concrete ledge above the water taps my father had installed so that local people who had no water could come and fill their buckets from our supply. When we stood on this ledge, we could see over the top of the wall, and we saw there were people rushing out of the house behind us; they must have been hiding just like us.

As we watched, one of the rebels began to shoot. He looked to be in his late thirties, slim, medium height, with dreadlocks and very, very dark skin. His eyes were red and he seemed unhinged, probably from all the drugs he was taking. I later came to know this man as Coal Boot – they all had strange gangster-style nicknames – and I would find out just how vicious he could be. On that morning, he shot our neighbours right in front of us. About ten people fell to the ground dead, just like that. I couldn't believe what I was seeing.

We ducked down and I closed my eyes and started to pray. But I could hear that the people from the house behind were still running out and then I heard rapid gunfire. Coal Boot had sprayed them with his machine gun. I started to pull myself up the wall to escape and caught a glimpse of piles of bodies writhing on the ground – among them our friends and neighbours, people we knew. I will never be able to erase that sight from my head.

I had to drop down behind the wall again; it was too dangerous. Then, as we crouched trembling behind the wall, Coal Boot walked away to the front of the house. This was our chance! We climbed to the top of the wall and jumped. We landed on the dead bodies on the other side and had to clamber on top of them.

My dad then ran in the opposite direction to me, around to our front gate. My brother Alieu and I and some others who were with us scattered in different directions. But there was no escaping; there were too many rebels. They rounded us up at gunpoint and herded us onto the open land next to our house. It was there I met up with Papa again.

The rebels next decided to burn our house down. On the ground-floor verandah, one of them poured petrol on my dad's brown leather chair, the one he always sat in and which everyone knew him for, and lit a match. As he held the flame over it I thought, 'This is it, our house is gone.' But then – more out of curiosity than any sense of compassion, I think – one of the rebels asked, 'Whose house is this?'

The reply came: 'It's Pa Conteh's house.'

Another rebel said, 'Oh, he's a nice man, he's a good person, he's the one who had the hotel with the refugees staying there.' And so, they put out the fire and they didn't burn our house. But they didn't ask, 'Where is Pa Conteh?' By this time I was holding my dad's hand tight, saying nothing, hoping they wouldn't notice us.

And then the rebels started picking girls. There were more than 50 rebels and the behaviour of each was completely unpredictable. The very young ones would just shoot randomly; older ones could be very cruel; and then there were those who wanted girls to join them. And all the time they were looking for more potential soldiers to recruit – fit young men mostly. I was terrified; a million scenarios were running through my head. Would they burn my whole family? Would they start hacking at us with machetes? Or was this the moment every girl in that field on that day was terrified of: was this when I would be taken?

The rebels were walking through the crowd with their guns and their machetes, looking for young girls who had never slept with a man before. They wanted light-skinned virgins. It was a warped superstitious thing for them; they believed it would bring them luck and increase their powers, so they could fight better. Knowing this, girls would put soot in their hair and on their faces so they looked older and they would wear baggy clothes that cloaked their bodies. No one wanted to stand out, no one wanted to look attractive.

My sister Tigidankay's fiancé, a man called Alhaji, was there when the rebels came and saw me with Pa Conteh in the field. He didn't know that Tkay had actually crept under the house and was hiding in the place where we used to keep firewood. She couldn't see us at all. Alhaji assumed Tkay was taken with the rest of the girls. I found out later that when they finally found her she was dressed like a grandmother with her head covered. Tigidankay was very attractive and would definitely have been chosen by the rebels, so she was smart to cover herself up. She told me that when the rebels pulled her out from under the house she said to them, 'I have a child – let me go and get her and then I'll come back with you.' Incredibly, they believed her and agreed to her request, and that's how she managed to escape. But her fiancé was with my brother Alieu, watching what was happening to me.

I was wearing cargo pants and a t-shirt. Like all the girls, I wanted to look like a boy so the rebels wouldn't notice me, but their attack had been so swift and unexpected that I didn't have time to prepare properly and make myself look older, and my hair was braided because that's how we wore it to school. This gave me away as a young innocent schoolgirl.

Back when the war was raging in the countryside, and it seemed unthinkable that the rebels would make it to Freetown, my friends used to joke: 'If the rebels come for us, you'll be the first one they'll choose.' When I asked why, they'd reply, 'Oh, because you're beautiful.' I didn't understand what they were talking about, because there were girls at school who were really stunning. And in any case, Papa had always taught me that beauty was something inside you. How could the rebels see that?

But as soon as I locked eyes with Daramy, I knew he was going to take me. Daramy was in his late twenties, very small and skinny, almost fragile. Like Coal Boot, his eyes were blood red from smoking. In some ways, he looked like a weakling, but of course he had a gun, which he loved to use. He smelled bad, too – all the rebels did. They never washed and so they had a strong smell of body odour, dirt, blood, urine and you could smell smoke on them. Even the young ones looked really dangerous.

Daramy stared straight at me and said, 'You! Come here!' He looked bewitched; the flame of his horrendous obsession with me had been lit.

At that moment, a woman spoke from the crowd. She had been one of those hiding in our house and was Daramy's mother-in-law. She said, 'Daramy, she's the daughter of the man who has been protecting us. Don't take her.'

Daramy replied: 'I will take her and protect her and bring her back safe. If I don't take her, someone else will and he will hurt her.'

Without a word, I let go of my dad's hand and walked towards Daramy. It was like my body told me that this was what I had to do. I was in a trance. I didn't look back because I didn't want to see my dad's face; that would have been too much. We both would have broken down and caused a scene, and I didn't want anything to happen to Papa. All my life he had nurtured and protected me, but for the first time in his life he was unable to. Instead, I had to protect him by handing myself to the rebels without a fuss. I had heard stories from friends about girls being raped by the rebels in front of their fathers. In some cases, they had forced the dad to rape his daughter and, if he refused, they would make the daughter kill him. This was all rushing around my head. I knew if they tried this with Papa it would literally stop his heart.

What surprises me most about that scene to this day is that Papa was totally silent as I dropped his hand and walked towards the rebels. He didn't scream, he didn't cry, he didn't make a sound. I was told afterwards that the neighbours held him back. Walking away from my father is the most painful memory from my kidnapping.

Daramy nodded his head towards the group of captives he had chosen, telling me to join them. In that group was a girl I had been at primary school with. I knew her by sight, but I didn't know her name, though later Frances and I would become very close.

I was numb, gripped with terror as I watched the other rebels choosing their girls and also some strong boys to carry the supplies they had stolen from the houses – food, clothes, ammunition. Some of the rebels also picked young children. I knew that this was to groom them into fighters. I'd heard rumours about this and now it was happening right in front of me. They would send the children to camps where they brainwashed them and transformed them into killing machines. These kids made the most terrifying soldiers because they didn't know what they were doing. You would hear them screaming or making noises as if they were rough gangsters. If you messed with them they would say, 'What are you looking at?' and then they would shoot you just like that.

Then there were the children whose parents had just been shot, their bodies lying in the nearby fields and outside the burnt-out houses. These little ones were in shock, deeply traumatised, and a lot of them just followed the rebels, not knowing where else they should go. Like lambs to the slaughter. It was heartbreaking.

After another ten minutes or so, the rebels took charge of their groups and started urging us up the hill away from my yellow house. We kept loosely in our groups, although you couldn't see where one group ended and another began. Certain rebels who were friends stuck together. In Daramy's group there were about fifteen or twenty rebels, each of whom had five or more girls, plus some wives. Then there were maybe ten child soldiers and also some children who were the sons, daughters and babies of the girls in the group. The size of each rebel group varied, but all together we numbered several hundred as we climbed the hill. Sierra Leone means 'mountain lion'; in Kissy we are surrounded by mountains, beautiful mountains, but suddenly they didn't seem so magnificent anymore. My heart was jumping with fear. I knew I had no choice but to stay with the group; if you tried to do anything else, to run away, to sneak off, to fight back, they would just shoot you. If a boy they had chosen to carry their supplies faltered at all, they just shot him and picked someone else to take the load. So I knew that I mustn't hesitate to obey their orders if I was to survive this.

I later found out that Derek had seen us walking past his house. He was on the rooftop. He said it was the worst sight in his life. He couldn't do anything, they all had guns, but he couldn't bear to just let me go. He told his dad he was going after me, and he headed out onto the street. He tried to follow us as we walked up into the hills, but it proved too dangerous. Daramy had me and he wasn't going to let me go.

★

While I write this today, I am racking my brains, forcing myself to go back to that moment, to recall what I was thinking, what was going through my head. Was I thinking about Papa, about Derek, about my siblings? But I have locked it away for so long, not wanting to relive that terrible day, that now I simply can't remember – my mind has blanked it out. From the moment I was taken I lost all sense of time. Hours, days, weeks, months went by, and I had no idea where I was. All I could do was stay in the present.

I know there were helicopters flying around as the rebels urged us up the hill; this was the government soldiers and the ECOMOG forces. They were determined to stop the rebels, to push them back out of Freetown, but now we were in the way. The rebels regularly used us as human shields in the coming months. They didn't care that we were girls and children; death and killing had become a way of life and they cared only about staying alive themselves. I don't think they even knew what they were fighting for anymore. They were out of their heads on drugs a lot of the time and had lost all reason or sense of humanity. This whole war had taken on a life of its own and now we were caught in its net.

When the soldiers in the helicopters saw people, they would drop bombs – or, if they were low enough, they would shoot at us. Knowing this, the rebels were moving really quickly, almost running, and pushing us to move faster up the hill to reach the jungle, where we wouldn't be seen. If a bomb dropped nearby, they would shout, 'Duck!', and we would immediately crouch down until they told us to stand again. When we got back up again we would zigzag a little to dodge further bombs as we ran deeper into the jungle.

If you tried to run off, you were shot. If you didn't move fast enough, you were shot. This was happening all around me, bodies falling. Sometimes I had to step over them. Every so often I would recognise someone: a neighbour, a school friend, the daughter or son of someone at the mosque or a friend of Papa's. But I couldn't stop. I just had to forge on or it would be me lying bleeding on the ground. The sight of dead bodies became normal but it always terrified me. I don't think you can ever get used to the sight of human life cut down indiscriminately.

As we were scrambling up the hill, we met another group. The rebels in charge of that group knew Daramy really well, and he left us for a few minutes to talk to them. When he came back, he had Fatmatta with him. I think he just liked the look of her. I knew Fatmatta vaguely because the girls from her school and mine had socialised together. We hadn't been friends back then – I was eighteen when I was kidnapped, Frances was a little younger than me and Fatmatta was only fourteen – but Fatmatta and Frances became my rocks during my captivity. We three kept together as much as we could, trying to support each other over the next few months. I couldn't have got through it without these girls, and even though we live in different countries now, we are close friends and I think we always will be. We share a unique bond of suffering; only we three understand exactly what we went through.

I later found out that Fatmatta had been taken two days before me. Her family lived in a big house in my neighbourhood and, like us, had opened up their house to families fleeing the rebels. They had a large basement and lots of people she'd never met before were hiding there, including a number of young girls. When the rebels came, they took her and a few other children away and held them up the road. Her parents were praying for her release and miraculously, after an hour or so, Fatmatta and the others were all let go. She ran back to the house and thought that was it, that God was watching over them and they had been the lucky ones who were spared.

But the next morning, the rebels came back, and this time they set the house on fire, forcing everyone to come out. When the rebels saw them all running for their lives, they said, 'Look, they have all these pretty girls in this house. It's a good thing that we set fire to the house or we would have missed them.' Fatmatta says she will never forget the feeling of dread that washed through her body.

★

We carried on walking for several hours. Sometimes we had to stop and go into hiding in the bush because we could hear a government truck coming or a helicopter overhead. We would stay there for a while, until it went quiet and we knew that our pursuers had gone, then the rebels would make us continue up the hill.

My mind kept on darting back to the yellow house and Papa. Was he safe? What was happening to the family I'd left behind?

I learned later that after the rebels abducted us, the people who remained in the field took my distraught, trembling father to the mosque. Many sought refuge in the mosques and churches during the war, hoping that the sanctity of these holy places would give them protection. But when my father and our neighbours entered the mosque, they discovered that everybody inside had been killed. The floor was covered with bodies, some still taking their last breath.

As for Baimba, my grandfather, he was trapped in his apartment at the back of our house. He was 107 years old, unable to walk, and as hard as they tried, it just wasn't possible for the people who'd sought shelter with him to lift him out. I think it was a couple of days after I was captured that I heard that he was dead. The rebels had little portable radios with them all the time; it was their only way to track where the government soldiers were and find out what was happening. We used to listen to the radio to hear who had died. Every day a roll call of names would be read out, and it was always a really tense moment. I was not surprised when I heard Baimba's name, but I was still devastated. I had been very close to my grandfather and I used to believe that I would be with him when he died. I remember him telling me all the time, 'Before I die, I want to leave you with something.' I didn't know what it was he wanted to leave me with, and now I never will.

I presumed he must have been shot when the rebels stormed our house, and that was the image I kept in my mind during the months of my captivity. But a few years ago, when I visited them in London, my sisters – the twins, Mabinty and Fatmata – told me the truth about what happened to Baimba. They hadn't been keeping it from me deliberately; they thought I already knew.

I still can't think about it without sobbing. It was so horrific. The rebels cut off all his toes and left him in the house to bleed to death. But he didn't die immediately. He was left there suffering in agony. Eventually, when people came into the house and found him, he was still bleeding. Baimba asked them to wash him and bind his feet.

They washed him, he prayed, and then he died.

I'm glad I didn't know how my Baimba died when I was in captivity. It would have destroyed me.

CHAPTER SIX

Daramy's obsession

It was evening but still light when we reached the place where we would stay that first night. It is a night I have tried to forget; it haunts me, and even though I long to be rid of it I don't think it will ever leave me.

We reached a group of houses on the far outskirts of Kissy. This was a poor suburban area up in the hills where families who couldn't afford to live closer in or preferred to be out of the city had built their houses. They were surrounded by tall trees because the town planners hadn't yet reached this area to clear the land. The houses were very basic, made of corrugated iron with cold, hard concrete floors. The people who lived there had fled, leaving their few possessions still in their homes. Daramy picked one and ordered Frances, Fatmatta and me to go inside.

We huddled close to each other on the floor, trembling, too terrified to speak or cry. We were all in such shock. We hadn't had anything to eat, our legs and arms were battered and scratched from running through the bush, and we were terrified because we suspected what was coming next. We had all heard what happened to girls who were kidnapped, and now we were those girls.

Although we hadn't properly met before, Frances and Fatmatta both knew me as 'Mommy', because this was what my sister and my family called me at home. The story goes that when was I born and I was brought home from the hospital, they said to Tkay, 'This is your sister Aminata,' and Tkay said, 'Mommy,' because Aminata was also her mum's name. The name stuck, and everybody called me Mommy from then on. (In Sierra Leone we don't call our parents 'Mum' or 'Dad'; we say 'Mama' or 'Papa'. So it wasn't confusing to us; it was just a cute name.) Frances and Fatmatta called me Mommy the whole time we were kept captive and sometimes today they use that name as well; it's like a link to our childhood and to our closeness throughout the ordeal that followed.

As we were whispering, it started to get dark. There was no electricity and it was pitch-black. At night there was never any light, because the rebels didn't want the government soldiers to spot us. So even when we found candles in some of the houses, we weren't allowed to light them. The rebels had torches that they used but just a flash here and there. They were very careful.

We sat in the farthest corner of the room, trying to hide in the shadows and make ourselves invisible. We were all shaking uncontrollably, still raw with the horror of being ripped from our families. My mind couldn't take in what was happening; there was so much confusion, with one thousand conflicting things going on. My senses were barraged: the smell of choking smoke, the odour of stinking bodies – alive and dead – and the noise of people screaming, gunfire right outside the door, bombs in the distance and above all this the rebels laughing and talking. I could sense that people were being hurt out there and feared they would be coming for us next.

Then Daramy appeared at the doorway and pointed at Fatmatta. I could only hope that the ECOMOG soldiers would attack right now – surely some of the bullets I could hear flying through the air outside were theirs. But they didn't reach us; our fate was sealed.

'You come here,' he said, pointing at Fatmatta with his gun.

She had no choice. Trembling violently, she followed him into the room. After a while, I could hear Fatmatta crying.

Outside, the other rebels were getting rowdy. They were high on drugs and drinking, smashing beer bottles on the ground as the alcohol took its hold. There was a big group of them making a lot of noise, having a party, shooting bullets into the air. They knew what was going on; I soon found out this was what happened every night.

I also knew what was going on: that Fatmatta, at just fourteen years old, was being raped by Daramy. Frances and I said nothing to each other. What was there to say?

Afterwards, Fatmatta came back to the living room and sat down on the floor with us. She was silent and shaking, tears rolling down her face.

And then it was my turn. Daramy called for me and quivering I walked towards the bedroom. The room was full of guns; they were everywhere, piled on the floor, propped up against the walls. Without these weapons, Daramy would have been nothing, just a pathetic scrawny man who smoked too much marijuana. But the guns, one of which was always slung over his shoulder, gave him power – that and his obscene cruelty.

He looked straight at me and as he walked towards me he told me to take off my clothes – I was still wearing the cargo pants and t-shirt that I'd had on that morning, and my hair was still braided. He was dripping with sweat and smelled really bad. I don't think he'd washed or had a shower for weeks. He was bare-chested and his pants were loosely belted. He had obviously just pulled up his pants after raping Fatmatta. He unbuckled his belt, forced me down onto the bed and raped me.

I had never been with a man before and at first I fainted with the pain. I was terrified. I drifted in and out of consciousness and I could sense that there were more and more different men on top of me, at least five or six who had come in from outside. After Daramy, they took turns, one after the other. This went on for a couple of hours.

When I woke up there was blood all over my legs and searing pain pulsed through my body. Daramy had left me alone and gone outside to be with his friends. I could hear them all out there talking, but I couldn't move, barely conscious, my head spinning. I hadn't eaten anything all day and my body was covered in bruises and bleeding. My rapists had been very rough, and as well as the bruises I realised I had a big bump on my head and a black eye. I had struggled against them as they pinned me down and they had hit me to stop me fighting back. I think they must have used the butt of a gun against my temple.

For a long while I just lay there on the bed. I tried to get up a couple of times, but my legs were very heavy and I couldn't lift them. Eventually I managed to stand up. I found a bucket of water in the corner of the room and tried to clean myself as best I could with a rag from the floor. I found a piece of cloth to cover myself up. I tied it around my body and pulled my pants back on.

I can't remember if I cried, but I do recall an utter emptiness.

Finally, in a daze, I made my way back into the living room to Fatmatta and Frances. It was quiet now. We didn't talk about what had happened; we just sat there in the dark until the early hours of the morning, when the rebels came in to tell us it was time to move again. My legs felt so heavy I could barely walk, but I knew I had to make them work or they would kill me. The men gathered up all the guns and we set off into the hills. Daramy insisted that I stay close to him. He wouldn't let me out of his sight. After that night, his obsession with me escalated, and became uncontrollable.

Less than 24 hours earlier I had been with Papa, holding his hand. He had protected me since I was born, but the cage he had built around us had been prised open in the cruellest of ways. That life was gone. My body belonged to Daramy now, but I already knew I would never surrender my soul.

Looking back, there was one positive: Daramy's infatuation with me meant that he didn't touch Frances after he raped me. In fact, he never touched Frances, and after that first night he didn't touch Fatmatta again either. After just one night, I had become his everything.

★

It was early the next morning – before the sun had properly come up, with the rebels, still high on the previous night's drugs, getting ready to move on – when I noticed two young men a little separated from the other rebels and realised that one was my brother, Alieu, and the other was Tkay's fiancé Alhaji. Having witnessed my abduction, Alieu had been discreetly following our group. When I saw him, relief swamped me. He waved at me but we both knew we had to keep our greetings to a minimum. I was excited and told Frances and Fatmatta: 'Look, my brother is with us!' Alhaji, not realising Tkay had managed to escape, had followed me thinking that he would see my sister. The two of them ran fast, hiding along the route, and didn't try to make contact with me initially. They didn't want to alert the rebels and were hoping they could help me escape with them.

But later, when it was clear that I belonged to Daramy, I think they realised that the best thing they could do for me was to stay close. Alieu especially was determined not to leave me. He didn't care that his own life was in danger. It was very brave, and when I saw him out of the corner of my eye, I felt a glimmer of hope knowing he was watching my back even though he couldn't help me directly.

When I saw my brother I could tell that he knew that I'd been raped because of the condition I was in. I was dirty, covered in bruises and broken. Alieu and I had always had a special connection. I was his baby sister, and when I was a little girl he had this premonition: he would always say to me that I was going to do something special, something to make our family proud. His role, he said, was to look after me. If a friend of his looked at me in *that* kind of way, disrespecting me, for Alieu the friendship was finished. He was even more protective than my dad.

I decided to introduce Alieu and Alhaji to Daramy immediately; I knew if I didn't they would likely be shot. And once Daramy knew they were related to me, he let them stay and protected them from being forcibly recruited as soldiers. Most of the time when you had young men like that within the group, they were supposed to fight with the rebels or they would be killed. But because Daramy was so fixated on me, he accepted my relatives as part of our group – he thought it would please me. That's why he kept Fatmatta and Frances with me – because he thought they were my sisters or related in some way. Daramy thought that taking in my relatives was a way to prove that he loved me. He really believed that what he felt for me was true love.

But the abuse didn't stop. Every time we stayed overnight somewhere, Daramy would rape me.

Daramy had a wife and son but I didn't know this then. He had sent them ahead with another group of rebels and they were camping further up in the hills. We joined them a couple of days after that first night. I knew she was his wife from the minute we met. She was relieved to see her husband alive and she quickly took control. Also their son, who was about eight years old, was the spitting image of Daramy. But I could see there was a problem. She sensed his obsession with me immediately. She could tell that he wanted me in a way that he didn't want the other girls. I soon realised that she felt deserted as his attention focused totally on me now, but she was also scared of Daramy, so couldn't do anything to harm me.

As the days went on I regularly overheard them arguing about me. It wasn't jealousy as such, more a fear on her part that she might be abandoned. I went out of my way to reassure her that I didn't want his attention, in the hope that she would not hurt me. She believed me, and could see I was not her rival at all, but she was frustrated that her husband couldn't see that I was never going to reciprocate his feelings.

I think they were married before the war and no doubt this was very far from the life she had expected to have with Daramy, who was in the army back then. It was very difficult because every day I had to let her know that I did not want this man – I loathed and abhorred him – but I had to avoid upsetting Daramy at the same time. When the rebels chose you, it wasn't just to have sex with you and then leave or kill you; they intended you to stay with them. Most of the rebels' wives started as women they'd abducted. Many had been with the rebels for years now. At first they were too scared to run away because they knew they would be killed if they were caught, and then they just got used to their new existence. They barely knew who they were anymore. They had lost their own families and now they were having babies by the men who had kidnapped and raped them. Even though Daramy's wife terrified me, I also prayed for her. She was just like us, doing what she had to do to survive.

★

After a few weeks, life began to assume a pattern. The rebels would occupy another empty house in a village they had occupied in the hills and then they would go off to fight, usually back towards the city. Sometimes they'd be gone for four or five days at a time. We didn't dare run away because we knew we wouldn't get very far. We were surrounded by soldiers, either other rebel groups or government soldiers. ECOMOG forces would assume we were with the rebels and kill us. But at least when the rebels were away we weren't being used as sex slaves. The most freedom that I would ever experience then was when Daramy went to war. I longed for these times.

But soon he stopped doing even that. He wanted to stay with me and build a relationship. He thought I could be his wife, that I would return his love. He didn't understand the life that I came from, what kind of values I was raised with. As far as he was concerned, he was caring for me: I was still alive, and now he was the only one raping me. Other rebels' girls seemed to accept this grotesque parody of a relationship quickly and saved their lives in doing so, but I didn't want that to be my survival skill. I could not bring myself to change my attitude towards him. He was my abuser and I despised him.

He was still raping me and hurting me regularly, but he tried to win my love in other ways. Most of the captured girls were barely fed, but Daramy would make sure we had food and when his wife cooked he'd tell her to give me a bigger serve than her own.

At this time, we were still constantly on the move, so when we stayed somewhere for a few days or weeks, it almost felt like home, like normal. In the towns the abandoned houses were more comfortable and had better facilities, so we could have a shower, and if there were shops around, the men – including Alieu and Alhaji – would break in and loot them, bringing supplies back to the women. We were always hopeful there would be a pharmacy that hadn't already been raided because, aside from paracetamol which we took as a painkiller, in Sierra Leone the pharmacies had biscuits, chocolate, lollies and dry food which we could carry and eat on the run for energy. The rebels told us to find and wear clothes that were black or brown or green to blend in with the trees. The government soldiers would shoot at anyone in bright colours, so it was for our own protection as well as the rebels'. We picked up clothes along the way from the houses we stayed in, the clothes people had left behind. Everything we ate, wore and cooked with was stolen. Mostly the rebels foraged for food, alcohol and medication that we would carry with us when we were travelling. In addition to rice and vegetables from the towns, the rebels would also catch animals like goats or sheep or a cow to kill so that we could eat.

When we were in the hills, Frances and Fatmatta and I would always go to the toilet together for safety. We had this funny thing we would do; it seems silly now, but it meant so much to us then. We would go into the bush and, because Fatmatta's dad lived in America and some of my family and Frances' family lived in the UK, while we were squatting down we would look up to the stars, thinking that somehow we could communicate with our families by a sort of satellite and tell them to come and save us. Then we would take a leaf and use it to wipe ourselves. That's a powerful memory I still have.

Every day I thought this could be the day I was killed. But I didn't think so much about death itself. It was just a fact, something that would happen. I knew I would be killed.

People were dying all around us and seeing dead bodies covered in flies became normal.

I remember there was a moment when that feeling was very intense. We were in a place that was almost like a desert. It was a beautiful setting, on a hill, with red dust. I remember helicopters coming, almost skimming the ground they flew so low, the chopper blades were whipping up the dirt and they were shooting at us. I remember a dead body fell on top of me and I stayed lying underneath it, pretending I was dead.

You know how in the movies a powerful honourable soldier, one of the good guys, drops down from the helicopter on a rope and scoops you up? That doesn't happen in reality. No one was interested in saving us; all the government forces wanted was to push the rebels away from the city, back towards the Liberian border where all this had started. The rebels, meanwhile, were putting us women out in front as human shields, so the government troops wouldn't shoot. If the soldiers saw lots of civilians gathered together their helicopters would turn around and fly away again, which was exactly what the rebels wanted. But it didn't always work, because lots of the longer-term abducted women also carried guns. The rebels gave them guns so that when they were running through the hills the soldiers would think they were rebel fighters and wouldn't try to rescue them. Possession of a gun was the only way to tell between a rebel and a civilian.

Daramy didn't give us guns, but one day Frances and I saw Fatmatta holding one and we were very scared. She had become friends with a rebel, and he had given her his weapon. I think she was looking for someone to protect her. Some girls changed when they were captured, and we hoped

Fatmatta hadn't changed. The rebels would start giving girls marijuana and try to get them to behave like them. They would brainwash these girls so that they would do things or witness things that changed them forever, their moral compass spinning out of control, so they could never go back to their normal lives. It happened a lot.

Perhaps for Fatmatta this was just a way to make a connection across the void between us and them. After all, the rebels were once our people – our neighbours, our friends. And now, after pushing for so long, most of them didn't seem to know what they were fighting for anymore. They were tired and lost. We were tired and scared. To our great relief, Fatmatta put the gun down. She was still with us.

Trapped together in this nightmare, Frances, Fatmatta and I became really close, so much so that other rebels thought we really were related. We would do everything together: cry together, pray together. Prayer became incredibly important to us. We were all Christians and had these tiny Bibles that we carried with us. Mine was a little blue pocket Jehovah's Witness Bible that I found in the house where we'd stayed on our first night of captivity. Through the worst times it was often our faith that kept us going, because without God there was nothing else for us to hold on to. We would come together whenever we could and pray, sing and hope – hope that one day we would not be in this bondage, one day we would be released and God would see us through. I think every prayer was a conversation for us; we just wanted God to know that we were there.

Naturally I asked, 'Why, why is this happening to me?' all the time, but when you met people around you and realised you were not the only person who had been kidnapped – that you were one of thousands – it brought a perspective that was impossible to ignore. This was so much bigger than my suffering. In my weakest moments I would think, 'Why, why, why me?' But then bombs would go off, or shelling would start, or I would hear shots fired and see people, ordinary people who had done nothing wrong, dead on the ground. Then I was left with, 'Why them?' Death was so arbitrary and instant. There was nothing we could do but pray.

The rebels prayed too. The ones that were Muslim prayed. The ones that were Christian prayed. That was the problem with Daramy: he believed that I was a gift from God, given to him so he could win the war.

I used to pray for my family. I didn't know if they had been killed. I used to pray most of all for Papa and for a miracle that would bring us back together.

Sometimes I prayed that I could just disappear.

I don't think anybody's faith can stand and not waver. That is impossible. During my captivity there were many, many times that I didn't even think about my grandparents or Papa or any love that I had in me; I just wanted to die. But the human spirit is an incredible thing, and just when I was sure I wanted my life to end, so this nightmare would be over, there would be bombs and shooting and I would be running for my life, fighting to stay alive. That's the irony. I really believe that we all have the same survival drive; I don't think I'm special in that. When somebody kidnaps you, takes away your freedom, your first instinct is to wonder: How do I get out of this? When you come face to face with death, no one surrenders.

CHAPTER SEVEN

My darkest days

As time went on, my desperation grew more extreme and I even tried to escape a few times, although I never got very far. After a while, it may have been a month or two or more – I spent so long trapped in abandoned houses, running through the night and collapsing exhausted that I had no idea of the passage of time – we settled into a barracks. This was a proper government army barracks that had been abandoned by the government soldiers and the rebels had now fully occupied the place. It was big and there were lots of us in the barracks' buildings and others in the surrounding houses. It was like we had our own compound. I'm not sure exactly where this was. We had been on the run for some time and all I can say for certain is that it was a long way from Freetown. I don't even know if we were near a town because we never left the barracks. I do recall that there was bushland around with lots of trees and wild vegetation. At that time there was a break in the fighting so Daramy was around much more.

Daramy was at the height of his obsession by now. Fatmatta and Frances had their own rooms, as did Alieu and Alhaji, but I didn't; I had to share with Daramy and he wouldn't leave me alone. He was forcing me to have sex with him all the time and all the time I would resist, squeezing my legs together, but the more I resisted the rougher he got with me, violent at times. Sometimes he would tie me up. I cried constantly until there were no more tears. I knew I was close to breaking.

One time when I was let out to go to the toilet I took the opportunity to escape. It was the first time I'd plucked up the courage to run away from Daramy, and stay away. When I left, I wasn't even aware of where I was going or what I was doing. All I knew was that I had to get away; my head was exploding. But I didn't tell anyone from the group that I was leaving, no one at all.

It was early afternoon and Daramy had gone out to find food, taking Alhaji and Alieu with him. Frances and Fatmatta had more freedom than me and on that day they were out, too, probably taking a walk. It was a very hot day I remember. The sun was punishing. My heart was beating so hard and I knew I was risking everything, but I couldn't stand it anymore, and if that meant I would be killed while running, so be it. Something had clicked; I had to get out.

I didn't go far, just to another building in the barracks compound about three blocks away. I had seen it from the kitchen at the back of the place we had occupied and had waved to some of the captured women there from the window. We were all in the same hell, at the mercy of the rebels. One lady there took me in. She was part of another group of rebels, the girlfriend or wife of one of the group's members. She was a little bit older than me, not much, and I had no clue if I could trust her. But when I explained to her why I was hiding, she said she knew of Daramy and his reputation for abuse, so she understood why I was running and let me stay.

I hid in that house for six days, not going out at all. I can't even remember if the woman gave me food – I don't think so. I was just hiding in a dark room, praying that Daramy wouldn't find me. I tried to stay alert, not knowing what would happen next, but couldn't help drifting in and out of sleep. There was a toilet nearby and I would sneak out at night to get to it, terrified that I would bump into Daramy. I was too scared to wash, even. I didn't want to draw any attention to myself.

I was right to be scared. Daramy was in a frenzy and was looking for me everywhere. He was crazy with anger. Meanwhile my friends were worried and looking for me also. But I didn't dare seek them out to tell them what I had done and where I was, because I knew if I told them anything they would be too relaxed, confident that I was safe, and Daramy would sense that. They told me later that they thought I had gone and killed myself. Daramy, realising that they were all really distressed, probably started to think this too.

I have to admit that when I was hiding in that room I did consider killing myself. I was just so exhausted, cowering in a dark corner all the time. My body felt numb. I had nothing left to live for.

And then I came face to face with Coal Boot. He was a friend of the rebel soldier who had abducted the woman who was sheltering me. I recognised him right away as the vicious leader who had shot all those people the day the rebels came to our house.

Coal Boot had heard that there was somebody hiding in his friend's house and he used to come into my room and make fun of me. 'Who are you hiding from?' he would tease. I suppose to him I looked a little ridiculous crouched in the corner. Somehow, I managed to laugh a little bit and he liked this. I remember him making a joke about how I must be a fortune teller or soothsayer because they're always in dark rooms. When he found out that my name was Aminata, he said to me, 'Oh, my wife's name is Aminata. You look like her.' His wife wasn't with him in the camp, so I think he felt that he should look after me because I had his wife's name. This was the sort of crazy logic adopted by the rebels. I was terrified of him.

In addition to this, a few times I heard Daramy's voice close to the building. He could walk in at any time, I feared. I pleaded with the lady who was hiding me to secretly pass a message to Frances. I just felt so alone and longed for my friend. Frances arrived and was overcome to see me alive. 'Your brother is in such a bad way,' she said. 'He's not eating at all and thinks you are dead. Everybody thinks you are dead.' They thought that if I hadn't killed myself, I must have been killed trying to escape. The rebels would shoot anyone they thought was running away.

I urged Frances to tell Alieu I was alive and that I was hiding nearby so he would start eating again and get better. She did this but, as I had feared, Daramy sensed that the attitude of my brother and friends had changed. He gathered them together and said, 'If you won't tell me anything, I'm going to kill you all. Tell Aminata I know she's alive and I'm going to kill her brother first if she doesn't come back.'

When Frances told me this I knew I had no choice. I had to go back. Coal Boot had said to me, 'I can protect you from Daramy. I'm senior to Daramy. He won't do anything to you. I can take you out of Daramy's hands.' I believed him because I knew he had more authority, but I also knew Daramy still had my brother and Fatmatta and Frances, who by now were like sisters to me. I knew Coal Boot wasn't interested in saving all of us and I was being pressured to go back quickly or my brother would be killed. So I went back to Daramy.

He was deranged with fury and determined that I would never escape again. He locked me in a room in the barracks for a very long time – more than two weeks. Sometimes he would tie me up and beat me. He said there was no way I was going out again. He didn't go to war anymore; he just hung around the compound, keeping me captive in his room. Every day he would come in and rape me again. He didn't think of it as rape, though. He said, 'Now you have to become like a wife.' As far as he was concerned, this was what a husband and wife did.

I didn't fight back. I just lay there, closed my eyes and took it, day after day. It was then that I started to get sick. At first I didn't know what it was exactly, but I knew a little bit about the sickness called sickle cell, a genetic blood disorder most commonly seen in people of African and Caribbean backgrounds. I knew people who had sickle cell and they said that their bones hurt. So I started pretending that I had sickle cell. I would put menthol drops in my eyes so they would look red and start streaming, and I would tell Daramy how ill I felt. Not only Daramy, but Frances, Fatmatta, everybody thought I had sickle cell. I reasoned that if Daramy believed I had sickle cell, he might stop having sex with me. And for a couple of days it worked. He was really worried, and I would just cry bitterly because of the menthol.

I was sick . . . but it wasn't sickle cell. I didn't recognise the signs at first because I didn't know what the signs were. I didn't know I was pregnant because growing up I never really had regular periods. Even now it's the same. I only suspected I might be pregnant when my pants started getting tighter. At this time I was eating hardly anything, but still I was putting on weight. I have no idea how far along I was. It could have been Daramy's baby or the baby of any of the other rebels who raped me. So many kidnapped women got pregnant and they just had to have the baby on the run. I never saw anyone in labour, but I did see these women with a growing number of kids.

It was around this time that I started to think more seriously than ever about suicide. I didn't really know that word or what it meant; I just knew I wanted to be gone. It came over me every time I was with Daramy because I knew he was going to force himself on me. People were dying around us all the time, so I thought I might as well die too. I started thinking about ways I could harm myself, both to miscarry the baby and to end my own life. When I was in school I'd heard that if you put aspirin in a fizzy drink, like Coca-Cola, you would miscarry. I didn't have cola but the one thing that I thought of (and I think I had seen this in a movie) was that I could pull a battery apart and put what was inside into a meal, as a sort of poison. We had batteries, so I tried that. Surprisingly there was no taste and nothing happened. I thought the battery acid would create some sort of reaction – that I would start frothing at the mouth or choking. It would have been an easy out for me, a quick solution I hoped. But it didn't work.

I also tried drinking bleach. This did have an effect: it made me sick and weak, though I couldn't keep it down long enough to kill me. I was throwing up for a long time and felt really, really terrible afterwards. But at least it made my sickle cell story believable.

It was probably the bleach that did it. I can't say for certain, but that was when I started bleeding a lot and I knew I must have miscarried the baby. I felt a slight sense of relief even though I was very unwell. The idea of bringing a baby into the world without even knowing who the father was – knowing that it might be the child of Daramy, whom I despised – was too much to bear.

My brother didn't know and Daramy never knew either; he believed the sickle cell story. But I think Frances knew. I later found out that Frances was pregnant herself. She had been pregnant when she was abducted and managed to hide it throughout our captivity. She gave birth after she was released.

Frances didn't mention my pregnancy but after my illness we talked more. Fatmatta had a companion – as I mentioned, she had become friendly with one of the rebels – but Frances didn't have anyone, so the two of us became really close. Frances knew how distraught I was because when Daramy was away – when the other rebels made him go back out and fight – I would cry, and then she and I would cry together.

★

Those weeks in the barracks were relatively calm and settled, giving us a chance to catch our breath. The rebels would send the youngest of the children to scout the district, wandering through the bush, looking for government troops. The rebels would then follow at a close distance behind observing what happened; this way it would be the children who would be shot first. One day the rebels knew we had to move on; the government soldiers were getting too close.

Suddenly it was on. We had to move fast, grabbing food, guns and ammunition, chased through the bush for days and weeks at a time. As we passed through villages we would search for more dark clothes that would camouflage us in the bush. At one point we found ourselves enveloped by swamps. In the past the rebels knew which areas had quicksand but now the government soldiers had taken over a lot of the ground and the rebels didn't seem to know where we were anymore. I only ever came across one patch of quicksand, but I'll never forget it. I had never seen this before. I didn't even know that such a thing existed in Sierra Leone. But then I saw those in front of me just going down and not coming back up. It was the worst thing I have ever seen: people drowning in front of you, screaming as they were sucked under. But survival instincts took over. As soon as anyone started sinking into the quicksand, the people they were with would let go of their hand and keep on running. There are a lot of things that happened that I have managed to push away, but that vision really has stayed with me and I still see it often.

After the day of the quicksand we settled in some clay houses in one of the rural villages. They were very basic with wooden windows and roofs made of straw or corrugated iron. There were no beds; people just slept on the floor. It was here that Coal Boot took me away from Daramy to live with him. I think Coal Boot saw that I was really sick and he knew that Daramy kept me locked up whenever he could. He told me he was going to protect me.

I didn't know what to believe but I prayed he meant it. And for the first couple of days, everything was fine. Daramy was angry – *really* angry – but he could not hurt my family and he could not hurt me, because he was terrified of Coal Boot, who had told him not to harm us. No one would ever cross Coal Boot; he was utterly vicious. He was one of those rebels who, for fun, would make somebody stand against a tree and then shoot at them until eventually they fell. I witnessed this on one occasion: a young man, shot repeatedly. We also knew that when Coal Boot raped a woman, he didn't keep her around afterwards like a lot of the rebels did – he would kill her.

There were so many stories about him around the camp, and I had seen what he had done to the neighbours who lived behind our house in Kissy when he mowed everyone down with a round from a machine gun. But for some reason – possibly because Daramy had become so repulsive – at that time I felt safe with him. He really made me believe he was going to look after me because his wife's name was Aminata and it was as if he was taking care of his wife. When he said,

'I can protect you from Daramy,' I knew he had that power. He didn't force me to go with him; he didn't say, 'You have to come with me,' but I just did. I felt some sense of security with him.

So I lived with Coal Boot in the hut he had taken for himself. There were various other rebels living there too. It was not far from where Daramy was staying, but even if he saw me – which he did a few times – he could not do anything. At Coal Boot's I was sleeping on my own in my own room. At last things were looking up, I thought.

But I was wrong. One day I sensed there was something different about the way Coal Boot was looking at me. I could sense his power and got really nervous around him. I knew so much of his story, I had seen what he could do, and when he looked at me, I thought, 'Oh, he's going to rape me and then he will kill me.' It was one of those times when I thought, 'Okay, I'm going to die.'

That night Coal Boot called me to his room and I remember thinking this was it. For the first time I saw lust in his eyes. I knew what was coming and that I wasn't coming out alive.

I was wearing faded black cut-off jeans and a loose black-and-white soccer shirt and he was fully dressed. The rebels wore hardly any clothes most of the time because it was so hot, but he had jeans and a shirt on. When he pushed me to the ground and lay on top of me, unzipping his trousers, I tried to resist. I squeezed my legs together tight, tensing all my muscles as hard as I could. That was when he took his pistol out of his belt. He forced my legs apart and he put the barrel of the gun inside me. I thought he was going to shoot me, right up through my vagina. My legs were shaking uncontrollably.

He didn't shoot me, but he did rape me. It took ten minutes. Afterwards he left.

I sat on the floor for a while, totally lost, unable to move. I must have fallen asleep eventually, because I woke up to find dawn was breaking. My first thought was to go and wash myself, but at the same time I was too scared to move, to leave the room. What if one of Coal Boot's friends saw me and tried to rape me again?

Then Coal Boot came back into the room and, looking at me on the ground, said: 'Why did you have to close your legs so tight? I did not mean to hurt you. You are so beautiful and all my friends like you too.'

I started to shake again and asked if I could leave the room to wash. He let me go to have a shower. I washed myself again and again. I wanted to wash his smelly sweat off me and I needed to wash him out of me, but he was already inside me. I called desperately to God, saying, 'This can't be my life. Why do I have to suffocate in this hell?' I picked up a piece of rock from the floor of the toilet and used that to rub at my skin, trying to erase every trace of him.

After showering I pulled on my clothes. I thought Coal Boot was going to kill me – this was what he was known for – but to my surprise he let me leave. I saw Frances outside and so I went back with her to the house where Daramy had put her, Fatmatta, Alieu and Alhaji. I didn't know what else to do. Daramy was installed with his wife and son in a house across the road, but he also had a room in Frances' house. He was furious. He knew what Coal Boot had done but he couldn't do anything to him, so instead he blamed me.

I remember crying and crying. I couldn't stop.

Frances was crying too and she said: 'Maybe we can try to kill Daramy and escape?'

If only. I knew it was impossible. They had all the power.

Rumours had been going around the camp the day before that they wanted to release some children to the government in exchange for food and medicine. I hadn't really been listening to the rumours; I was in a frozen state, numb. Barely there, barely alive. And in any case, it was just a whisper. To be honest, I didn't believe it, because nothing like that had ever happened before. But then it was as if something came to me from the heavens: this idea that I was going to escape. Today, I was going to be freed.

I remember saying to Frances: 'Have you heard that they're releasing some children?'

Frances said yes, she had heard that.

I said: 'I think I'm going to go with them'.

Frances, crying, said, 'I'm so sorry, Mommy. If anybody's going to go, it won't be you. Daramy is too obsessed with you. He will never let you go. Anyway, the exchange is just for children.'

She was really sad about it because she thought I was deluding myself. I said it with confidence, but I didn't actually believe I would be released.

Daramy heard us talking and called me into his room. He had this crazed look on his face and he shouted at me: 'You're only running away because you have feet to run on.' As far as he was concerned, I had already run away twice:

first in the barracks and then to Coal Boot. All of a sudden, he pulled out his gun and fired seven shots right at my feet. I closed my eyes, screaming in terror. When I opened them I could not believe I was still standing and my feet were still there. He just intended to scare me, I think, but I honestly thought he was going to break my feet.

He fired some more shots but then, as abruptly as he had started, he stopped. He was boiling over he was so mad and he turned and walked away, consumed by his own rage. He went into the bush to blow off his anger. Before he left he ordered, 'Go to my house and don't come out.'

I knew I had to go. I was limping across the road to Daramy's house, crying, when I saw about fifteen or so children with Coal Boot. I stood under a tree watching the kids, tears running down my face.

The rumour was true. It was happening. Coal Boot was choosing the kids for the exchange. He had organised for the other rebels to gather children whose parents or families had been killed and who had followed the rebels. The children released were not to be soldiers; that was part of the deal. They were all young – eight, ten, twelve.

Coal Boot saw me watching and he said: 'Hey, you – come here.'

I walked towards him, wondering if this was when he was going to kill me. But instead he looked at me and said: 'Do you want to go with the children?'

I just nodded my head.

He said, 'Okay, go.'

He couldn't look me in the eye. There was a sense of remorse in this savage man. This was so unexpected, so unlikely coming from him. Clearly I wasn't meant to be included. I was not a small child. But I saw a moment of humanity in him. Perhaps letting me go was his way of saying sorry. Or perhaps it was all a ruse to shoot me as I walked away. I had no way of knowing, but I had to take the chance. So without a word I followed the children.

I never saw Daramy or Coal Boot again.

CHAPTER EIGHT

Don't look back

I don't know what day it was but it wasn't a church day, so it must have been a weekday, and I thought it was right at the end of March, although Frances has since told me it was more like April. It had been cloudy that morning but now it was full sun: a typical Sierra Leone day, the air hot and dry blowing in from the Sahara. But it felt unreal; it still feels unreal today as I write this.

That moment changed my life. Within twenty minutes I was heading out of the camp with some of the rebels and children, on our way to the exchange point. It was afternoon by now, and I felt as if my mind and my body were separate somehow, my legs moving but my head not able to comprehend. It had all happened so suddenly, which was lucky, because I knew if Daramy had been there he would have tried to pull me back. But he didn't even know I had gone.

We started walking along an unmade road, dust blowing in the hot breeze. Along the route were clay houses, peoples' homes, now empty. After a while we joined another group at a second location. This was a house where more children were waiting to join us. Nobody really knew what was going to happen, but we all hoped it would be our way out of this nightmare. Now a new rebel leader was in charge, one I hadn't seen before. His nickname was 05, which everyone pronounced as 'Oh Five'. They loved these tough-guy tags, the rebels – as if changing their names could change who they were, from boy to gangster; or perhaps it was more than that: the crass names excusing what they were doing.

05 was even more important than Coal Boot. He was more highly educated and he was the one who had organised the exchange with the government. By this time, I would learn later, the RUF was flagging. They had only managed to hold on to Freetown for a few weeks, and by February 1999 the government and international forces had pushed them back into the hills. They were running out of ammunition and arms, they were tired and hungry, and their leader, Foday Sankoh, was under house arrest. He had actually been sentenced to death in 1998 but received amnesty in return for a peace treaty which was still being negotiated. I think this exchange paved the way for the peace accord which came in July 1999. But the rebels didn't stand by that accord and the war limped on for another couple of years.

But while the government saw the exchange as symbolic of a march towards a ceasefire, for the rebels it was about refuelling with desperately needed food and supplies. I think 05 must have been negotiating this exchange behind the scenes for a little while, and there was very little trust between the government and this arrogant rebel chief. ECOMOG insisted the hostages in the exchange had to be children; they didn't want to take adults in case they were really rebels trying to get behind enemy lines.

05 had decided that I would be the one to hand over their letter of demands, which the rebels wanted read on television. For the RUF this was a major part of the deal and really important. In the letter they stated that they would grant peace in return for their freedom. The rebels were tired of fighting; they hoped to negotiate an end to the war that wouldn't end up with them being imprisoned. This letter was the rebels' opportunity to put their case to the nation.

Meanwhile, my brother Alieu had seen the conversation between me and Coal Boot and then had watched me walk off with the children. He decided to follow us and ran around the other side of the pathway so he was able to bypass us, hiding in the bushes along the route, always keeping me in his sight. But then one of the rebels saw Alieu and asked him what he was doing. He said, 'That's my sister,' pointing at me. By then 05 had given me the letter; it was already in my hand. I desperately wanted Alieu to come with me so, thinking on my feet, I said, 'I have the letter to give to the government but my brother is very smart and very intelligent, and he will be able to talk to them better than me.'

05 started asking us questions. He wanted to be sure we were definitely related and that we would do what he wanted with the letter. He asked which tribe we were from and was pleased when we said we were Susu, the same as him. Then, after a few more questions, he realised that our dad was Pa Conteh, the man who owned the hotel. I sensed

that he knew of him and believed that Papa was a good man, and that was when he agreed my brother could join me.

05 said: 'Okay, he can go with you, but if this letter is not read on television, if it's not talked about on the radio news, we'll kill all of your friends.'

Alieu took my hand and we set off; it felt as if we were walking a tightrope of uncertainty. I didn't dare believe it was happening. I kept expecting something to go wrong – for us all to be shot, or for Daramy or Coal Boot to come and grab me and take me back to their torture chambers. But I was feeling so bad that, whatever happened, I was prepared to risk it. Nothing could be worse than what I had already been through.

We were walking out in the open now and no one was shooting. We were just moving forwards to the place where the exchange was going to take place on a road in a clearing. There were seventeen of us in total, including my brother and me. Alieu and I were side by side, shaking but defiant, with the children following us.

There was meant to be a total ceasefire. That was the agreement on all sides. And, incredibly, that was what happened. After all the ugliness of the war, the inhumanity, the random senseless brutality, here on this day, in this spot, for this moment, there was peace.

We came out onto a main street – a really nice proper street with beautiful tarmac, the like of which I hadn't seen for a while. (I later found out that the exchange happened in Grafton, which is east of Freetown and not that far from the city.) There we saw the ECOMOG soldiers and the Sierra Leonean government forces with their truck. That was a good thing to see. I felt a wave of relief wash through me, even though either side might have broken the ceasefire at any moment. In my head, I was praying hard to God that this was it, that I was really walking away from my captors. Could it really be over?

It was like a scene from a movie. The government soldiers reversed their truck down the street and we walked in the middle of the road towards them. When they had us all safe with them, the soldiers handed over the promised food and supplies to the rebels.

Alieu and I were holding on to each other, holding on to hope. The soldiers were surprised to see us, I think, because they were only expecting small children. Later, the ECOMOG soldiers questioned me and Alieu at length; they wanted to be sure we were actually brother and sister and that we weren't rebel soldiers trying to ambush them.

We wanted to drive off straight away and head back home to Freetown, but that's not what happened – I don't know why. Instead, we had to join the government soldiers in their camp and stay there in tents through the night. We were driven to the camp in trucks and the soldiers were very kind to us. They could see we had all been through a terrible ordeal. They gave us packages of food – the sort of rations the soldiers themselves carried. We were starving and ate everything.

I was petrified the rebels might come in the night and I didn't sleep at all. I was listening to every sound in the bush. The exchange had happened so quickly, but for us that night felt like ten years because we were so desperate to see home. We all stayed close together in the tents, like sardines. No one wanted to be apart. And yet throughout that long, wakeful night with my brother by my side, he and I didn't talk about what had happened. To this day we never have. I don't think that's even a cultural thing; I think that's an abuse thing. You just can't talk about it. Writing about it now is the first time I've allowed myself to put it all down in words. It was twenty years ago, but as I write it's like I'm living through it again. I suppose this is partly why I've locked it away for so long. But there is also a release in letting the words run freely on the page.

Meanwhile, Daramy didn't know I had gone until I was far away. Even Frances and Fatmatta didn't know that I had gone. They didn't find out until later in the evening, when they went to Daramy's house. Frances was really in shock, because she remembered that I had said earlier that I was going to be released and she hadn't taken me seriously.

After shooting at me and then heading off into the bush consumed with rage, Daramy had been hanging out with some of his rebel friends – no doubt smoking – and he didn't come back until really late. When he found out I was gone, Frances told me, he went crazy. He grabbed his gun and started looking for my brother to kill him. Then he realised that Alieu had gone with me and that made him even more furious.

That night, our names were read out on the radio in the news about the release. Frances told me later, 'I did not believe you were gone until I heard your name on the radio.' She said that in the days afterwards Daramy became really sick and fell into a depression so deep they could barely recognise him. I think that's when I understood the depth of his obsession with me. In a strange way, it was as if he had lost the love of his life.

★

When we finally left the army camp it was still dark, probably in the early hours of the morning. We sat in the back of a truck which had high sides but was open to the stars. We wished the truck was on a plane, because still we did not feel safe. We knew that the rebels couldn't get at us because we were with the ECOMOG soldiers now, and they were more heavily armed than the rebels, but I was still anxious that something might go wrong and I didn't let myself fully believe that I was free.

Although we weren't that far from Freetown, we'd had to stop at so many checkpoints along the way that our journey took a long time. I ached for it to be over. More than anything, I wanted to see Papa. We were huddled in the bottom of the truck, in case stray bullets might be flying around; this was second nature to us now. I only put my head up when I noticed we were driving through Wellington, where my dad's hotel was. As we passed familiar landmarks, I felt like I was dreaming. People had lined the route and were shouting and clapping as we drove past, all hoping they might see their loved ones among us, but also celebrating the lucky ones who had escaped.

And when we drove through Kissy I saw my house. It was there – my yellow house! I was relieved to see that the house was still standing, that it hadn't been burned, but I didn't know what I might find there, if Papa and my sister and brother were alive. But, still, I was exhilarated to be free from Daramy. I didn't dare believe it and kept having to pinch myself to be sure I was awake and that this was really happening.

At first they took us to an army barracks. It was a small clay building, painted pink and caked in dust. There was a large crowd standing around, and as those of us who had been captive climbed down from the truck, people started screaming. Our release had already been mentioned on the news and people were coming to see the army truck arrive. The whole country was watching, thousands wanting to be reunited with their stolen children. But there were only seventeen of us here. The media were also awaiting our arrival. This was a huge deal in the journey of the war. It was the first time there had been an exchange like this between the rebels and the government. Everyone hoped it could be the start of peace and wanted to hear the news.

I found it all very overwhelming. I was still in the cut-off jeans and football shirt I'd been wearing when Coal Boot had raped me and Daramy had fired bullets at my feet. I was having trouble taking it all in. They lined us up for photographs – all the kids and me and Alieu – and the TV cameras filmed us. That was the first time Papa realised I was still alive. All my friends and family were listening to the radio, or watching the TV if they had one, and when they saw the footage and heard our names read out, my dad, Derek, everybody thought, 'Aminata and Alieu are really back with us.' This was indisputable evidence. This was real.

After the flurry of our arrival, we were taken to a room upstairs in the barracks for TV cameras to capture more footage. It was then that Alieu and I handed over the letter with the rebels' demands. I think others had forgotten about this part but I was very anxious. It was starting to dawn on me that it wasn't over, and although everyone wanted to celebrate, it wasn't really a celebration for me because I knew my friends were still there in the bush. I needed the letter to be read on television or radio so the rebels would know I had kept my promise and my friends wouldn't be harmed. The demands were later read out on TV by a newsreader with the ECOMOG soldiers standing around. We were filmed also, but I can barely remember this part. I can't even see the TV camera when I try to recall the scene. Now that I had handed over the letter, all I could think was: Where's Papa?

After the filming we all went back downstairs and within a few minutes my stepdad came rushing over. Anfah Condé, my mum's second husband, was a member of the ECOMOG forces. He was crying and hugging me so tight. It was a glorious moment seeing Anfah. I knew I was home safe now and he would take me to Papa.

Ever since my kidnap, Anfah had been going to Guinea whenever he had a break from the fighting to check on my mum, who was still living there. She had no idea I had been kidnapped; they kept it from her because they knew she would be desperate. He had to lie to Mum all the time, and often she would come into the room and catch him crying, because as the days went by he knew that the chances of me still being alive got less and less. She would ask, 'Why are you crying?' And he'd say, 'Oh it's from the tear gas from the war.' So when he was squeezing me and squeezing me,

I think all the emotion of those months of lying and praying and hoping was wrapped up in that hug.

Anfah had been at the front throughout the war and many times entered rebels' camps. He told me that he would scour every house, every tent, every piece of ground, hoping to find me. He didn't have children, so I was like his daughter and he really loved me. He and my dad were very close, too, and throughout the war, when there was no food in Freetown, he would bring bags of rice over from Guinea for Papa and our family. The two men had huge respect for each other.

It was quite an operation hiding my kidnap from my mum. She kept on saying that I should come to Guinea to safety with her, and Anfah would reply, 'She loves her dad so much, she would never leave him.' That made sense to Eleas, because she knew Papa and I were inseparable, and there were no phone lines during the war for her to talk to me so she just believed what she was told. But she told me later that she just couldn't understand why I didn't want to come and why my dad didn't insist that I go to Guinea, where it was safe.

It's strange because, during my kidnap, I had a feeling that my mum didn't know, and it gave me a little bit of peace in all that horror. At least I didn't have to worry about her. I worried about Papa constantly and how he would cope with me being taken away, especially because it happened right in front of him, as I was ripped from his hands. So the first thing I asked Anfah was: 'Is my dad alive?' Anfah told me he was, that everyone apart from my grandfather, who I already knew about, was okay. I was so relieved. But Papa was in his sixties and not so strong. I didn't know if he could cope with all of this.

There were no medical checks or doctors or anything like that. At that time in Sierra Leone abductions like this were commonplace. It was not like it would be in the West, with specialists and counsellors for survivors. Families just had to identify their children and then they took them home. Anfah had a big army truck, and less than twenty minutes after he'd found us in the crowd Alieu and I were back at Macauley Street. Our yellow house was still intact, with only a few bullet holes in the walls.

Papa was downstairs, sitting in his chair on the verandah. A lot of people in our community realised that we were coming, so there was a big crowd waiting; so many children had been kidnapped, it was a miracle for him to have two children returned. When we got to the gate, my father saw us. He stood up, his body was shaking. He looked surprisingly small to me. He was crying. He was always a very emotional person, but this time his crying was different: he didn't cry loudly, but very softly. It was like he wanted to show us he was happy, but at the same time he couldn't control his sobbing. Papa put out his hands to draw me near; they were still shaking with the Parkinson's, and it took me right back to that day when I had last held his hand – and let it go. We embraced, holding on tight but not saying much; we were both too traumatised to speak. I felt that something had been taken from both of us. It was as though all of his joy, the very essence of what made him who he was, was gone. I could feel it. I could sense it. The energy around us was different: I felt his vulnerability, and somehow that gave me unexplainable strength. The memory as I write this is still raw: I could feel that his heart was both whole and shattered at the same time.

I was home, and everything, everyone, was all right. But I knew that nothing would ever be the same again.

CHAPTER NINE

Home but not free

When we went inside the house, Papa could no longer control his anguish. He started to cry so loud it was like a howl. He couldn't stop, he was so hurt. He hugged me and then he hugged Alieu, squeezing us both to make sure we were real. Now the three of us were sobbing hard. All the pain, all the emotion, all the fear and the desperation came out in that moment when our family was reunited. It was devastating for me to see my father like this, because I really did not recognise him. His joy in life was gone. He was not the same person. He had always been my beacon of strength, but this man before me was a shell. I was not the same person either. We were both lost in our own trauma. He knew that his little girl was gone and that thought destroyed him. Every day of my captivity I had dreamed of being back with Papa, but this wasn't how I had imagined our reunion. We were both consumed with an overwhelming sense of loss and pain.

That night, I didn't sleep at all. I was upstairs in my room, and all night I could hear my dad crying downstairs. Later, my friends told me that while I was in captivity Papa had cried every time he saw girls in my age group. It was just too much for him to bear. Eventually my friends stopped going to see him because they upset him too much.

Meanwhile, in Guinea, my mum's family had heard of my release. My mum tells me that she first heard the news from her husband. At that moment her feet went numb and she collapsed to the floor. She kept repeating: 'They released who? You can't mean *my* Aminata.'

When Anfah told her that I had been kidnapped, she says, she wanted to die, because she knew what would have happened to me. Everyone knew that girls were raped and taken as sex slaves by the rebels. No one ever asked what had happened to you, it was just a given, one of many dirty truths about the war that all Sierra Leoneans lived with but no one talked about. I'm not saying that was a bad thing – it was our way of moving forward and it was part of our culture. Later, when I came to Australia, I realised that talking about it can help, too, and is part of healing.

My mum was very shocked, learning about both my kidnap and my release on the same day. She'd had no clue. But then she started to think back over the previous few months. She remembered that she would hear her own mum crying all the time but she wouldn't explain what was wrong. And then she remembered that all her friends and neighbours had been really gentle with her, making sure she wasn't bothered with anything. She had sensed something was up and that it might involve me. But whenever she asked my stepdad if I was okay he would say: 'Oh, I just saw Aminata when I was in Freetown. She's with her dad. She says hi.' It's pretty extraordinary that they managed to keep it from her, but I'm glad that they did. I don't think she would have been able to take it. I honestly believe it would have killed her.

Anfah managed to telephone my mum after he took me home to Papa. He said, 'Aminata is back.' Through her tears, she asked if I had been hurt, if my arms, my hands or any of my fingers or toes had been chopped off. Anfah assured her I was okay. But she said she couldn't believe him until she saw me with her own eyes. Although she and I have never discussed what happened to me, I think that as soon as she found out I had been taken, a pall of sadness engulfed her which has never gone away.

Alieu and I stayed with Papa for three days. It was a strange time. I knew I wasn't safe there. I sensed that Daramy would come for me and that made me really fearful. He didn't have a criminal record, so he was able to walk the streets of Freetown without being arrested, and there was no guarantee that the police would help us if he should turn up. There were rebels walking freely around the city. It was a very dangerous place. I knew in my heart that I had to leave and I had to do it immediately.

Papa didn't want to lose me again and was very conflicted. But as well as being concerned for my safety, he was also thinking of Eleas. Now that my mum knew everything, he believed it would be unfair not to send me to see her. I think he was wracked by guilt; it was written all over his face. Protecting me was everything to him, and in his eyes he had failed. I hated to see him so defeated.

Although I understood that my mum was also suffering, I was reluctant to leave Papa. I was worried about his safety. My family didn't know the extent of what Daramy had done to me nor how obsessed he was with me. We kept on hearing that the ceasefire was imminent, and I was concerned that Daramy would come to the house to find me and would hurt my family if I wasn't there. It was a very difficult decision to make. In the end, Papa was the one who decided. He said that I needed to go to Guinea and that I should go right away.

But first I had to see Derek. Derek and his family were now living at his aunty's house on the other side of Freetown. They had hidden in their house in Kissy as long as they could, but eventually they were told by the soldiers that it was far too dangerous and they needed to go westwards, where the ECOMOG forces had more of a stronghold. They escaped in the nick of time, but it is a day that still haunts him. 'When we left our house that day it was the most gruesome sight I've ever seen,' he told me when I spoke to him recently. 'We had to walk over piles of charred dead bodies. There was a child who had sought refuge in our house, a little girl who was about five or six years old. She ran after us and then suddenly some rebels came around the corner and saw us leaving and started shooting. People were just falling down all around me and this child, who was the most lovely little girl, was shot in the back. After she fell to the ground she started trying to crawl but she couldn't. I went back and tried to pick her up but they were still shooting and my dad said, "Keep running, don't look back, just keep running!" I had to leave her there. It was devastating.'

Derek and his family had heard about my release on the radio and then watched it on TV. Derek was desperate to see me. He had prayed every day and his parents told me that he didn't eat and he would cry all the time I was away. He kept my photo with him and would talk to me, willing me to be okay.

Anfah had asked his driver to take me wherever I needed to go over those three days before I left Freetown. Papa knew I would be safe with anyone who worked for Anfah, so he was happy to let me go. My friend Safie, who lived near our house in Kissy, knew where Derek was staying with his aunty in the city, and together we decided to go and surprise him with a visit. Our meeting was very emotional. I could feel Derek's sensitivity towards me – he had tears in his eyes and was so gentle in his behaviour – whereas I was mainly excited and grateful to see him. But we had hardly any time together at that meeting, so we organised to meet again the following day in Kissy.

When I saw Derek the next day at his family house we tried to pick up where we had left off. We hugged and kissed and we lay on the bed talking, but even though it was amazing to see him, I had changed so much. Derek wanted to protect me, to provide everything for me, to make everything better. I understood, but it didn't feel right. Growing up with my dad, that was what I expected from a man, but Papa had also taught us girls not to be dependent on men; that was why he thought our education was so important. And then, when I was kidnapped, I'd had to protect myself, to think independently.

When I was released I kept on thinking about my grandfather, and how he used to say to me that I was going to do something great with my life. He always used to call me Bahteh Guineh. In the Susu language that means 'the most powerful woman'. These words had always given me a sense of confidence. And even though that was not what I was feeling now – quite the opposite in fact – I think that sense of my own strength was still there, deep down inside.

Derek, on the other hand, wanted to wrap me in cotton wool. He wanted to fix what had happened to me, and I would never be able to get away from that. I needed to put the past behind me. At that moment, lying on the bed and talking, I realised that I would have felt held back. It would have been in a beautiful, gentle, kind way, but I couldn't have that – not after what I'd been through. For me it is this idea of small thinking. I didn't like small thinking then and I don't like it now: when somebody decides that I'm not able to do something, puts obstacles in my way or wants to tell me who I can be. I think I gained a sort of inner confidence from my experience and I didn't feel like Derek would be able to let me embrace that. He wouldn't have wanted me to talk as I do, to share my story, to lead. I didn't have the words back then but now I do. I wanted to be a woman who runs with the wolves.

It was then that I made a conscious decision that if I was going to marry, it would not be to an African man. This wasn't about what Daramy had done to me nor was it about my relationship with Derek. It was about me wanting to control my own life and not always be the girl who was kidnapped. I didn't want protection and I didn't want to be pre-judged and defined by what I had been through. Also, an African man would not have wanted me to be open with my story. In our culture there is a sense of shame attached to rape which imprisons women who have gone through abuse. An African man would not want people to know that his wife had been raped because she would be seen somehow as less respectable. I had big plans; I didn't know yet what form they would take, but I knew I wasn't prepared to be held back by anyone, especially a man. I really liked Derek – more than that, I loved him – and I wanted to make him happy, but I knew it could never work.

Saying goodbye to Derek was difficult, but it felt right.

★

Meanwhile, in Guinea, my mum was crazy to see me. From the moment she had heard about my release, she couldn't sleep and she wasn't eating either. Anfah called her to say he would be putting me on the ferry to Guinea. She was full of nervous excitement.

But then I missed the boat. This time I called her myself. I found it hard to talk. I had so much going on in my head, so many feelings, but on the outside I was very quiet. My mum thought that we were hiding something, that I wasn't really okay or, worse, that I wasn't coming at all. But the next day I boarded the ferry in the early evening and we sailed through the night. Anfah had put me in the care of a group of Guinean soldiers who were returning home. I felt safe with them, especially as the soldiers were given preferential treatment. We were all in cars and I stayed in the car throughout the journey. I had never travelled by boat before and being on water made me anxious.

The main deck was crowded with people weighed down with bags. They were fleeing the war, taking as many of their possessions with them as they could carry. During the war hundreds of thousands of refugees fled to camps in Guinea. While relations between people from Guinea and people from Sierra Leone have always been friendly, during the war they became tense. Everyone was running for their life and Guinea was the nearest place to go. Guinea welcomed refugees – in fact, it was the most generous country towards our people – but the locals were worried that the fighting might spread to their country and there was a lot of mistrust. Looking back, I can see why. People did desperate things in the war – whatever they needed to do to survive. And there was no way to tell if the refugees who were flooding across the border had collaborated with the rebel forces or even taken part in their vicious reign of terror.

In 1999, following that day when the rebels broke through into Freetown, Guinea hosted the largest refugee population in Africa – in some parts of the country the number of refugees was greater than the number of Guineans. More than 300,000 of these refugees were from Sierra Leone and, of these, 65 per cent were children. The things these children had seen were horrific; some had seen their parents killed right in front of them. Guinea's refugee camps ranged in size from a few thousand occupants to more than 20,000 and while the UNHCR, the UN Refugee Agency, did its best, donations from international governments were desperately inadequate. It was as if the rest of the world was turning its back on us. As a result, the camps were dirty, dangerous places to live, although you did have a better life expectancy than trying to hide from the rebels in Sierra Leone. Women and children were particularly vulnerable and sexual abuse was common.

Tigidankay and Ibrahim, my half sister and brother, had been among those fleeing to Guinea. They both had family there and had left Sierra Leone as soon as they could after I was kidnapped. Tkay lived in the Conakry refugee camp when she first arrived, but it wasn't good. There were hardly any resources. It was a jungle of tents and everyone was packed in there. So then she moved in with her relatives. Tkay's mother had very influential relatives in Conakry. One of her maternal cousins was married to a government minister who was very powerful. Ibrahim was staying with his mum, who had a big house in the centre of the city. Both Tkay and Ibrahim were trying to get refugee visas to America. This, they hoped, would be their escape. There were no jobs in Guinea and, in any case, there was the language problem: they didn't speak French.

★

When the ferry arrived in Conakry the quay was bustling with activity. As we drove off the ferry in the car I caught sight of my mum waving at me. When I saw her swollen eyes, I understood her pain. We pulled up on the quayside and I got out of the car and ran over to her. She grabbed hold of me and looked me up and down, checking that I was in one piece, feeling down my arms and my legs. I too was crying, but I was also withdrawn. Everything that had happened was making me shut down. I wanted to be quiet. I wanted no one to notice me.

Pa Conteh.

Mama in Guinea as a beautiful young woman.

Left: My parents Yayah and Eleas when they first met in Guinea.

Below left: Papa and Mama on their wedding day. Papa is totally smitten!

Below right: The yellow house on the hill (photographed recently), where Mama came to live with Papa. It felt enormous when we lived there but when I go back now it feels much smaller. The floors are now rented out separately.

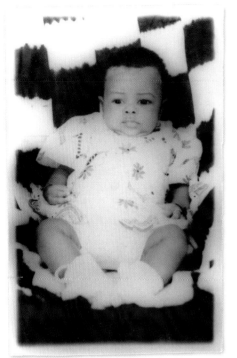

Top left: Me as a baby – Mama loved dressing me up.

Top right: Me as a toddler looking very like my daughter Sarafina.

Left: Me (front left) with the three siblings I lived with in our yellow house. Ibrahim is next to me with Alieu and my sister Tkay behind.

> *Opposite*: Me (left) and Tkay (right) with our beloved Baimba.

Left: All dressed up
for my school band.
I loved that uniform.

Below: In my bedroom
in Kissy. This was my
special place.

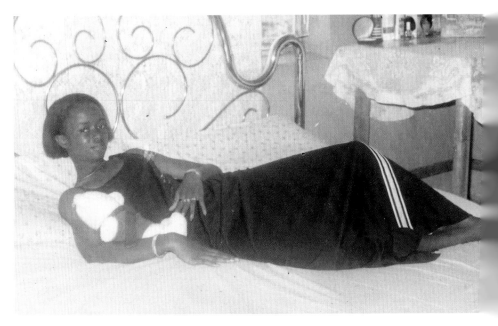

Freetown: the red red earth of home.

.ebel soldiers during the war.

After I escaped from my captors I went to safety in Guinea-Conakry to live with Mama. Here I am eating a meal outside with family friends.

Celebrating my birthday with my cousins at Mama's house in Guinea. I later sponsored these cousins for residency visas to come and join me in Sydney.

Left: A bittersweet day as Mama sees me off at the airport in Guinea-Conakry.

Below: Tkay and I with Tkay's great-aunt's family on the day we left Guinea for Australia.

My new life in Australia: in my school uniform on the balcony of Liz's apartment in Penshurst.

Above: It took some time but eventually we settled in to Australia. The first sofa we bought for our new apartment in Beverly Hills, Sydney, made me think of the brown leather chair Papa had in our Kissy house.

Left: Tkay and I, proud Australian citizens.

Below: With my friend Marion, who I sat next to on that first flight from Guinea to Sydney.

Left: My first try at modelling for a test shoot in the streets of Sydney that proved to be a scam. Even so I love this photo.

Below left: My model card for the talent agency Coffee Coloured Characters.

Below right: Testing make-up for a cosmetics company. This is the most make-up I've ever worn and even though I like the photo I washed my face immediately afterwards.

Working as a Special Representative for Australia for UNHCR is truly a privilege.

Above: Speaking on a panel for Australia for UNHCR.

Right: With the wonderful Dame Quentin Bryce at the Australia for UNHCR World Refugee Day Breakfast at which we both spoke. This was one of my earliest speaking engagements for the organisation.

Meeting my husband Antoine was one of the most important moments in my life. Here we are outside the Sydney Opera House a few days after we first met there in 2007.

The night Antoine proposed in Réunion.

Aminata,

Hey u its antoine, i know you since now 24 day
and its gööd always cause your are my sunchine
When i am whith you, the time is to good and i
forget all.
When i'm whit you i'm happy ☺
J'adore te regarder car tu est trop belle.
(tu comprend)
I like to take you in my arms.
Ma petitte animata, tu est vraiment gentil, Je t'adore ☀

Je t'adore my princess. 🌹

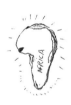

Antoine.

Above: Antoine's wonderful love letter.

Right: The Coca-Cola ring Antoine
proposed to me with.

Above: Our wedding was the most magical day. I loved every minute of it.

Right: Pastor Matthew Waqanivalu watches over us as we sign the register in church.

We got in the car, Mum sitting next to me and holding me tight. The driver took us to my mum's house, a journey of about 30 minutes through the dusty streets. While there wasn't the same tension as on the streets of Freetown, Guinea was full of refugees from my country. To me, Guinea always felt a little richer than Sierra Leone, with less visible poverty. There were nice, well-maintained houses and a sense of industry among the people. Of course, at this time the country was struggling with the influx of Sierra Leonean and Liberian refugees, but the atmosphere for those of us coming from Freetown on that day was of a safe haven where we could take a breath and work out our next move. There were still soldiers in evidence, but there was no conflict here or fear of shooting.

My mum had a ground-floor apartment with four or five bedrooms in a flat-roofed cement house. It was in a big compound with a fence all around and felt safe and secure. She was living there with her mum and her sister's children. When my mum came home all the children would run into her arms. And I really admired this. She loved looking after other people's kids. I think, as I've said, because she didn't have me to care for she instead looked after every child who came into her world. She was like Papa, in a way, and would put them into good schools and help to raise them. I saw this side of my mum a few months later, when I brought home about six friends who had come from our community in Sierra Leone, girls who had arrived on the boat and didn't have anywhere to stay in Guinea. They didn't want to stay in the refugee camp, understandably, so we took them in. The house was full of Sierra Leoneans who spoke English and Guineans who spoke French and we all stayed together for a year or so.

★

Physically, I was small but healthy when I arrived in Guinea. You would not think that I'd just been released from months in captivity, because even though there were times in the bush when I hardly ate for days or sometimes weeks, I didn't look emaciated. Even so, it was only recently that my mum told me she could see then how deeply traumatised I was. She says she asked me what had happened and I wouldn't talk about it. I don't remember her asking, but I do know that we didn't have a mother–daughter conversation about it. And, yes, that was probably my choice. To anyone who asked, I just said I was kidnapped. I didn't want to upset people, especially those who were close to me. The extent of it, the horror of what had happened, I could not put into words. It was just too much.

Perhaps what was more odd was the fact that I really didn't feel any anger after being released. I knew something physical had been taken away from me, but I didn't feel completely broken by it. Instead, I felt at peace with myself: something new was rising in my heart.

The whole time I was with the rebels I knew that a higher power – which for me, is God – was looking after me, but it was not faith that I was feeling now. I think it was about forgiveness. I started to feel that when I first saw my dad. The gift of seeing Papa again, his face, even if it was for one minute, meant the world to me. Then, when

I went to Guinea and was reunited with my mum, I made the decision to forgive Daramy, Coal Boot and the other rebels. I kept on thinking about the prodigal son and the father forgiving. I said to myself, 'I'll forgive, because I don't want to be consumed by anger. I want to have joy, I want to live without fear or hate, I want to enjoy my life.' Not that I really forgave them or even understood the notion of real forgiveness. I just wanted to be free of them.

A few months after I was released a ceasefire was brokered, but then shortly after, the thing I most feared came to pass: Daramy turned up at my house in Kissy looking for me. It was Alhaji who phoned from Freetown and told us.

It was chilling to hear; all of a sudden I was that terrified girl again. Memories tumbled into my head, dark moments from my captivity. I felt sick with fear, not because I thought Daramy would kill me, but because of what he had done to me and could do again. I despised him and just the thought of him made me remember his smell, his stinking body, and how much it repelled every part of me. Even though I had 'forgiven' Daramy, I was in no way saying that what he did to me was okay. For me, forgiveness was about liberating myself from what he had done to me. I wouldn't let it define me, although it is always with me. I still can't think of Daramy without that smell coming back to me and it makes me shudder. It was when I heard that Daramy had been looking for me that I made a momentous decision: I would have to leave Africa completely.

My mum supported my decision, even though she would miss me terribly. She had been urging me to leave the region, and hoped that I would join the twins, Fatmata and Mabinty, in London. Then she too could move to the UK and we could all live together. But I didn't want to go to London. I didn't want to be recognised. There is a big Sierra Leonean community in Britain and I thought a lot of people would know me from seeing my release on television.

No, I was aching for a new life away from anyone who knew what had happened to me. And I needed to get as far away from Daramy as was humanly possible.

CHAPTER TEN

Out of Africa

I stayed in Conakry for a year and a bit while I threw myself whole-heartedly into the lengthy process of seeking asylum in a new country via one of the various resettlement programs run by the UNHCR.

Everyone was desperate to get out and each case was treated individually. Just having fled the war wasn't enough; people were judged on their educational standards, their language competence, their perceived needs based on what had happened to them and the urgency of their case. There weren't enough places for the vast numbers applying, so for most, these were nail-biting days with your future and your family's future hanging in the balance. The whole process was painstaking and involved endless queues and forms and waiting, and all the time people were trying to get through each day in a country that was bursting at the seams.

For most people, the first step involved queuing up at the refugee camp to get an ID number, which would place you in the system. Your personal details would be recorded and filed under this number, and families were mostly registered together, so if they secured a visa they would be placed together. The biggest programs were run by America, then there was Canada, the UK, Ghana and a new program sending people to Australia. Most people in the camp didn't care where they went. They literally had nothing. In many cases their houses had been burned down and they had escaped over the border with nothing more than the shirts on their backs. Just coming to Guinea was like a hallelujah for them, let alone boarding a plane to get them out of Guinea. They just wanted a new life in a safe place.

I was lucky: I didn't need to go to the camps and I wasn't living with the same level of desperation. I had a secure, comfortable home with my mum. I wasn't scrapping for food in the refugee camp or constantly watching my back in case the person in the makeshift shack next door was a rebel. I wasn't sleeping on the streets or having to feed and clothe my family. I wasn't trying to get work in a place where there was no work and I didn't speak the language. But, looking back, I can see that I needed help.

This must have been clear to others, too, because one of the United Nations representatives took a special interest in me. Sidney, an American, was in charge of the resettling of asylum seekers. He immediately understood that I was in deep trauma and should be resettled as soon as possible. Even though I thought I was coping it must have been painfully obvious that my experiences had damaged me in ways I didn't yet realise. Sidney seemed to look out for me right from the start, probably because of the high profile of my case. He took it very seriously. I was also aware that, unlike others, I had a choice of where to go, since I would fit the requirements of most refugee programs as a person at risk in their own country.

If I had chosen to settle in America, I could have left Guinea-Conakry almost immediately, but I was intrigued by Australia. I didn't know where it was or anything about the country except that there were hardly any people from Sierra Leone there, since the resettlement program was so new. And that appealed to me a lot. When I finally made it to Australia I also discovered that Australians had no clue Sierra Leone even existed or any concept of the war, which was perfect for me. I thought I would be able to slip in under the radar, which, as it turned out, proved rather naive.

Sidney wanted me to get out of Guinea urgently and knew that placement on the Australian program would take much longer to process, but I felt safe with my mum and rarely went out to public places, so I wanted to wait to see if I could get a visa for Australia.

I didn't live in fear that Daramy would find me in Guinea because I didn't go out into the community. There was a place in Conakry city by the Sierra Leone embassy where all the Sierra Leoneans gathered to hang out together, but I never went there. I was fearful mostly that somebody would recognise me as the girl who was on television. I didn't want that sort of attention and I didn't want any chance of a rebel seeing me and it getting back to Daramy.

I did have friends in Guinea, like Zoff, a really good friend and neighbour, and his girlfriend Mam. We spent most of our time at my mum's house, drinking tea and talking. I wasn't scared of men when I was in Guinea, because I knew this place from visiting my mum before the war.

My Guinean friends vaguely knew my story but they didn't treat me any differently which I was relieved about. A lot of the Sierra Leonean community, or people who have been through what I went through, never feel as if we have the luxury to dwell on our experiences, because we are surrounded by people who have gone through similar things. They might not have been kidnapped like me, but they'd had their family killed in front of them or watched as their children's limbs were mutilated or their house was razed to the ground with people inside. Everyone needed to forget.

You can't spend your life being disgusted and angry; that solves nothing. You have to move forwards. So as I went about my life each day, I barely thought about what had happened to me. I know that is hard to believe, but except when I was in the UN offices with Sidney, I never had to think about it and I didn't talk about the kidnap or the abuse.

What I quickly learned is that every pain is the same. So people who had seen their whole family burned alive, leaving them the only survivor, they carry the same pain as I carry. It was only the organisations – UNHCR and the refugee bodies – who treated my story as a big deal. It wasn't how I saw it, and for me it was something I wanted to leave in the past.

I wasn't scared to be alone. Growing up, I'd always loved being around people, but I think after my experience with the rebels I wanted to be by myself to reflect, and to heal.

★

When I'd been in Guinea for about three months, Papa came to visit. I felt anxious, distressed. I didn't know how my relationship with him would be now, after all we'd been through. How should I behave? He was on his way to the UK. He was very sick and was going to London for treatment. We thought it was to do with his Parkinson's, and he'd also had a stroke, but it turned out to be much worse, though I wouldn't learn this for a long while yet. Fatmata and Mabinty in London would look after him as he went through treatment; they were eager to be of help after all our family had been through.

The twins had first left for the UK when they were fifteen, just before I was born. They were sent to a private boarding school in Edinburgh. We have talked about it since and both feel my dad's biggest gift to us all was education.

'Back then, they didn't educate girls,' Fatmata told me when we caught up on my last visit to London. 'Our dad said that educating us was the property he could give us that nobody could take from us; even if you got married, we'd still be self-sufficient.' He was right.

At boarding school the twins were the only two black students on the campus, and they were sent to elocution lessons to fix their Sierra Leonean accents. They remember when they would go on trips to places like Glasgow everyone would stare at them. After their exams, they moved to London and went to university, Fatmata studying computing and Mabinty accounting. By the time the war started in Sierra Leone, they had already finished university and were working. During the war, they couldn't get in touch with us and feared we had all been killed. They told me that our Papa's health plummeted after I was taken and they were pleased he was coming over to them for treatment.

In Guinea, I felt overcome with emotion when I saw what Papa had been reduced to, because he wasn't really with us. He didn't have dementia, or anything like that; his mind was still sharp. But he was lost. Everybody wanted to be around him because in Guinea they loved him so much, but he wasn't the same man. He and I didn't talk much. Papa was never a big talker at the best of times, but now he was very quiet. I think the Parkinson's had affected his speech but mostly he was just extremely sad. He would be like this for the rest of his life. What happened to me broke him into pieces and he never fully recovered. I feel the pain of that deep in my heart, and though I try to lock it away, it does come to me from time to time with an intensity that stops me in my tracks. When that happens, I have to be by myself.

I was withdrawn then also, and I think in general in our culture we tend to back away from facing our emotions. My dad and I didn't talk about my time with the rebels or the time when he went to hide in the mosque and it was filled with dead bodies. We didn't spend any time alone together, which was a shame, but it was probably not something either of us could have handled at the time.

He stayed with us for almost a month before flying on to London. It was hard to see him go, but I wasn't tempted to get on the plane and go with him. I didn't want to live with my sisters. It's funny, because I had grown up with Papa taking care of us kids in every single detail. From buying our undies to making our food to choosing our schools and our teachers, it was Papa who did it all. But after the war I didn't want anybody to take care of me anymore. This independence was something my dad had instilled in all of his children. He wanted us to make our own path; he didn't want us to have to feel obligated to family, because he felt this would be an added burden on our shoulders. And I didn't want the pressure of having to depend on people all the time. After surviving the war, I wanted to keep building my resilience. I wanted to stand on my own two feet.

I really wanted to go to Australia on my own, but Sidney was concerned. I didn't know anything about trauma; I'd never heard the word and it took me a long time to understand what it meant, especially in relation to me. But Sidney was an expert in it. He had seen it again and again in war victims, and from the moment we met he recognised that I was severely traumatised. I was very quiet back then and spoke only to Sidney. I found it really hard to speak in front of people and if I tried I would physically shake and my palms would be drenched in sweat. I think it was for that reason that he was so determined to protect me.

So he told me that he thought I should take somebody with me to Australia. I was still very young, and I was the only person in the program who was by herself; everybody else had applied with their family. I told him that I wanted to make this journey alone, but Sidney was adamant. He said: 'I don't want you to go by yourself. It'll be too lonely for you. Australia is very far away. Do you have a friend that you're close to, or a sister?'

I could see that he was serious and that this might be the difference between going or not going. I was silent for a bit; I needed to think. Finally I said, 'Well, I have a sister in Guinea. Could I talk to her and see if she wants to come with me?' Sidney was pleased by that possibility, and suggested I ask her.

I actually didn't know much about what Tkay was up to when I was in Conakry. Although she visited the refugee camp regularly – I later learned that this was to check up on her visa status – she was actually living in the big ministerial house with her cousin. I thought she had said she was trying to go to America, but that was all I knew.

When I went to see my sister at her aunty's house, she was packing her bag. She had been turned down for the America program and was ready to go back to Sierra Leone. So when I said to her, 'Do you want to come to Australia with me?', she didn't hesitate. She said yes right away. She wanted to run to the other side of the world, too.

No one in my family or group of friends knew at that time about my plans to go to Australia. I was very discreet and hadn't talked to anyone about it. Tkay didn't even ask about the program or Australia; she just knew she wanted to get on that plane.

I remember one of her aunties was there and she said, 'How do you know Aminata is telling the truth about Australia?' and she said to the aunty, 'Oh, if Mommy says she's doing something, then she's doing something.' She was right of course. Even though my sister and I were very different, we knew each other well.

And so it was decided. We would apply to go to Australia

together. I took Tkay to the UN and we started filling out all the forms.

She was living in the moment, and this was our moment.

★

If you were called for the medical assessment, you knew you had been accepted into the Australian program. Looking back, it is surprising how healthy Tkay and I both were. I was very small for my age, but miraculously I hadn't contracted AIDS and neither of us had malaria or any other tropical diseases.

It was at my medical that I first met Marion, who would become one of my closest friends in Australia. Recently I was present at the birth of her first child in our local hospital in Sydney – a beautiful daughter, Ariana. It was a truly joyous moment for her and her Australian partner, and for me too. For us to be together at that special time when she was bringing new life into our new world after the journeys that had brought each of us to this faraway island meant the world to me.

Although Marion and I hadn't known each other in Sierra Leone, I later discovered she knew about me. She said her sister had seen me on TV and immediately recognised me as Pa Conteh's daughter, the girl who was kidnapped by the rebels and then handed back in the exchange. She remembers that when we met I was very quiet and shy and never talked. We were going through the asylum preparation process together, which involved lots of talks and interviews. Even at the interviews, she recalls, I wouldn't say a thing.

When I compare that girl to the woman I am now, we are totally different. Today I would be the first asking questions; the first to speak out.

Marion was eighteen when we met in the camp in Conakry and was with her sister and her sister's children – there were eight of them travelling together in total. Her home had been in Kenema, a big city in the Eastern Province of Sierra Leone, and when the rebels came she and her family had fled, eventually ending up in Freetown and then Conakry. They had lost everything and had some dark, painful experiences along the way. Initially they had hoped to go to America, but Marion tells me they were just as happy when they were picked for Australia. The UNHCR felt that Marion and her sister would be safer in Australia. Like me, Marion knew nothing about Australia, only that this country was welcoming her to its shores and that was enough. They had been in Conakry for just over a year and had immediately applied for asylum. They were not living in the camp, but with people in the city, and Marion says going through the processing proved agonising. Every day she and her sister would go to the refugee camp to see if their names had come up, hoping that something would change for them and they could embark on the future. 'So whatever country would accept us, we were happy about it,' she remembers. There were so many of our people who were refused asylum and the reasons were never explained. Marion says she often thought, 'Why me? Why not them?' when she saw the queues of our countrymen and women who had been rejected. As we prepared for our lives on the other side of the world, we knew that we were the lucky ones. We really believed that.

Getting ready to come to Australia was both invigorating and confusing. There were so many firsts, so many new experiences. I had never been on a plane before, even though my dad travelled often; I used to think he was waving down at me whenever a plane went over. I didn't even know what it looked like inside the cabin. But I was not frightened. I knew zero about Australia and didn't make any effort to find out more about it. I hadn't even heard of Australia before Sidney mentioned it to me. Tkay knew as little as I did, but she had at least heard of this distant nation. The Olympic Games were approaching, and because she was living in a house that was full of ministers, they were talking about the Olympics quite a bit.

My mum was sad about my decision to leave, but she understood I had to go and part of her was relieved to see it happen. She learned more about Australia than I did. Without telling me, she found out about the culture and the government and the people and the laws, and that gave her comfort because she thought it was a good place and we would be safe there. Also, hearing that I was going with my sister was a relief.

Sidney suggested that I might like to change my identity. He was worried that Daramy could search for me, and if I changed my name it would be more difficult for him to track me down. But I didn't want to change my name. Conteh was Papa's name. I treasured it.

Sidney brought a woman into our planning meetings to assess me. I think she must have been a psychologist or counsellor or something like that. They both knew I struggled with writing and reading – years later I was diagnosed with dyslexia, but I had never heard of the condition then.

This lady was helping me to write down my story to submit with the paperwork. As we talked, they both feared that I would be completely lost at first in Australia. I wouldn't know anyone and, even though I was travelling with my sister, they suspected I would struggle. By the time I arrived, I might be too old to fit into school, and Sidney believed that my trauma would have prevented me from attending university or finding a job.

Because of the war and changing schools, I hadn't sat exams in Sierra Leone, and when I was in Guinea I was too scared to go to school, which would be a strange environment with lots of people I didn't know – now I realise I was suffering from severe anxiety issues, which considering my situation was totally understandable. My mum wanted me to go to school so badly while in Conakry. There was a French school, an international school and schools specifically for Sierra Leoneans. She thought at a French school I would learn her language, but I refused to enrol.

In Australia, I could fix that. I knew that I was behind with my studies, and in the back of my mind I heard Papa's voice talking about the importance of education. The idea of going to school in Australia didn't seem as daunting as in Guinea. Also, since it turned out there was to be no help for us on the ground in Australia – the refugee program was in its infancy – the structured and nurturing environment of a school would be very helpful for me. It would turn out that in Australia I had no case worker, no one to rely on; my sister and I were very much left to fend for ourselves. But at school the teachers supported me, and this was crucial for me in my early years in Australia.

Tkay, on the other hand, was super intelligent and had already finished high school. In fact, she ended up being the first one on the refugee program to go to university in Australia.

*

By May 2000, we were all set.

My mum and Tkay's aunties wanted us to take a lot of our traditional African clothes, even though Tkay and I barely wore them. They said there wouldn't be any in Australia, which was true. So our suitcases were packed with beautiful clothes, many pieces handmade by my mum. We call them bazin dresses – they are colourful and long and flowing and make you walk like an empress. I only wore them once or twice to church in Australia, as I felt too conspicuous in them. I also had photographs from my time in Guinea, of me and my mum and my friends, but otherwise I had nothing from back home to take with me.

Before we left Conakry my mum held a small celebration. I had developed a tight group of friends who lived in our area, and we had become very close. The boys didn't speak any Krio, and I didn't speak any French, but somehow we all clicked.

The party was held at my mum's home and her friends were invited too. There were about 50 people in total and we had lots of Guinean food, music from my mum's sound system and dancing. We all loved to dance. Everybody was really excited for me. It was a very beautiful way to say goodbye.

CHAPTER ELEVEN

A brand-new life

My mum, my aunt and lots of family and friends came to the airport to say goodbye to me. I could see sadness in Mama's eyes and I could tell that she feared we may not see each other for a very long time. But it was a happy parting because I think everyone understood that this was what I needed to do. That certainly didn't make leaving home any easier. I was conflicted: excited to be on my way to a new life but sad to be leaving everything that I had known and loved.

Every refugee had a bag from the International Organisation for Migration. It was a white plastic carrier bag with I.O.M. in big blue writing on the outside. We were told we must have this bag with us at all times, so everyone was holding their bags super tight. This was our passport to our future. Actually, it literally was. Inside the bag was my Australian ImmiCard, which was a special visa for those who didn't have a passport, my medical records and other important documents that the authorities in Australia would need to process my arrival and that I would then need to live in Australia. I was being admitted to Australia under refugee category subclass 204, the visa for women at risk. While I didn't like being labelled as such, it was true. Daramy was still out there. On the visa it stated that Tkay and I were 'permitted to remain in Australia indefinitely', which was good to read. This was a proper, official new start with no danger of our being sent back to Sierra Leone.

Of course, because we were holding these bags people knew straight away we were refugees, and in the airports and during the journey we were generally gathered together in one place. I don't know if people put two and two together and realised we were escaping from the war in Sierra Leone. Probably not. In the coming months, I would learn how little people knew of what was going on in my country.

When Marion came through customs to the departure lounge at Conakry airport, she says she saw me straight away. I was wearing black jeans and a white t-shirt and my hair was in long braids. She remembers I was clutching my I.O.M. bag in the departure lounge and was quiet and withdrawn, just sitting there with Tkay. The reality of what I was doing hit me at that moment. My mum and friends were no longer with me. There was no looking back now. I remember feeling that I was closing the door to Africa, my homeland, and that made me sad. I was running away from my people to be safe, and I knew I had to do that, but my heart still belonged to Sierra Leone.

Marion and I didn't actually speak until we were on the plane, when we discovered we had been allocated seats next to each other. Papa travelled a lot when I was growing up, regularly flying off to Europe, and I had this feeling when I sat in my seat near the window that I was sitting with Papa. It was as if he was there, holding my hand,

We were the first group of refugees from Sierra Leone to resettle in Australia. There were about six different families and we totalled 27 people. It still felt unreal, like someone might take it away from us at any moment. But once everybody settled into their seats on the plane you could sense the relief and you could almost hear our group sigh as the plane finally left the runway and soared up into the cloudless sky. After you've tried so hard, overcoming so many hurdles, and then you finally leave, the relief is overwhelming.

It took us three days and three plane journeys to reach Sydney from Conakry. We spent eight hours in Paris airport and then more time in transit in Singapore. And all the time I was thinking, 'Are we really going to Australia? Is this a trap?'

I don't remember much about the flight, but Marion tells me we chatted about the airline food, which was strange to us, and we tried each other's meals and swapped things we didn't like. We talked about Australia and what it might be like. We didn't talk about the war or what happened to us. We all wanted to put that behind us now.

When we stopped in Paris, I remember Tkay and I mused about whether we might see people we know. We had a lot of family members in France because of our connection to Guinea, and we genuinely wondered if we would bump into one of our many relatives. It was wishful thinking – of course that wasn't likely: we were stuck in transit. But we didn't know about things like that then.

Most of the refugees didn't have money with them, but Tkay and I had dollars with us, and I remember I bought some perfume and my sister bought Calvin Klein Eternity, which had always been her favourite. We also bought chocolates. We roamed around the airport for hours, looking in the shops and cafes. Looking back, it might have seemed pretty frivolous, but we were just having fun, enjoying our freedom and marvelling at all the beautiful things everywhere.

Eventually we left for Singapore and then for Sydney. It felt so far away from Guinea. And it was. I don't remember flying in to Sydney, which is a shame, because that approach over the sparkling harbour, with the Sydney Harbour Bridge and the Opera House below, is something I love to see now when I am flying in. All I remember from back then was coming in to land and finally hitting the tarmac.

It was early morning on 11 May 2000 when we arrived at Sydney airport, and we thought we were going to be greeted by a crowd of people making a big fuss of us, but the only person there to meet us was a man called Mr Condé and his beautiful Singaporean wife Linda. I was immediately struck by her poise and elegance.

Even though our welcome was a bit of an anticlimax, Mr Condé, who was a lawyer, was very friendly and helpful. He was originally from Sierra Leone, had studied in London and then ended up working in Australia, where he had lived for a long time. He was our first point of contact and seemed to have everything organised.

Going through customs didn't take long because all our medical and visa entry documents were already in the system and we had all the paperwork in our trusty I.O.M. bags.

We were expected by the authorities and it all went pretty smoothly.

It was sunny but chilly, especially compared to Guinea, as we walked out of the terminal to take our first breath of fresh Sydney air. Mr Condé had already rented accommodation for all the families. Tkay and I climbed into his minivan with two other families – the others from our group were in separate vans – and he drove us out to our new homes.

Sydney was a million miles from Freetown in every way. The streets and buildings were so different, and everything looked big and perfect. But it didn't feel shocking to me, because I knew this sort of place from my James Bond movies. It was early in the morning and there was a little bit of traffic on our drive to the city's western suburbs. I think the Australian government's immigration department had given Mr Condé money to rent places on our behalf until we signed up with Centrelink to receive our government allowance. We were all located around the Bankstown area.

My sister and I had a unit on King Georges Road in Wiley Park. It was a ground-floor two-bedroom place in a two-storey red-brick block of six or eight units. The apartment was basic but clean. The front door opened straight into the living room and we had a kitchen with a fridge, a bathroom, and there was a mattress on the floor of each bedroom. This was the only furniture. There were no chairs, no table or sofa. The idea was we would buy household furniture ourselves with our government allowances and some vouchers which we could use in charity stores like the Salvos or the Smith Family. This was a shock. In Guinea we had been told that our new homes would be all set up with everything we needed, including some clothing, but there was nothing. The only clothing we had was the Guinean clothes we had brought with us.

We deposited our bags and then headed straight out again. Mr Condé and his wife spent that first month helping the families that had arrived. They would arrange appointments so we could register with the government bodies and helped with transport, either driving us themselves or pointing us in the right direction for public transport. On that first day, we had to sign up with Centrelink, and then buy some food, and pots and pans to cook it in, as well as bedding. I was not tired at all; in fact, I felt wide awake. But everything was very confusing. And there was so much paperwork.

We received a welfare allowance from Centrelink which was paid into a bank account. The allowance was scaled depending on your age. I was given $270 a fortnight, although some fortnights it was $280. I never queried it. I was just thankful for the unexpected extra ten dollars. This money had to pay for everything. Our rent was $240 a fortnight, so $120 each for me and Tkay. Mr Condé made sure we paid the rent directly out of our Centrelink allowance as soon as it hit our bank accounts so we didn't get in arrears. On top of that we had to cover electricity, transport, food and everything else, including clothes, which we also bought mostly from charity stores. It didn't go very far.

I remember the first time I went to withdraw money out of the bank. It didn't go well. I had never seen Australian notes before and dealing with money felt very strange to me. My dad dealt with these sorts of things in Sierra Leone and my mum in Guinea. I took out the whole $270 and then somehow I lost it in the shopping centre. Tkay was so mad. But when we spoke to Papa later on the phone he told her not to be too hard on me. He said to think of it like an offering of thanks to this country that had taken us in. I'm not sure Tkay was in agreement, but after speaking to Papa she did lay off me a bit and I never did it again!

In the supermarket we bought the sort of food we knew from home – rice and ingredients for a stew – and this was pretty much what we lived on. Our stews were made from chicken or lamb, onions, fresh tomatoes, carrots and potatoes, flavoured with some spice and a little water and oil. We would serve it with steamed rice. I had done home economics at school, so even though I was used to being cooked for at home I did know how to cook. That said, it was Tkay who did most of the cooking. My sister didn't let me pay for food either. She had to get a job and she got one quickly in a nursing home. She was doing cleaning and smaller caring jobs around the facility while training to be a nurse. (Most refugees end up doing menial jobs, because our qualifications mean nothing in Australia.) I realise now that this is what Sidney had anticipated when he encouraged me to bring Tkay with me. There is no way I would have been employable. I didn't even understand what the process of getting a job meant. But, more than that, I was in no shape to work. I needed Tkay there.

We would sit on the floor to eat because we didn't have any furniture for a very long time; we couldn't afford it. Looking back, it was a bleak existence. It would never have occurred to me to ask Papa for money, that wasn't something we do in our family. In any case, after the war, like the majority of businessmen in Sierra Leone, my dad suffered financially and certainly had no ready cash to fall back on or hand out.

That first week I suffered terrible jetlag, which I didn't understand at all because no one had explained to us what that was. I'd fall asleep in the day and then at night I was wide awake, so I would go out for a walk along the nearby streets or along King Georges Road. This is a major multi-lane transit road and there were all these big trucks speeding by. I would sit on the kerb and watch them. It was the first time I had ever seen trucks carrying cars on their trailers. I would just sit and stare at them. By now I was starting to wonder what I was doing here in this very strange place. I don't know what I expected and I quickly realised I hadn't thought about it nearly enough. This wasn't what I was hoping for at all and I wanted to go back to Sierra Leone. Homesickness was beginning to consume me. I was missing Papa terribly and longed to be back with him in our yellow house on the hill in Kissy. What I wouldn't have given for an afternoon sitting at his feet on our verandah.

At that time, we were the only African faces in Wiley Park, and right from that first night I felt extremely scared. I didn't feel at ease here at all. As a nervous newcomer, it seemed to me like there was no sense of community here, no warmth. A group of men who lived nearby started harassing us, and I was really frightened. I think it was mainly because of my sister, who, as I have said, is very beautiful and always attracts attention. I was still small like a child. But they would just look at us all the time and then they started banging on our door at night. It took me right back to my time with the rebels and soon I couldn't sleep at all.

That time was really frightening and so isolating. Coming to Australia, I felt like I was still in a war zone.

We ended up staying in Wiley Park for just a few weeks and never had any furniture in the unit. I was too terrified and I could not live there. Fortunately, there was a family acquaintance in Sydney, Mr Raymond, who knew my dad because he used to live in Macauley Street in Kissy. He had heard from Mr Condé that two girls were having trouble and were too scared to live in the two-bedroom apartment they had been allocated. Mr Condé was trying to move Mr Raymond and his family in to take over our lease. When Mr Raymond came to see the place and realised it was Pa Conteh's daughters who needed help, he kindly agreed. Even in Australia my dear Papa was watching over us.

For a little under a month, my sister went and stayed with a friend and I stayed with Marion and her family, just while we sorted ourselves out.

Before the war I was very sociable and loved talking to people and helping out with their problems. Tkay was more discerning about her social circle. But the war changed all of us and in Australia it was as if our personalities had swapped a bit. I was probably suffering from post-traumatic stress disorder, only then no one recognised it as such. I didn't want to be around people and was becoming quite isolated. Tkay, however, made friends easily within the growing Sierra Leonean community and fitted in quickly. We loved each other very much but we were going in different directions. I avoided contact with people because the conversation would always lead to Sierra Leone and the war. It became part of my identity in other people's eyes and I found that hard.

The way people in Australia saw me was new for me. People didn't understand my accent and would laugh at my pronunciation, so I just stopped talking to them. Their laughter made me feel I was stupid which, even though it probably wasn't meant that way, hurt and was also confusing. I realised I stood out: I was black, which had never been a thing for me before. And that made me feel not just alone but very small, especially because it would happen again and again. It still happens to this day, in fact. It may seem like a tiny, harmless thing, but these constant small paper cuts – these constant suggestions that I am 'different' – have a cumulative effect that is hugely hurtful.

I couldn't stay with Marion's family indefinitely, so Tkay and I ended up renting a room from a woman called Liz. She was from Papua New Guinea and I think she understood a little about how we were feeling. Also, she was dating a Sierra Leonean man, so she was very accepting of our culture.

The apartment was in the suburb of Penshurst, further south along King Georges Road. It was away from the main road – a huge improvement on our Wiley Park apartment – and in a quiet street with a few trees. Liz had two bedrooms and rented one to Tkay and me to share. With all of Liz's furnishings her unit was more welcoming for us; it felt like a place we could live in.

Liz was very carefree, and a lot of fun. She loved us being around, and she especially loved it when Tkay cooked African food. My sister is the best cook in the world. I love her jollof rice – just the smell of it takes me back to Africa. It's like an African pilaf: a spicy tomato-based rice dish with puréed red capsicums and onions and beef or chicken.

Liz was totally into the cultures of Africa, so it was good for us to be with that kind of person when everyone else saw us as something strange. But when she said, 'Oh, I love Africans,' I really didn't understand. Why would you not? It's like when people would say to me, 'I love black people.' I was even more bemused by this comment. 'So there's a thing about *not* loving black people?' I would ask myself. People still say this to me today, and it still confuses me.

It was really cramped for me and Tkay at Liz's flat, though; sharing a room wasn't ideal for either of us, and after six months of this we realised we needed more space. We had put our names down with the Canterbury Bankstown Youth Service. Run by Mission Australia, a Christian charity, CBYS helps to find housing for young people who are homeless or in need. A genuinely kind man called Patrick (we are still close friends today), who was especially concerned about us, had been looking for something for us for a while. At first he came up with an apartment in Punchbowl, which is next to Wiley Park. But even though I was grateful for Patrick's help, I knew I couldn't go back to that area, and when I told him why he understood. Then Patrick heard of a new apartment block being built in Beverly Hills, which is a nice, quiet suburb just fifteen minutes by bus from Penshurst. The block had six units – two per floor – and was government-owned for social housing. It was perfect for us, and in 2001 we moved in.

We were on the top floor and had two bedrooms, a living room with dining area, kitchen, bathroom and balcony. From our balcony there was a distant view of the city: we could just make out Centrepoint Tower rising up to the sky.

The apartment was brand-new with wall-to-wall carpeting and felt right. By this time, Tkay, who had been working every spare moment, had earned enough money to buy us some furniture and for the first time we were able to create our own space with our own things. I bought a second-hand single bed from the Salvos and Tkay bought a new double bed for her room. Then she bought a fridge and a microwave and eventually, after a couple of months, the apartment was fully furnished. We had a tan leather sofa with a matching chair, which made us think of Pa Conteh back at home. In fact, without meaning to do so, we had furnished our new home much like our apartment in the big yellow house.

Our neighbours in the building were mostly older. Most of us moved in at around the same time, and we became a close-knit community. There was one lady, Helen – we called her 'Mam' – who was originally from Israel and lived on her own. She became a good friend and I still pop in to see her.

Beverly Hills was a wonderful place to live. King George's Road, with its lively strip of restaurants and a cinema, was within walking distance of the apartment, as was the train station. The whole area felt so peaceful and safe. Our unit was warm and clean, and it felt like our home. But I was still a long way from feeling like Australia was home.

CHAPTER TWELVE

Finding my way

When I first arrived in Australia, I needed to go to school and study for my HSC. And I wanted to go to school. It had always been such a happy place for me, so I thought it might help me adjust to life here and fit in. And I could hear Papa's voice in my head drumming home the importance of education. I enrolled myself in Penshurst Girls High School, just down the road from Liz's flat. I had to fill out all the registration forms myself, which I was surprised about; I had thought I would get help. In the end, it was Liz who helped me with the paperwork. (When I spoke to Marion recently, she told me that her schooling was all organised for her.)

I was really excited to start school. I needed a focus in my life and I hoped this would be it. There was a uniform – a blue dress – and I loved the idea of wearing it and being smart and looking after my appearance. But while I thought I looked just like everyone else in my uniform, I was an object of intense interest – from afar – and the other students stared at me all the time. I suspect they had never had an African person in that school before. Before I came to Australia, I didn't even know I was black; in Sierra Leone we didn't recognise colour like that. I didn't even picture myself as being black. I was just a human being. The fact that the colour of my skin seemed to mean so much was very strange for me.

There was no abuse, no one hit me or called me names – at least not in my earshot. But I was treated as an oddity right from that first day. The teachers knew that I was a refugee from the war and that I had been kidnapped and released, but not the detail. So they were very aware of me, and probably made sure no one bullied me, but I would always sit by myself in the schoolyard because most of the girls didn't want to sit with me. I do remember one lovely girl who would sit with me – Erin. We still chat on Instagram. But the other girls saw me as a 'bush girl' from Africa. They were only children, of course, and had possibly never met anyone from Africa before. They didn't know where Sierra Leone was; they had no idea there had been a war, and they didn't ask. They weren't curious about anything like that. Instead, they asked questions like, 'Do you see lions all the time?' or 'Have you touched a snake or eaten a rat?' in much the same way, I suppose, that some people might think kangaroos hop across the Sydney Harbour Bridge. I think it was based on what they had seen on television about Africa. They thought that I had lived like Tarzan in the jungle; they didn't seem to realise that I came from a home with walls and furniture and all the things they had in their houses. Their questions made me feel like I was different and that there was something wrong with me. I didn't understand, because I'd never seen a lion or a snake – the first time I saw those things was in Taronga Zoo. As a result, I didn't talk too much to other girls and kept myself to myself.

Lessons were different for me here too. In Sierra Leone we sat in one classroom and the teachers would come to us for each subject. Here, it was the pupils who moved, and I was in a new classroom, often with a different group of students, for each subject. The subject and curriculum were similar to those in Africa, but the history and geography came from a whole different standpoint, and to be honest I never really caught up – the gap was too huge. At boarding school I had really enjoyed performing: playing the trumpet and being on stage, that was my thing. But in Australia I couldn't find a way to fit in to the drama and music on offer; it seemed so far from what I could achieve.

Things were different outside the classroom, too. For example, I had to prepare my own lunchbox for school. At boarding school, we had lunch cooked for us and served in the dining room, and when I was back in Kissy Papa always prepared our school lunchboxes, so I had to catch up quickly. In Sierra Leone, we spent our lunch hours playing games and laughing and singing together. At my school in Australia, everyone separated into their cliques and sat in groups talking. There were no games going on.

On the bright side, there was a lovely teacher, Mrs Harper, who was originally from India. Her husband was a principal at another school. Mrs Harper took me under her wing – as an Indian Australian, she was sensitive to how I was feeling.

I think the principal, Ms O'Brien, helped with that, too. Mrs Harper was the first person who really understood what I was going through. She was very strong on discipline, which I felt comfortable with because my dad was like that, too. She would invite me to her home over the weekend and treated me like one of her children. I would join in setting the table for dinner and cleaning up afterwards. She would also ask me out to dinner with her friends and I was included in the conversation. With Mrs Harper and her friends, I felt accepted for being me.

But, still, it was very lonely. I was the loneliest I've ever been in my entire life. I cried a lot and most of the time I didn't want to go to school at all. And when I'd come home from school I was alone there, too. My sister was working hard and going out with her new friends. Our schedules didn't overlap, because Tkay was doing shift work. Often she would be sleeping when I came home from school and then she would go out to work; she was busy providing food for us.

★

It was not only at school that I felt isolated. Australian life is all about enjoying the great outdoors – the beaches, the ocean – and the fantastic cafes and restaurants. But not for me.

I remember once I went with Marion and a couple of others from Sierra Leone to Manly, a famous beach in the north of Sydney. We went to a nice restaurant because we wanted to treat ourselves. As soon as we arrived, everyone started staring at us. When we tried to sit at a table inside, the staff said we had to sit outside. The plates were dirty, so we asked for clean ones, but they wouldn't give them to us. I think they knew they couldn't refuse to serve us, so they just took the coward's way out and treated us with contempt, in a way that showed us we should leave. I didn't go back to Manly for almost a decade after that.

Looking back today, I realise that most people meant no harm. It was simply that I was different to them and a new face in that world. The effect on me, though, was at first bemusement and then hurt. It wasn't so much that I felt a lack of belonging in Australia, it's that I was totally lost. I knew I was coming to a country where there was no one here that looked like me, but I didn't understand why they didn't like me when they didn't even know me.

When I was growing up – and this is possibly something Papa taught us – my siblings and I never felt as if we were excluded from anything: we had the right to be there. Whether I was with people who were very high up – leaders, politicians, teachers or people from the UNHCR – I felt that I could pull up a chair at their table and sit down with them on their level. Yes, of course it was my place to do so; it didn't occur to me it wouldn't be. But I can also sense when somebody doesn't want me to be around. I can sense it even if there are 200 people there and just one person doesn't like me. When that happens, I excuse myself and get up from the table. I don't leave entirely, I will stand and listen, but I won't stay around for them to abuse me.

Now, it felt like I needed to excuse myself everywhere I turned. It didn't seem to matter what I did in those first few years, I couldn't find a place for myself in Australian life.

I wanted to leave so badly. My head, my whole body, was screaming.

Since then I have learned how to deal with the racism I face daily. I know it is rarely about me but more about the person doling out the abuse, but it hasn't abated. Recently, when I was in my car in a Sydney suburb I know really well and feel comfortable in, I pulled out from the kerb and the man in the four-wheel drive behind didn't see me and sounded his horn. I held my hand up to apologise, but he was really mad and followed me around the corner. When he saw I was black, he threw an apple at my car and called me a nigger, holding up his middle finger. In that moment I felt scared – not of him, as such, but of the heat of the situation, the idea that someone who didn't know me could be so angry and abusive. Had my children been in the car I would have reported him to the police, but in that moment I refused to let this man ruin what had been a lovely day. I turned the music up and turned the other cheek. I have discovered that this is what I have to do for the most part.

★

At school, Mrs Harper and the principal sensed that I was struggling, and they were worried about me, but I don't think they really understood the depth of my story. How could they? They just knew that I was a refugee from Sierra Leone. But they recognised that I was in trouble and organised for me to see a counsellor who had an office in Rockdale. I would go by train to see her and she would try to get me to talk. She knew a bit of the back story about what

I'd been through, and obviously she would have researched Sierra Leone and read about what generally happened to girls who were kidnapped, and from that she would make assumptions. She would always start by saying the same thing and I remember it so clearly, because to this day I don't get why a person would ever say this to someone in my position. She said: 'I understand. I understand what you've been through.' How could she? *I* didn't even understand what I'd been through. It made me angry and I couldn't get on with her at all. I didn't challenge her, because I didn't know how to back then, but I never talked. Never. It went on for months. I would keep the appointments, because that's what the school wanted me to do, but I was silent.

Marion told me recently that her school also sent her to a counsellor and, like me, she'd felt unable to open up. I don't blame the counsellors – they were just trying to do their job and, in retrospect, I can see the cultural divide between African and Australian girls was gaping. They just couldn't appreciate what it was like for us in this strange place.

I've never really felt a need for people to like me, so it didn't worry me that I wasn't getting along with the counsellor, and although it was a lonely life back then it wasn't being alone per se that was the problem for me. I like my own company and being by myself. I can see now what the problem was: I was sad. Sad from the experiences I was having at school and the places I was visiting; sad to discover that humans are like this. I was experiencing racism for the first time. My sadness had nothing to do with what had happened to me back in Sierra Leone; it was about the shortcomings of *this* life, this place that was going to be my fresh start.

I couldn't afford to phone my family much because it was expensive, but I knew they needed to hear from me because they were concerned. I bought phone cards but they were expensive and didn't last for long. When I talked to my mum, first in Guinea and then in London (she moved there alone in 2002), it was not really like a chatty talk; it was more just checking in to tell her how we were doing and to give her peace of mind. It was a bit different with Papa, who was sick and still in London going through his treatment. He was very worried. He would talk to my sister and ask, 'How is she?' Tkay would say I was fine, but he didn't believe her. I knew Papa could tell something was very wrong.

The only light I found in those dark days was at church. My faith had been the thing that helped me most when I was kidnapped and now I needed it more than ever. It kept me sane and helped me to believe in my life and my future after what I'd been through, which I really could not process at all – and to some extent I still can't. I had seen so many things that I can't even begin to describe: walking over hundreds of dead bodies, or hiding underneath them, using the corpses to shield myself from bullets. People wouldn't think what happened was possible, but it was real. So many vicious things. But I had to believe in something good because I'd come from something good. My father was good. Everything around me when I was growing up was good. The source of the goodness that I needed to seek out when I first arrived in Australia, and which I will always seek out wherever I am, was the word of God. So I found a church right away.

At first I went to a Methodist church in Penshurst, but I didn't feel anything there. It was different from the Methodist church in Africa. People kneeled to pray and to take communion. It was more about the process and that didn't feel right for me. I didn't understand the difference between all the churches – Methodist, Catholic, Pentecostal, Seventh-day Adventist. I did not have a clue. I just thought all churches were the same. I thought Australians were Christian. I didn't get that there were different forms of Christianity.

Then a Sierra Leonean churchgoer suggested I try the Revival Life Centre. I liked it. It gave me a sense of something bigger than myself and that was what I was after. It's a Pentecostal church, part of the Australian Christian Churches, and it felt the most like my church in Africa, although the building was nothing like those at home. From the outside, it looked like a big English house with mock Tudor beams and a pitched roof. Inside was a big hall where the services are held filled with rows of chairs in front of a platform where the pastor preaches. On one side is the band which plays at every service. It had a joyfulness to it, with lots of singing, and was much freer than the Methodist church with all its rules and rituals. In Sierra Leone, we like to worship in a celebratory way, with praise filling the church, and here I could do that.

I loved the church services, but I have to admit it was tough to start with. The other parishioners were very curious and kept asking me where I was from. But I couldn't talk about it. I didn't want to. This was my new start, putting all that behind me. I would just say I was a refugee and then, after the service, I would slip out as quickly as I could. I still liked going there, though; I found a peace in it, and this was the only place I could find such peace at the time.

I was fortunate that a couple who lived near me, Robyn and David, used to give me a lift to church, which was really nice and made me feel more welcome. After the service, they would drive me home again, or sometimes I would walk the fifteen or twenty minutes home. I love walking, and it cleared my head so I could think about what I had heard in church and try to apply it to my life.

It was at church that I met Michael Dwyer. I call Michael my spiritual father, and I really believe it was God who brought him into my life at that crucial time. In those days Michael was the CEO of First State Super, the biggest superannuation company in Australia, but he was also on the board of Australia for UNHCR and he no doubt recognised that I was a refugee. I am also really close to his wife Janelle, who I think is an angel on earth. Michael and Janelle have four kids – Daniel, Sarah, Jess and Joel. Today they would say they have five children, because I am like their fifth child, which is a great feeling for me.

When I first met Michael and his family, they tried to talk to me like the others, but I didn't give anybody the opportunity. I would sit by myself and then I would leave. It took a long time before I connected with other people there, and I think it was really the love of the Dwyer family that made me open up. The whole family would look over at me in church and smile, and after a while I started to smile back. I knew they were talking about me because you could see them all huddled together, but I felt as if they were saying nice things. Then one day, as I was about to leave after the service, Michael came up to me and said, 'My family and I just think that you're the most beautiful girl we've ever seen.'

I was so surprised. I said, 'Oh, thank you,' and I just ran. I was taken aback and didn't know how to respond. To be described as beautiful is a compliment that I have found hard to accept since the time I was kidnapped by the rebels in Sierra Leone. I had been abducted and raped 'because I was too beautiful', the men said. It made me feel so ashamed and I still find it hard if anyone calls me beautiful. But hearing that word from the Dwyers was a turning point, because this was the first time I had heard myself described as beautiful and felt it was a good thing. I remember I went home and I called my mum and told her what Michael had said. Eleas agreed it was a good thing, and from that moment on I felt really welcome at the church. I joined the youth group. There I forged an immediate bond with Janelle: we talked about our lives, about faith, about anything and everything. We both felt an instant togetherness from the moment we met. It was like we'd each found something we didn't even know we were missing. She is my confidant and we have a very special connection, one that's difficult to describe: I call her my spiritual companion. She's the first person I call with the happiest and the most challenging news. I wholeheartedly adore her.

I think the one thing that really made me open up to Janelle and the rest of the family was that they never asked me about my past, and that was very rare; they were the only people who were sensitive in that way. Everyone else wanted to talk about the war and what had happened, but I couldn't and wouldn't talk about it. The Dwyers understood that.

Michael and especially Janelle saw a light in me, and that felt really special. After a while, Janelle assumed the role of my spiritual mum in Australia and naturally Michael became my spiritual dad. It wasn't a formal role, just a reflection of our closeness.

It was at the Revival Life Centre that I was baptised in early 2001. I hadn't been baptised in Sierra Leone and I think it's significant that this happened in Australia, because it was all about me taking control of my life, following my heart. Even though I had been a Christian for some time, this was the affirmation that I was moving away from my family's religion and making up my own mind.

It was something I asked the pastor to do when I felt ready. I didn't think I needed it to feel holy, because I felt that anyway, every minute of every day. And I didn't think I needed to have my sins washed away, as some people do when they are baptised. But I did want to make peace with what happened to me.

Mine was the only baptism that day. There was a baptismal pool at the front of the church which is usually covered over during services. On this day, it was filled with water. I wore a long white robe, held my nose and was completely immersed in the water, emerging dripping wet. It felt really good, as if I had been cleansed of what happened to me. On that day, I told myself that I would not be with a man until I was married. A friend had said that if you didn't have sex for a long time your hymen would grow back and you would be 're-virgined'. I wanted this so much. I wanted my virginity back, and for me the baptism was the start of that process.

Afterwards I was taken into a room to get changed. I felt no different towards God, we were as connected as ever, but I felt differently towards my body. I felt new, pristine, unused. It was an important moment.

Being baptised also meant that more people became aware of me, but I still wasn't ready to share a great deal of my story. All they knew was that I was from Sierra Leone, a recent refugee who had been kidnapped and needed asylum. That was all.

★

Another person who was helping me a lot at that time was my teacher, Mrs Harper. I was at a different school now; Penshurst Girls School had become part of the Georges River College and we moved to a new campus in Oatley for our senior studies. My principal from Penshurst, Ms O'Brien, had moved there to run it. She took some of the key teachers with her, including Mrs Harper, which was brilliant for me because I was still close to her. From the weekends I sometimes spent with her and her family, she knew what was happening in my life and how much I was struggling.

Mrs Harper was teaching me how to speak better English, because even though I understood the language well, at home we had spoken Krio. I was still very shy speaking English, and I could tell people were having trouble understanding me. It was easier not to speak at all than to deal with people's laughter. Mrs Harper would make me sit at the far end of her dining table because she wanted me to speak clearly and to project. She was great, and it is thanks to Mrs Harper that my English improved so quickly and today I am able to give speeches and go out to schools to talk to Australian students. She really boosted my confidence, which I sorely needed then.

But things were about to get worse before they got better.

CHAPTER THIRTEEN

My beloved Pa

I was in my final year of high school at the Oatley Senior Campus of Georges River College when I heard from Fatmata and Mabinty in London that Papa needed to see me. He had been very sick for some time, but they had been keeping it from me because they didn't want it to affect my new start in Australia. Even now they didn't reveal to me how serious it was. They realised I was not in great shape myself, struggling to adapt to my new life in Australia, and knowing how close I was to my dad they didn't want to upset me further.

I was at school, I reminded them when they called, and I couldn't afford to fly to London. And that was when they told me: Papa had liver cancer and he didn't have long to live. He wanted to go home to Sierra Leone for however long he had left, but he wouldn't go until he had seen me. I was shocked; I'd thought he was in London having treatment that would make him better. I don't think I really believed that he was dying, though. Of course death was ahead of him at some point, but at that moment I didn't realise how very sick he was, even when I spoke to him on the phone and he said, 'You have to come, Mommy.'

Tkay was working and earning money, and she was able to pay for a flight, so she flew to London. When she returned, she said I needed to get there quickly. Still, I wasn't thinking Papa was about to die. I just thought he wanted to see me in London before he went back to Sierra Leone, and of course I wanted that too.

Mrs Harper knew how anxious I was about my dad, so she did this incredible thing: she spoke to the principal and they hatched a plan. They knew I didn't have enough money and that Papa was passing and I might not get to see him. So the school raised the money for me to fly to London, and then the principal topped up the amount with her own money. Just when I thought I wasn't fitting in, I realised people cared deeply and wanted to help. It was a good feeling in a very dark time.

But it took a while to organise the flights. Papa had already seen Tkay and didn't understand why I wasn't with her. He accused the twins of stopping me from coming and not telling me the extent of his illness. He was pretty cross with them. Fatmata tells me that when Papa heard that I was coming, he started to get better. He sat up and started to eat food after days of eating very little, and it was then that the twins truly understood how close Papa and I were.

Eventually I flew to London on a Qantas plane on my own from Sydney. It was only the second time I had flown and the first time I had flown to London. I don't remember much of that flight. I was worried but also thrilled that I was going to be seeing Papa. I had felt so alone in Sydney and was longing to see him.

Mabinty and my mum came to pick me up at Heathrow. Mum had been going to see Papa every day to help with his care. It felt right to me that they were together again.

It was good to see my mother and sister when I got off the plane, but all I could think about was my dad. They hadn't told Papa that I was arriving that day because he had been in such a state about me and they wanted to make sure I was actually in London before they raised his hopes. Just before we got into the car to drive to the house, they called to tell him I was on my way. I remember my sister on the phone saying that he had just then started talking again, because his speech hadn't been good. They told him, 'Mommy's here,' and then they put him on the phone to me. He was very excited and so was I.

Papa was in the house in Catford, in south-east London, where he used to live when he did business in London. Fatmata and her husband lived there now, and Mabinty lived not far away in Elephant and Castle. While we drove through London, Fatmata washed him and dressed him ready for our reunion; he was very sick indeed and couldn't do anything for himself, so Fatmata's husband would carry him to the toilet and bathe him, but I didn't know all that until later.

Everyone had been concealing from me just how gravely ill Papa was, so when I finally saw him I was totally unprepared. I so wanted to see Papa, to touch his face and hold his hand again. When we arrived at the house, my sister and mum knew that I was going to be shocked, so they stood and

waited in the doorway like soldiers on guard. They told me
he was in the bedroom and I went at full speed up the stairs.
I opened one door, two doors, but I couldn't see anyone.
And then I opened the door to the third bedroom and I saw
somebody asleep in the corner, but it wasn't him. I closed the
door and I went downstairs and they were all standing there,
hardly able to breathe – it was as if they were waiting for
something to explode. I said, 'I can't find him. He's not there.'
And my sister said, 'Oh, Mommy, that's him in the bed. That's
Papa.' I couldn't believe it. That wasn't my dad; it couldn't be.
He was so small. So very, very small.

★

I spent three days with Papa and then we took him to the
airport for his flight back to Freetown. In that time, he
started to talk again and the cheeky little smile of his that I'd
always loved so much came back. My sisters said that seeing
me had given him a new lease on life, he was so happy. It was
an incredible transformation from the man they had been
nursing the past year.

They were precious days. He and I had lots of conver-
sations. I would go to him in the middle of the night and
talk to him, and sometimes I would just sit with him on the
couch and hold his hand. He used to have these chubby
little hands – when I was little I used to love pulling his
fingers – but now they were so skinny. His fingers felt so
fragile. I had to be careful not to break them.

He found it hard to talk, but when he did it was to
reinforce those life lessons I still carry with me deep in my

heart. He knew I loved giving and I loved people, and he told me that was a good calling but that I must also take care of myself. Most of all, he underlined the importance of treating people right – all people, whomever they are.

We didn't talk about the war at all or what had happened to me, but we did share happy memories from my childhood. He told me one story again and again that really summed up our connection. My dad was a very emotional man and would cry at the drop of a hat, often happy tears. When I was a little girl and I saw him crying, I would burst into tears too, to share his tears with him, and then everyone would laugh at us and we would laugh too. I love that memory.

As we talked we cried a lot as well, every night, and these were sad tears. He used to say to me, 'You have to stop crying because you're going to make me sad. I know you're fine.' I told him that I was a practising Christian now and that I was going to church, and I tried to tell him some of the Bible stories I loved, but he just thought it was kid's stuff. I could tell he wasn't taking me seriously, but I didn't mind.

He said he couldn't die until he had seen me and he had said to my sisters, 'If I go without seeing Mommy, I will never forgive you.' I believe he wanted to see me to make sure I was okay. I wanted him to have that peace and, even though I was far from okay, I told him I had lots of friends in Australia and that I was doing well at school, and he believed me. It put his mind at rest and I could tell he relaxed a bit.

Before he left for Sierra Leone, Papa told my mum that he was sorry for abandoning her all those years ago when I was little. It was the first time he had acknowledged her pain, she tells me today. I think this was a time for him to settle everything and put things right.

I went with him to the airport and there he was put into a buggy because he was no longer able to walk. My sisters had dressed him in lots of clothes to keep him warm but also so he didn't look sick. They didn't want to risk him not being allowed onto the plane. As the buggy drove off we followed it right up to the departure gates. At the final moment Papa turned around and waved. I was sobbing; this was the last time I was going to see my beloved Papa, and I knew that now. That was our goodbye.

★

We thought that he would die as soon as he arrived home, but back in Freetown he suddenly had all this energy. Mabinty had flown back with him, thinking he might not even survive the flight. In the end, she stayed in Sierra Leone for a month before she had to return because she had to go back to work.

I stayed in London for a couple of weeks. This was my first time there, but I didn't really take it in. I had an affection for the city, because I knew it had played such a key part in Papa's life, but those days were overshadowed by his departure. Fatmata wanted to show me the sights and took me to the London Eye and to the market stalls along the South Bank. We rode around on red double-decker buses and I saw Buckingham Palace. I tried to seem enthusiastic, because I knew my sister wanted both to lift my spirits and to show off where she lived, but I was consumed with tiredness and ached to lie down and sleep. When I flew back to Sydney I slept most of the way. I kept on playing my dad's words over in my head and tried to pull myself out of my sadness.

Back in Sydney I returned to school as normal, but I cried every day. Every time I got a phone call and heard that Papa was still alive, it upset me more; all I could think of was how much he was suffering. That really broke me, because I felt I didn't have anyone to share my pain with. Tkay was there of course, but we were so different, and not very close emotionally. I didn't really know how she or my other siblings were dealing with Papa's decline. We all adored him, but we didn't talk about our feelings to each other. I cried myself to sleep every single night until my dad died, and when he did it was such a relief.

Alieu was still in Sierra Leone then – he's in the US now – and he looked after our father in his final days. Papa died on 6 May 2003, three years after I had arrived in Australia. He was buried in the graveyard just down the road from our yellow house. Alieu was the only one of Papa's children who was there at his funeral.

CHAPTER FOURTEEN

Where is my home now?

When I finished school at the end of 2003 I went into a panic. What was I going to do with my life? I knew I couldn't work in an office – for that I would need to use computers, and to do that I needed to be smart. I wasn't smart like the rest of my family – at least, that's what I believed back then. I had struggled with my lessons all through school. I didn't understand why I did so badly in the exams because I was extremely attentive in class. I would sit right in the front of the class and concentrate as hard as I could, but nothing went in. It just went straight over my head. And when there was an exam I would get so panicked I couldn't write anything. It was only years later that I was diagnosed with dyslexia.

Tkay, however, was doing really well. In 2004 she went to the Australian Catholic University to do a Bachelor of Nursing. She studied for three years for a degree and then an extra year for honours and graduated in 2008. She was flying. Today, Tkay is a mother of three and works as a qualified nurse in hospitals around Sydney and I am so proud of her.

My path would prove much harder. I would go through the newspaper employment ads and call up for jobs, but as soon as people heard my name, Aminata Conteh, and my accent, they would put down the phone immediately. It took me a while to understand that they were just reacting to my accent, because it felt really rude. But I can't change how I talk. It was impossible: no one would employ me.

I liked performance and the arts, but I didn't think it would be possible to find a job as an actor. I used to go to the cinema by myself a lot. I'd watch every movie that came out and sometimes see two back to back. But to act in a movie I would have to read scripts, and I knew that I couldn't do that; what was later identified as my dyslexia would make it too much of a challenge.

But even if I couldn't be an actor, it occurred to me that I might be able to model. I had always loved fashion, and although I was well aware by this time that I didn't look like the average Australian – whatever that was – people would often say to me that I looked like a model, so I thought I might have a chance of finding a job in that industry. I could use my interest in performance without having to take on something as big as a movie. It would be perfect for me.

I saw a listing for a modelling agency in Sydney in the local paper and rang the number. They immediately invited me to their offices in Surry Hills for an interview. At the reception was a svelte young woman who looked like a model herself. She gave me a form to fill out with my details and showed me into a waiting room. It looked exactly as

I expected a modelling agency would look. There was a TV screen sitting on a table with a constant video running of models on a catwalk and framed model shots all around the walls.

After about twenty minutes I was called in to another room to meet a group of three men and a woman. The oldest man was in his late thirties or early forties and smartly dressed – he introduced himself as one of the managers. Then there was another man around the same age who told me he was a photographer, and his laidback vibe fitted with my picture of what photographers would be like. The remaining man and woman were models who had worked overseas. They were apparently going to be training me.

I was asked to strike some poses and walk as if I was on the catwalk. Then the photographer took a portrait shot; I stood against the wall of the office and he snapped away. They said they would review the photo and call me, but they assured me I had what it took to be a model and asked if had a passport and was able to travel. I was certain that in no time I would be on a plane to Paris. I was so excited. I believed I was on the brink of an international modelling career.

About a week or two later the agency phoned me to say that I had won a free photo shoot on the following Saturday and that I should arrive with some different outfits to pose in. This was fantastic news . . . or so I thought. I turned up at the offices and we headed out into the streets of Surry Hills for my first-ever modelling shoot. There were no hair and make-up artists, nor a stylist; it was just me and the photographer. But I had no idea what a modelling shoot should look like, so I didn't think this was strange. It took about two hours and I wore a sheer floral off-the-shoulder top and tailored tan pants in one look, a red dress in another and a short black skirt and one-shoulder top in the final look. I thought it went very well.

A few days later I received another call asking me to come in to the office. At this meeting, they said the shoot was really successful and they wanted to put me on their agency's books. They presented me with a folder which had letters all about the company regulations for overseas travel, suggesting I would be staying in top hotels and flying all over the place. There was also a small flip book of my portraits from the photo shoot, which they said would be made up into a portfolio if I decided to sign with them.

But in order to join the agency, I would have to pay a fee. I can't remember exactly how much it was, but it was quite a significant sum. I went off proudly with my folder, and over the next few months I saved and saved from my Centrelink allowance until I had enough money to pay them. I went back to the offices and paid in cash. I was made to feel really special. I would be hearing from them soon, they said. But I never did. At first I called them every few days, then every few weeks, then months. No one had booked me yet, they said.

When I look back now, I realise I had been tricked. It was a scam and, in my naivety, I had catwalked right into it. But all was not lost, because I was now determined to find modelling work and eventually came across an agency called Coffee Coloured Characters. It was run by a lovely Australian lady called Lisa who was married to a Ghanaian. She had all Latino or dark-skinned people on her books and she signed me up immediately without asking for any money. I was thrilled. This was a turning point for me. I landed a lot of jobs through the agency, but they weren't modelling. I was shooting commercials and was regularly hired as an extra in movies or TV series. Australia was not yet ready for a model with my skin colour; even today it is rare to see a black model on the front of an Australian magazine.

I shot a campaign for Fanta, the soft drink, and for the sportswear brand New Balance. And I did movies, including *Superman Returns*, which was four months of solid work. It was a really big-budget movie shot in Fox Studios and around Sydney. We used to film night scenes in the city, which was so amazing. I was floating on a cloud. One of the things I liked the most was the wardrobe. I had to dress in classic vintage costumes; they were chic and elegant and made me think of my dad. That whole shoot was exciting and easily the coolest thing I had ever done. There was something in me that enjoyed being a part of the entertainment industry. It was frothy and frivolous and nothing like real life. It was a million miles away from my normal. The wonder of it enthralled me and every day I met new people who all wanted me to be there and treated me like I was one of them.

My roles were all non-speaking 'blink and you'll miss it' parts, and my appearances often ended up on the cutting room floor, but for the first time since I arrived in Australia I was having fun and I was earning money. It wasn't much, but I was starting to gain a bit of independence and a sense of worth and it felt good.

I used to be cast in a lot of extra parts in the Aussie TV soap *Home and Away*, which is shot in Sydney, and also the hospital drama series *All Saints*. I was always a patient – ironically suffering from diseases like sickle cell – but that didn't bother me. I would be lying in a hospital bed and I'd actually fall asleep, a real deep sleep, while they were filming. A few times the director would tell people, 'Don't wake her up,' and they'd go off to lunch. He would laugh and say to the cast and crew: 'She looks so peaceful!' I'd wake up and there was nobody there in the studio. I confess I did a lot of that. I clearly felt at ease around these people!

There were a number of American commercials being shot in Australia at the time and I was perfect for the US audience, so I pretty much cornered that market. At last my skin colour was working in my favour. Also, there was catering at the shoots, which I devoured. I even got to take some food home. I did this kind of work for a few years, and in a way it saved me. But I knew that it was not something I wanted to do forever and the work was sporadic. I was just exploring what I might do with my life.

★

Meanwhile, Tkay was still forging ahead. She had been dating a Sierra Leonean, and in 2005 they married. He was Christian and she was Muslim, so they opted to have a small civil ceremony rather than a religious one. Tkay had wanted her husband to move into our apartment in Beverly Hills with us, but I didn't want that. In the end, they moved to the suburb of Granville, to the north-west of Beverly Hills, and I took over our apartment on my own.

It was the best outcome for me. I needed my space as

I started to build my adult life and I enjoyed living alone, and it felt really nice to have the whole place to myself. Plus I loved living in Beverly Hills.

But I was still trying to find a place for myself in Australia and a job I could do that would mean something or teach me something. The modelling agency work was fine, but I knew there was no future in it. I thought I might make a good flight attendant. I didn't have a partner, so I thought I would travel around the world and meet new people. I was very naive, but whenever I have wanted to do something in my life I've always just gone ahead and done it.

I didn't know what the procedure was or the requirements for the job. For example, I had no clue that you had to be able to swim – which I couldn't – or speak lots of languages – which I didn't. I simply drew up my résumé, went to the airport and dropped it off at every airline office, announcing, 'I want to be a flight attendant,' as I proudly handed over my documents. I then went home and waited for the companies to respond. Most of them didn't, of course. I think Qantas was the only airline to acknowledge my application with a letter to tell me they were considering it. Now, I know it is a standard letter that they generate, but back then I believed them. I was surprised that I never heard from them again.

In my heart, I still felt my purpose in life was going to be helping others; I just didn't know how, and it was frustrating me. In fact, I was starting to get that lost feeling again, like I was stuck in a tunnel and every exit from the tunnel was blocked. My new world was closing in on me and I couldn't see a way forward. In Australia you couldn't do anything without a certificate, a degree, a diploma . . . and I had none of these. What was ahead for me?

The war in Sierra Leone had been officially declared over in 2002 and by now it was 2005. I'd heard that Freetown was a good place to go these days and that people were heading back to have parties on the beach. Everything was better, the country was alive and beating, or so I was told. My heart was aching for my country, my culture, my people.

So I decided to go back, just for a visit. With the money I was making from the commercials, I had enough to pay for a flight. I was thinking I would stay for a couple of months. I didn't want to pay the extra for the flexible round-trip fare, so I bought a one-way ticket. It sounds like a dramatic move, but it really wasn't; I just needed to find some direction, and at that moment the right direction was to go home.

It was December 2005 when I boarded the plane in Sydney bound for Freetown. The last time I was in Freetown I was running for my life, but now all I could think of was the Freetown of my childhood, a place of security and certainty. I knew I couldn't wind back the clock, I really did, but I needed a restorative dose of Africa. Now I realise what I was feeling was homesickness, which seems a pretty natural emotion considering what I had been through.

I didn't know what to expect. I thought I would just go and reconnect with my city. I wasn't scared and I didn't think of Daramy at all. I hadn't talked to anybody about him since I came to Australia, so there was no one to tell me I should be scared, and it honestly didn't occur to me.

I arranged to stay with Abdul Kpakra, a friend who lived not too far from where I was raised and was now working for the US embassy in a really good job. It was a very safe home with his mother living there and his sisters also. My plan was to stay with them for a few days and then stay on my own in a hotel. I didn't want to go back to my house, the yellow house. Now Papa was gone, that didn't feel right, and in any case it was rented out to tenants.

Abdul picked me up from the airport and made sure I had a chauffeur who would drive me around while I was in Sierra Leone. It was night-time when I arrived, and pitch-black, so I couldn't make out anything at all as we drove home to Abdul's place. In Africa, when there are no electric lights the darkness is impenetrable; you can't even see your hand.

I showered and went straight to bed, expecting to be tired after my long flight. But I couldn't sleep. I was so excited to find this vibrant culture that everyone had been telling me about; this big party that was making Africans leave their new homes in the West to spend Christmas in Freetown. I could barely contain myself as I waited for morning to come. I thought it would be heaven.

At dawn, I pulled on my clothes and went outside to see the sun rise and watch the beautiful change in my home town reveal itself to me.

It started with a few people moving about in the grey-black of the early morning darkness. They were emerging from their houses and making their way to the mosque as they did every day. I longed for this place to be bright, for the golden sun to take me home.

And then the sun emerged and I saw the scene in broad daylight . . . It looked like a war zone.

My vision of Freetown was of how the city had looked before the war. I was really stunned. What were people talking about? Coming here, to this place, to have a good time? Sierra Leone, my Africa, was completely destroyed.

I saw kids carrying buckets of stones to their school. They wore scrappy uniforms and no shoes and looked really poor. When I asked them what they were doing, they said they were taking stones to rebuild the school. Everything had gone backwards.

I felt a huge wave of fear wash over me. How could I talk to these people? They were trapped here whereas I had a choice: I could go straight back to Sydney.

I saw people who had no hands. I saw people limping along with only one leg, their bodies emaciated. The legacies of our war were stark and ugly. I couldn't talk to anyone, there could be no pity for me. Compared to these people, I was living like a goddess. And yet I felt so sad and bereft.

I went to see my old house only once. I was with my brother Alieu, who by that time was living in the US but, like me, had come to visit Freetown. He wanted us to take part in a prayer ceremony together for Papa. He had arranged the full Muslim ceremony, killing goats to prepare for a feast, but he started early and when I arrived the whole thing was inching towards its end and I had missed most of it. This was for our dad, but somehow it wasn't working for me.

I suspect my vision was clouded somewhat by a family rift that had opened up after Papa's death. My dad had arranged his affairs really carefully before he died, so that all his children would benefit equally; he didn't want us to fall out over money. But it wasn't to be. The yellow house was left to me, Tigidankay and Alieu, while Baimba's building was left to Ibrahim. Papa told us that we must never sell the house and he left a chunk of money so we could maintain it. Today none of us lives there; instead each floor of the house is rented out as a separate unit. I give my share of the income straight to my mum, to look after her, and so if there's an emergency she has money in reserve. Personally, I didn't want anything from Papa; I had inherited so much from him that was nothing to do with money.

The hotel in Wellington became a bit of a problem after the war, though, because at first we couldn't persuade the residents who had been living there rent-free to move out. Papa had intended for us to sell it and give the money away. He had written out a list of where he wanted the proceeds to go and none of it was to us directly. The most important portion was to be used to build a mosque. When the sale went through, my sister Fatmata put the money in an account which was under the control of three imams and Alieu, as well as herself. But the mosque was never built. Papa was so determined that the money from his estate would not cause a rift between us siblings, but it happened anyway. Today my sisters have no contact with Alieu and I have very little, which is sad, because he and I were so close, especially during my kidnap.

After the prayers, Alieu and I went to the yellow house. It looked exactly the same except about 90 times smaller. So small. I walked in the gate and thought, yes, this was our house – but was it? I said hello to two neighbours and then people started to recognise me. It was too much for me, so I left.

Now I realised that staying in a hotel alone wasn't such a good idea, so I remained with Abdul and his family. I was loved there, and his mum looked after me as if I were a daughter. But I decided I had to do something to help.

I asked Abdul if there was an orphanage nearby, because I knew that so many kids had been orphaned by the war. He told me about a Muslim orphanage that also had a school attached. If I wasn't using my money for a hotel room, I thought, I should give it to the people who were looking after these kids. The idea just came to me, and instantly I knew that was what I had to do.

Most people in Sierra Leone at the time were not in a philanthropic mood. They were either struggling or, if they were visiting, they were spending their money on partying. They had worked hard overseas and now they wanted to have a good time with their family and friends and just live life. They wanted to forget their troubles and enjoy themselves.

I wasn't interested in that. I was here to give back. I knew that now. It was a powerful emotion I couldn't control. I was so unusual in this that the newspaper took my picture and wrote a story about me helping the orphanage.

It was really beautiful with the kids in the orphanage and at last I felt some peace. We have this belief in African culture that when the sun is shining and then there's rain, it's a blessing. And at the orphanage it was sunny and then it rained a little bit. I remember it was so hot then all of a sudden there was this fresh rain. Every day I would go and see the kids and help out. It was like therapy for me.

But then I got sick. I hadn't been thinking at all when I left Sydney. I didn't have any inoculations and I wasn't taking malaria medication. The mosquitoes in Sierra Leone transmit malaria all year round; it isn't seasonal. I had never had malaria before and I thought I was going to die. I couldn't move from the bed, not even to have a shower. It was terrifying. The only food I could keep down was sweet rice. I didn't call my mum or anyone I knew to tell them that I was sick; I felt really foolish for not having taken precautions. So I suffered in silence, and when finally I was better I flew back to Sydney. I had been away for three months.

When I arrived back in Sydney, my heart was aching for my country. But I also felt a light growing inside me. I knew I couldn't do anything in Sierra Leone, I couldn't stay there, but I could do something for my people from Australia. I didn't know yet what it might be, but the spark had been lit.

CHAPTER FIFTEEN

My 'yay' moments

After my experiences in Sierra Leone, I felt a powerful connection with the Aminata Conteh who wanted to be of service, to help people: the girl my father had raised. So when I returned to Sydney, I decided to start volunteering at Canterbury Bankstown Youth Services, the agency that had found my unit in Beverly Hills. I went to see Patrick, my contact there, and asked how I could help.

Patrick and his colleague Nashmeer were very happy to have me. I was especially helpful with the refugees, because I could connect with them easily. I understood their problems because they were my problems. Refugees feel intimidated all the time. Asking for help is very hard, not just because it's a matter of pride but also because in the West there is the pressure to look downtrodden, sad and defeated all the time – as a refugee should look – and then to be eternally grateful for anything coming your way. Of course, in order to be a refugee you have to have a horror story, but constantly having to retell it in order to prove you deserve assistance is degrading and traumatic. Financial help is the most common need, but the authorities always require a lot of detail in order to give that support, and many times a refugee would rather stay quiet and suffer than parade their pain in order to be accepted. My role was to talk to these refugees on a more human level and give them the confidence to take control of their own destiny.

I also helped with the other young people in need. We used to receive referrals either from schools or from family members for at-risk children who needed emergency accommodation. I was an assistant in the office and some-times we would go out in the car to collect the children and bring them back to the office, or we would take them to lunch so we could talk to them. Eventually CBYS started paying me small amounts for my work there.

I was also still doing some jobs for the talent agency, but they were starting to dry up and I knew I had to find proper employment. But the same old barriers kept on plaguing me.

I went to Sydney's University of Technology (UTS) and signed up for a community management course. It was by correspondence, which wasn't ideal as it required a lot of reading and writing, and with my dyslexia still un-diagnosed I just couldn't get through it. I dropped out after three months.

By this time, I had learned how to drive. A good friend taught me; we would go on long drives out of Sydney and I learned in a couple of months. I passed my driving test first time and bought a brand-new car – a sky blue Toyota Yaris – with a windfall; the Fanta ad I'd appeared in was replaying internationally and I received some unexpected royalties. The car gave me a wonderful sense of independence and the option to look further afield for a job.

Then a friend of mine, a Ghanaian called Ibraham who worked at Sydney airport supplying food to all the catering outlets, called me. He told me that a new fashion store had opened at the airport. He had spoken to the girls running it and they had said I could drop off my résumé. The minute I heard the words 'fashion store' I thought, yes, this was for me. I had always loved fashion.

The next day was 24 November 2007. I remember the date exactly because it was election day and everyone was going crazy. But even though it was the weekend, I knew I had to get in there quickly; opportunities like this were rare, and I had to grab it before it slipped away. So I drove with my cousin Isatu to the airport. I was allowed to sponsor visas for some family members to live in Australia, and Isatu and her sister Fatmata had moved to Sydney in 2005. I left Isatu in the car outside the Qantas domestic terminal short-term car park – I had parked really badly, but I didn't care. Clutching my résumé, I ran inside. Something told me this was going to be my day.

Ibraham had said that the shop in question was the first fashion store that I would come to after security. I rushed through security, throwing my bag in the tray to pass through the X-ray machine, and emerged in the departure area. There I spied David Lawrence. When I spoke to Ibraham afterwards, he told me I was actually supposed to go to Witchery, which was next door and also new. But later, having met the staff at Witchery – the ones whom Ibraham had spoken to for me – I don't think I would have got the job there. I believe that my mistake was fate.

In David Lawrence I met two sisters who were Lebanese. They didn't judge me at all. They didn't see my skin colour or my accent; they just saw a girl who loved clothes and wanted to work, and miraculously they were looking for staff. When I walked in, I said, 'I understand you're hiring and my friend said to drop in my résumé.' Linda, the elder sister, was the manager. She looked at me, smiled, and said, 'Can you start now?' Just like that. My heart was singing. This was a new David Lawrence outlet, and they weren't even selling things yet, they were still unpacking boxes. I could see they needed help. But I had left my car outside with my cousin in it and I couldn't just leave her there, so I explained that I had to return to the car but asked if I could start the next day. And that was it . . . I got the job.

On my drive back home, I was praising the Lord so loud. I couldn't believe that these girls who had never met me before said, 'Yes, work with us, it'll be fun.' It was a real 'yay' moment for me. The job was a miracle. I really felt that deep inside.

I went back to the airport the following day and started working at David Lawrence. I had no experience in retail, and didn't know how to use the computer, but the girls were warm and caring and taught me how to do everything. Nothing was a problem or too hard; I didn't even pause to worry about how it was going, because they made it so simple. I learned really quickly and I took the job very seriously. It was everything to me. After three months they both left to move to other branches, so I was left on my own and ran the store for the next nine months, almost like a manager. I had cracked it.

I was working seven days a week but I didn't care. I was in heaven. There was a close-knit community at the airport among all the retail staff. We would have lunch together and swap stories about our customers. This felt right for me. I liked meeting all the new people every day and I loved talking to them and giving my opinions on what would suit them. I was really honest – why wouldn't you be? I wanted people to be happy with their purchases. We used to have menswear as well and the men were my favourite customers because they would just buy immediately.

The clothes were beautiful and to me seemed very expensive. Coats cost between $700 and $1000, and at that time David Lawrence sourced all their fabrics from Europe. I turned out to be a natural saleswoman and was paid a bonus most months because I was selling above the expected quota. Eventually the company realised this outlet had potential and brought in a manager. Amelie was German and she was very good, but she also had lots of rules. She needed me to know that she was the boss, and I guess after my time running the show, it wasn't always easy. I wanted to do more than the minimum and I had lots of ideas to make the store better, to help the customers and, ultimately, to sell more clothes. But Amelie wanted me to stay in my box, to be a salesgirl doing exactly what she asked me to do and nothing more. It was frustrating.

At the same time, Ibraham had moved to a job away from the airport. When I started at David Lawrence he had managed to secure a parking spot for me, but when he left this arrangement ended. The train journey wasn't too bad – the station near my house was on the same line as the airport stop – but the tickets were very expensive. So what with this and the extra pressures from the new manager, I asked the David Lawrence human resources manager if I could be transferred to another branch. To my delight they agreed. They moved me to the city and I worked in the concessions in both David Jones and Myer. The customers here were more diverse and many more people came through the stores, including lots of tourists speaking different languages. It felt exciting, like I was properly part of the city. It was incredible, my dream job.

I worked at David Lawrence for ten years and loved every moment. It was a great company and the HR department was especially good. The company looked after me, they valued me. My reputation with customers was excellent and the company recognised that.

I think this job more than anything else that happened to me back then changed my life. At last I was worth something and I was fitting in for being me. David Lawrence clothes are extremely elegant, with an emphasis on quality. I wore so many beautiful dresses because we were given a big clothing allowance to wear the store's clothes. On top of the allowance, we had a 50 per cent staff discount, so pretty much all my wardrobe was from David Lawrence and all my friends' too, because every time I had to buy a gift for someone it came from David Lawrence. I learned about all the different fabrics and textures: wool, cashmere, silk. It was all so exciting.

My dad had taught me the power of clothes and the importance of dressing well. When Papa dressed, you'd think he was one of the most educated people in the world. You would never know he didn't go to college. Today when I go to events I always take care to look my best so that when I walk into the room I feel equal to everyone else present. It shows that I respect myself, and that I respect the people I'm meeting with. Papa taught me that.

★

At the same time as I working at David Lawrence I was also volunteering with Australia for UNHCR. When I was away in Sierra Leone, Michael Dwyer's son Daniel had somehow come across the article that was published in the local newspaper about my work at the orphanage there. He had shown it to others at our church, and Michael felt I had a spirit of giving. So every time they had an arrival of new refugees, he'd say, 'Come with me,' and I'd tag along. I liked going. It was easy for me to talk to the refugees; even though our stories were different, our experiences in Australia bound us together.

Michael would also take me in to Australia for UNHCR offices in the city, and pretty soon I got to know everyone there. It felt like a place where I not only fitted in but also mattered. It was almost like a second home, my special place. I would help out, doing things like stuffing envelopes. I didn't care what I did; I just liked being there. When I talk to Michael today he says that there was something emanating from me which he calls 'the joy of living', and I'm pleased to hear that, because it is how I feel – even in the darkness there is always joy. Now I was finding that joy again.

I was also attending Australia for UNHCR events, where I would see refugees getting up on stage and telling their stories. It transfixed me. I thought the speakers showed immense courage, and hearing them touched something deep inside me. Pretty soon, I had this sense that I should be on a stage too. I don't know why I felt that. I loved performing, and I really came to enjoy talking to groups of people, but when I look back on that moment today, I wonder if it was a calling. Was God guiding me to use my story to help other girls?

Certainly I didn't have any fear of standing up and speaking in public. In fact, it felt very natural to me. But I would never share my story – at least, not then. So many of the refugees had experienced rape and sexual abuse. In some ways, it was a secret language between us even though we never talked about it. Was it time to let the world hear us, I wondered, to break through our joint trauma?

Michael never asked me to speak, never. He took me there to watch and listen. I know he never intended for me to become a speaker; that was my decision. It took me a long time to take that big step forwards, but in 2009 I finally took the plunge and I'm really pleased I did.

I can remember the turning point clearly. I was at the 2008 Australia for UNHCR Christmas Party at Parliament House in Macquarie Street, Sydney. I was Daniel Dwyer's date for the night. I couldn't believe I was in this venerable building with so many interesting people. It was intoxicating. I was dressed in a beautiful silk polka dot dress, one of the most glorious outfits that David Lawrence had in store that year. I still have it. There I met a lady called Maureen Collins, who was the donor manager at Australia for UNHCR and has since become a good friend. In fact, many of my close friends are people I met that night. Daniel introduced me to Maureen, saying, 'Meet Aminata Conteh – she's a refugee from Sierra Leone.' Maureen looked at me and said, 'Oh my gosh, no, you're not. You look like a model.' It was a lovely compliment, meant sincerely, but it made me think. What was a refugee supposed to look like? It is something I have encountered since, this idea that refugees should look somehow less than everyone else. This wasn't what Maureen meant at all, I know that now, but it is a concept I have struggled with when others raise it.

'Oh yes,' I said, 'I *am* a refugee from Sierra Leone.' And almost at once we started talking.

Maureen had just watched the movie *Blood Diamond*, which is all about the war in Sierra Leone. A large part of it is set in Kissy, my home. Even though *Blood Diamond* is a Hollywood movie, it's very accurate. I tried to go and see it but could only stay for the first five minutes before I walked out of the cinema. It was all too real for me. But I do think it is important that it is out there recording my country's story. When I heard that Maureen had seen the movie I knew that she understood what being a Sierra Leonean refugee meant. We chatted for ages and I remember afterwards she gave me her card. She suggested I email her so we could arrange to catch up for coffee. I think it was the first time I said I would catch up for a coffee with somebody in order to talk about myself. It was the first time I opened my mouth to tell my story. Something had changed and Maureen was the catalyst.

When we went out for coffee not long after that first encounter, I felt her warmth immediately. She was so chatty, she was so in my space, she seemed to understand me and what I was about, and I really enjoyed her company.

It was Maureen who told me about the Australia for UNHCR Mother's Day event coming up. She said they needed a speaker. 'Do you want to tell your story?' she asked. 'You won't have to write a speech or anything – it will be like an interview on stage.' Before I knew it, I had agreed. I don't know what made me say yes, but I was sure. Sometimes huge decisions can only be made in a second, but it wasn't just any second. Behind my shy, 'Okay, I'll do it,' was eight years of coming to terms with my kidnap, with leaving my country, with Papa's death and with my new life in Australia. I was ready.

In May 2009, I returned to Parliament House as a guest speaker at the Mother's Day lunch. There was a room full of elegant people all sitting at tables which were decked out in crisp white tablecloths with vases of flowers. There were close to 300 guests in the audience, including TV personalities like David Koch from Channel Seven. It was a big event.

There was no run-through beforehand, I just went up on stage. Strangely, I wasn't nervous. It felt right. I had bought these beautiful black high-waisted pants which I teamed with a blue, off-white and red top. My hair was long and in curls, and the red alligator-print shoes I was wearing became the talk of the day. Never underestimate the power of good shoes!

The MC, broadcaster and comedian Julie McCrossin, was a great interviewer. She made sure I didn't have to go into too much depth about what had happened to me; I think she sensed that it was my first time sharing my story, and her sensitivity stopped me from feeling frightened or anxious. I remember I said I was kidnapped – I have never liked using the word 'rape' in speeches – and that I was used as a human shield. As I walked off the stage, it felt really natural. I was sure now that this was my calling.

I could feel the mood of the room; the audience was really quiet, and I drank in that sense of silence. I remember everybody coming up to me in a rush at the end. I don't know what I said to people, but they all had tears in their eyes as they told me, 'You were so good.' I was overwhelmed. I didn't expect that to happen. I didn't think my story would affect people so deeply. Since then, I've never stopped talking. I've never stopped talking and I always feel the same presence I felt on that first day when I talk. Something takes over. It comes from deep inside me, a combination of Papa and God and my own joy shining through.

I became a special representative for Australia for UNHCR, and not long after that event I was up on stage again, but this time with then Australian Governor-General, Quentin Bryce, for a World Refugee Day breakfast. It was 19 June 2009, and there were 500 people at the Westin Hotel. The reaction was very big. Her Excellency told me you could hear a pin drop when I spoke. It was funny, because I had never heard that expression; in Sierra Leone, we were always quiet when people spoke. But then she explained what she meant: that this was a compliment. That not only did people want to hear my story, but the way I spoke – with such passion and conviction – was really impressive. I took the compliment, but inside

I was thinking, 'Hmm, if only they knew.' I didn't think I was eloquent or had a presence or any of those things. I thought you had to study to be like that and I had struggled so hard in school. But public speaking really did come naturally to me and I wasn't nervous at all.

★

My work with Australia for UNHCR was thrilling. After my disappointments at school, it felt good to be achieving.

I started to wonder about work beyond David Lawrence. I have always been drawn to motivational speakers and to inspirational books with a message, and I started to see that I could use my story to help other girls, to lift them up, to give them confidence.

But there was still the problem of qualifications. In Australia, all the jobs I was interested in needed university degrees or diplomas. I loved studying and going to classes and was happy to do these at night, but exams were a huge sticking point. I tried to stay positive and not beat myself up about it, but the cold, hard fact was that, on paper, I wasn't able to fulfil my potential, which was really frustrating.

It was around this time that my dyslexia was finally identified.

I was at a friend's house; she was a journalist who later worked for the government. We met when she wrote a story about me, and we stayed close. I used to spend a lot of time at her house just hanging out and chatting. One time I was there when her brother, who was a diplomat, was visiting. He was discussing issues he was having with his young daughter. The two siblings were talking about it in the living room; I was in the kitchen and I overheard their conversation. It was the strangest experience. Everything my friend's brother was saying about his daughter's problems made perfect sense to me. I was mesmerised and just sat there straining to hear it all. I didn't want to interrupt them, that would have been impolite, but I was bursting.

After he left I asked my friend, 'What is that word – that thing called "dyslexia" that you were talking about?'

She explained that it was a common learning disability, one that lots of people had, although it often took a long time to be diagnosed. The word comes from the Greek and means 'difficulty with words'. People who have dyslexia find reading and writing troublesome; there's a comprehension breakdown which is linked to how your brain is wired. It has nothing to do with your ability to learn, but it can, and usually does, affect your writing and reading. She said that her brother thought his daughter was probably dyslexic.

The more she described it, the more excited I became. 'I think I have it too!' I declared.

She smiled and said: 'Oh no, you don't. I've heard you speak and you're really eloquent.'

In Africa they say you're bright if you can read and write; speaking doesn't come into it. I couldn't read or write very well at all and now I knew the reason.

My friend wasn't convinced at first. She felt I might just have chosen the wrong course of study, and she suggested communications would be a better subject for me since I was so good at talking to people. She said the best course was the one at UTS, where I had earlier attempted further education. I wasn't convinced but was prepared to give it a go. So my friend and I went back to the campus for an open day. But when we started talking to the tutors, they said that for communications you had to have an excellent command of spoken and written English. I sighed: 'Ooh, that's a problem.'

My friend was still perplexed, so over lunch I explained. I said, 'When I talk to you I'm fine, I can express myself clearly. When I talk to a room full of people I'm more than fine, I shine. But if you ask me to write anything down I get stuck. It's like my brain freezes.'

Afterwards I had a meeting with Michael Dwyer. He had a friend who was involved with Australia for UNHCR who thought he could get me a scholarship to study at university. It was heartening that everyone was trying so hard to help me, but they simply didn't get how hampered I was. I guess I had been doing such a great job of covering up my problems that now no one believed me. I told Michael what I had discovered at my friend's house: that I was dyslexic. I said it would be a waste of money to send me to university, money that other people could be using. I would not do well at university. I knew that for sure.

Michael understood immediately and counselled me to look after the gift that I knew I had, which was connecting with people and inspiring people. He advised me to forget university and go to the less academic, more vocational TAFE college and study for a public relations qualification that involved a lot more presenting and less theory. There would only be two written exams on the course and the rest was all practical.

When I enrolled at the TAFE in Ultimo, Sydney, I sat a test to assess my communication skills. At first the examiner was impressed: 'You speak so confidently.' But when he saw what I produced with pen and paper he said, 'Yes, you have dyslexia.'

It felt good to finally have a name for what was going on inside my head. When I told Michael, he said, 'Do you know, most of the smartest people in the world have dyslexia!'

It was a one-year course and I not only finished it, I passed. I graduated with my husband-to-be, the beautiful Antoine Biger, by my side.

CHAPTER SIXTEEN

Antoine, *ma puce*

My husband, Antoine Biger, was born on 1 June 1982 in a town called Landerneau. Landerneau is in Brittany, in the north-west of France, not far from Brest. Antoine is the middle child of André Biger, who works in a bank, and Marine Biger, a hairdresser. Antoine's parents divorced when he was twelve and the three children scattered. Antoine's older brother Franck moved to Marseilles to become a firefighter, Antoine stayed with his dad, and his younger sister Eva chose to live with their mum, who moved to Paris two years after the break-up.

I have no doubt that the divorce affected Antoine. He says back then he always believed he could bring his parents back together, but of course he never managed it. Such is the wish of many children in this situation, no doubt, but Antoine is a peacemaker and I can imagine it cut deep when he couldn't fix his parents' problems.

André was also hurt by the split. Antoine recalls his papa

being devastated and going into a depression. Antoine neglected his studies when he was in his early teens, which I suspect was also in reaction to the divorce. While Antoine didn't do brilliantly in school, he was good at sports – especially basketball, which he played at competition level. He credits basketball with keeping him on track as a teenage boy. Also, André loved to talk to his son about travel and geography, which sparked a passion in Antoine. He, too, loves to travel and see the world, which is just as well – if he didn't, we wouldn't have met.

In 2006, Antoine arrived in Australia with his friend Julien and travelled around Queensland before making his way south to Sydney.

I met Antoine on 3 February 2007, and it is a day etched in both of our memories.

I was studying for my UTS course by correspondence and still doing some jobs with the agency, while becoming more involved with Australia for UNHCR. That day – a Saturday – I should have been at a birthday party with a man I was sort of seeing; everybody, including his family, liked us together, but we both knew it wasn't really working and we were probably better just as good friends. I knew how it would have been between us if I'd gone to the party: the same looks, the same feelings, but the same 'Are we, aren't we?' thoughts which went nowhere. So I decided not to go. And imagine if I hadn't.

Instead I opted to spend the day on my own. I love going out by myself. I really enjoy the feeling of walking around the city alone and I still do it. I caught the train and bus to Bondi and went down to the beach and sat on a rock, enjoying the sunshine and the fresh air and watching the people. I put my feet in the ocean and felt the cool water lapping against my skin. I had a Walkman and was listening to music through my headphones and reading one of the inspirational books I like to bury my head in. I was in my own world. After a calm, gentle day I was heading for home when I thought, 'Why leave now? It's a beautiful summer evening!' I hopped off the train at Circular Quay so I could walk past the ferries and follow the walkway up to the Sydney Opera House. This is a favourite place for me: that view of the Sydney Harbour Bridge stretching across the sparkling harbour, green and gold ferries chugging past and the thriving happy bustle of everyone. I just love watching people move by. All life is here and I love being a part of it.

At around 7 pm I was starting to think it really was time I went home. But as I strolled back towards the station, strains of a jazz song reached me, hanging in the air like some glorious scent. The singer sounded like Aretha Franklin and she was backed by a live band. I turned and followed the music to the Opera Bar. This is a famous Sydney hangout, an outdoor eating and drinking venue under the sails of the Opera House where they host live musicians. But you don't have to go into the bar to hear the music; you can lean against a railing above and look down on the band. I just wanted to listen. I love music – the rhythm, the melody, the joy. So I was standing there, enjoying the jazz, when out of the corner of my eye I noticed someone walking past. I had a glimpse of him but didn't really register anything. It was Antoine's first time at the Opera House; he had just arrived from Cairns. Then, no more than 30 seconds later, he rushed back and said hi to me. I thought he wanted a photo, so I asked if he wanted me to take it for him.

'*Non*,' he said.

'You're French!' I exclaimed, recognising the accent.

He was delighted. 'Do you speak French?' he asked.

'No,' I said, explaining that I had lived in Guinea so I knew a few words.

Antoine has this babyish smile which I have grown to love so much. He can't keep a secret, or hide what he is thinking and doing; it always reveals itself in that baby-boy smile. At that moment, his eyes lit up and he smiled that smile at me for the first time. He had told his friend to wait while he came back to try to speak English with me, to find out if I was alone. When I confirmed that I was, he said, 'Can I stay with you tonight?'

I said: 'What!'

'*Non, non, non,*' he said, dismayed that his terrible command of English was letting him down at this crucial juncture. He tried again: 'Can me and you stay here and talk?'

Relieved, I said, 'Oh yes, no problem.' I had been planning to leave, but he was very friendly and his twinkling eyes and that baby face won me over.

He said, 'Wait here,' and ran back to tell his friend to go on without him.

We stayed for three hours talking. I don't know how we managed, since he didn't speak much English, but I could understand a little bit of French, and we used gestures and we listened to the music. Then we started playing this kind of musical game, where I would hum something, like a Whitney Houston song, and he would have to guess the artist.

He was really looking at me, into my heart, smiling the whole time. Eventually I said, 'I have to go now or I'll miss my train.'

He walked with me to the station, and I remember as we said goodbye he put his arms around me and gave me the biggest hug, holding me for quite a while. He said, 'I'd like to see you again.' I gave him my number.

Then he went to the other side of the tracks, because he was going in the other direction, towards Bondi Junction. And he stood there smiling at me from across the tracks, mesmerised. The Bondi train comes more often than the Beverly Hills train; the trains came and went but still he didn't move. He just stayed there, smiling. I was hoping my train would come soon; I didn't want him standing there all night. He waited until I boarded my train before he left.

As soon as I got home I had a message on my phone. 'Hi, Aminata, it's Antoine . . . I'm very happy to meet you. Do you want to catch up again?'

When I talk to Antoine today, his memories of that day are similar to mine, but more intense. He tells me, for example, that I was wearing white linen pants and an orange singlet – I don't remember. He says he felt this strong uncontrollable urge to give me that hug. It was a symbolic thing for him, he adds. Afterwards, he says, his head was filled with questions. He had never felt this way before, and he immediately knew he wanted to have me in his life. He knew it was probably impossible, but that just spurred him on.

Antoine was on a working holiday visa and his plan was to go back up north to Cairns before he returned to France, but after meeting me he changed his plans and stayed in Sydney instead.

We became friends right from that night. It was instant. We would see each other most days, Antoine made sure of that. He remembers he was very demanding, but I didn't mind. The Opera House and the Botanic Gardens next door became our place. I enjoyed his company, but I wasn't looking for a partner. I remember that on Valentine's Day, which was not long after we met, I had made him a CD of zouk, a French Caribbean style of music that I had heard in Guinea and loved. It is beautiful to dance to. He came with chocolates and, even though we were not dating, we must have looked like a couple. I guess that, even though we hadn't discussed being an 'item', we did naturally become one.

Today Antoine says he sensed something in me he had never known before. He describes it as 'an inner freedom, an independence of spiritual mind'. He says I was unlike anyone he knew and that he felt I was already my own self. I think I know what he means, because he met me at a time when I really was coming into myself and finding my light. We loved to talk about every little thing, from really big issues to silly stuff. We talked about music, but we also talked about injustice and race, and it was good for me to have someone to share those thoughts with.

Antoine knew nothing about the war in Sierra Leone and I didn't tell him anything about me and what had happened. All he knew was that I had come to Australia as a refugee. I did mention the film *Blood Diamond*, though, and he ended up watching it on the plane back to France. I think it was a bit of a shock for him. But in many ways, it was refreshing not to have to discuss the war or to have it as the background to everything about me. Antoine knew literally nothing. There was something fresh and innocent about that, and when I was with Antoine it was almost as if it had never happened.

I knew he was serious and that I was not ready for a relationship. But we had such a good time together – sometimes I wondered (and still do) whether it was really possible for someone to be as happy as he was, all the time – that for the last few weeks he moved in with me in Beverly Hills. He had been staying in a place in Bondi, and when I saw it I said, 'You live here? It's terrible. Come and live with me.'

I knew that he had told his parents all about me, and that his dad was surprised that Antoine had met an African woman in Australia. I had this photo from one of my agency jobs and I gave it to him. He sent it to his dad, who thought that his son was pulling his leg.

Antoine was raised in the Catholic faith, but he wasn't a practising Catholic. Soon he started coming to church with me. I hadn't asked him to, he just wanted to go – mostly, I think, to be with me, but he ended up really enjoying the services. He met the Dwyer family and they loved him instantly. I think they could see he was a good and sensitive man and really good for me. He loved to see me happy and to share my joy.

We did start sleeping with each other, which was difficult for me. I still hadn't told Antoine anything about what had happened to me. I wanted to forget about all that when I was with him and I didn't want his behaviour towards me to be changed by my past. But after my experience with Coal Boot

I would find it hard not to close my legs together tight as a sort of reflex reaction. And afterwards my legs would start shaking uncontrollably and feel really heavy. But Antoine never made an issue of it.

In the end, though, I think I did get a bit claustrophobic when Antoine was living with me. I remember I had a study session for my course over the weekend for a group assessment and I left Antoine at home. And when I came back and he was there in my face, I was thinking that I wanted my space back. Antoine was due to leave in a couple of weeks to go back to France because his visa was expiring, and I remember looking forward to him leaving. I think if I had asked him to stay, he would have started applying for residency right away. But I didn't ask. I wasn't there yet, even though Antoine was.

Then, when the day of his departure arrived, I was overcome with sadness. I dropped him at the airport, and when I came home I felt as if something was missing – not just in my apartment, but in my life. It was a very strong emotion and I think it was the first time that I realised there was really something between us.

As he waved goodbye, Antoine had said, 'I'll call you,' which I honestly didn't think he would. It was very expensive to call from France and our relationship was about being together and having fun. I couldn't see it working long distance, and with our language issues phone calls would be frustrating. But once he arrived home, he called me straight away.

Antoine was hurting too. Unbeknownst to me, he had been trying to tell me how he felt about me: that I was the one and he wanted to spend the rest of his life with me. But language and opportunity and probably my reticence got in the way. He didn't say this in that first phone call, but I knew he was missing me. I was missing him too.

That day when I had gone out to study, Antoine had written a letter to me. I didn't know he'd written it, and I had no idea how deeply he felt. I knew that he liked me, but I was not thinking forever love. I just thought, 'We have such a good relationship,' and I told him, 'If you come back to Australia, let me know, and we'll hang out.' I can see now that I must have sounded pretty half-hearted about our relationship.

Antoine had written a beautiful, innocent love letter, in which he had poured out his heart. He then just folded the page in half without writing anything on the outside, and left the letter inside a wooden drawer by my bed where I used to keep my passport and important papers.

When he called after arriving back in France, he was hoping that I'd read the letter and would respond to it, but I said nothing. He must have been so disappointed. I blush when I think about it today. But I really hadn't seen the letter.

It was four and a half years before I found it, and in the interim Antoine must have thought I didn't feel as he did and so he tried to move on with his life. At first, he called me a lot, and then it started to drop off to every three months, then every six months. In all that time, he never mentioned the letter and I still hadn't found it.

Antoine says that every time he heard my voice on the phone his heart would skip a beat, but as time went on he tried to accept it was never going to happen. Back in France he landed a job selling windows. There was a lot of pressure to make a sale and Antoine hated the idea of forcing something on people they didn't want. He has a strong sense of right and wrong, and he told me he hated the job. Then a friend of his who was going to Greece to work in a hotel offered Antoine a job dealing with the French customers. As I've said, Antoine adores travel, so he was off like a shot.

All the time in Greece Antoine says he couldn't stop thinking about me and longed to come back to Australia, but knew he wouldn't be able to get another visa. Also, he knew I wasn't sure enough to make a strong commitment, so there was no point exploring emigration options. Antoine stayed in Greece for a summer season and then returned to France to plan his next move.

André told me that on his return his son had enlarged the photo of me I had given him and hung it on his bedroom wall. He also carried a smaller version with him in his passport (it's still there today). I think it's safe to say he wasn't over me!

Antoine had never wanted to get married, because the divorce his parents went through was so painful, but when André saw Antoine transfixed by me, he said, 'I think my son has fallen in love.' Apparently, Antoine told his dad and his best friend that if he was ever going to get married it would be to Aminata, and only Aminata.

He decided to distract himself by going travelling again, but this time he went further afield. He settled on Réunion Island in the Indian Ocean, just east of Madagascar. Because it's a department of France, he didn't need a visa. Growing up, Antoine had lots of friends who had lived on Réunion, and the island's coral reef, rainforests and beautiful beaches were just what he craved. Réunion is a melting pot of different cultures, with people from China, Africa and India as well as France, and this also appealed to Antoine, who was now especially interested in Africa. And it was situated halfway between France and Australia, so it meant he would be significantly closer to me.

Antoine saved up and flew to Réunion to start his next chapter. He loved it immediately and quickly found a job working for a custom furniture maker. He would go out to meet the clients, measure up their houses for the furniture, and then draw up plans for them back at the office. Antoine loves people and he's a very good technical artist, so this was a dream job.

Once he was settled in Réunion, Antoine phoned me and we started to become close again. I remember he was the reason I joined Facebook. I had never been interested in it before, but Antoine said it would be easier for us to share photos and chat. My neighbour came down to help me set up my Facebook page and she was screaming when, within seconds, Antoine accepted my friend request.

Even then, we didn't chat much, hardly at all, in fact. I wasn't interested in dating, preferring to go out with my friends. I enjoyed my independence, and whenever I thought about love, I decided that if it happened, it would have to be with somebody who shared my dad's qualities. I'm actually really glad I spent that time getting to know myself and finding out what was important to me; it meant that later, when I did get married, I was certain it would be for life.

My best friend Marion had met and spent time with Antoine when he and I were together in Sydney. One day we were having a chat about relationships, and she told me she thought Antoine and I were meant for each other. I said,

'No, you're wrong, he might be dating a girl in Réunion.' But the conversation made me think about Antoine, and I emailed him late one night, just to say hi. I honestly had no romantic intentions or even expectations at that point, but even so that email set things in motion. Antoine wrote back quickly, delighted to hear from me. Then he called, and very quickly after that we started talking more and more. And, just like that, our special connection came to life again.

We talked to each other on Facebook and then by Skype and planned to get together. It was just like when we first met; we reconnected immediately. The idea was that Antoine would come over to Australia and then, a bit later, I would visit him in Réunion. He booked a flight that would land in Sydney two weeks to the day after I had emailed him. It was all set.

In the days before he was due to arrive we were talking on the phone about arrangements and I was sitting on the bedside sorting through my passport and papers as I was chatting. I unfolded a piece of paper that was in the pile and I knew straight away it was Antoine's writing. I said to Antoine, 'Have you ever written a letter to me?' He paused. I could hear him breathing. And then he said, 'Yes, I wrote it to you when I was last there and left it in your house. I thought you chose to ignore it.' He couldn't believe I had only just found it.

The letter was annotated with little drawings – one of a sun coming out from behind a cloud, one of a flower, and another was the map of Africa emanating rays with Sierra Leone picked out. It was written in a mixture of French and English. This is what it said:

Aminata,

Hey it's antoine, i know you since now 24 day and it's good always cause you are my sunshine.

When i am with you, the time is so good and i forget all.

When i'm with you i'm happy

J'adore te regarder car tu est trop belle. [I love looking at you because you are so beautiful.]

(tu comprend) [Do you understand?]

I like to take you in my arms.

Ma petite aminata, tu est vraiement gentil, je t'adore. [My little Aminata, you are truly kind, I love you.]

Je t'adore, my princess.

Antoine

★

So, four and a half years after Antoine had declared his love in that beautiful, sweet, naive letter, I gazed right into his soul. When I picked him up at Sydney airport it didn't feel like it had been so long. It felt like we'd been together all those years, and he had just been away on a work trip. This time I knew that, yes, I was in love with Antoine.

To me, Antoine is simply perfect. I love him more and more every day – his kind, tender heart, his intelligence and his glorious, sweet smile. I have learned so much from his love and commitment to family and friends. Waking up next to him is my favourite part of the day. He is my 'person': my best friend, my lover, my spiritual partner in this life, *ma puce* (this means 'Antoine, my flea' and is a term of endearment in French – truly!)

I always knew that if I was going to marry anyone, it would be not only someone who made me laugh, but also someone who would allow me to fly. Antoine doesn't only allow me to fly: he flies with me.

CHAPTER SEVENTEEN

Bahteh Guineh — Powerful Woman

Back in 2009, on that life-changing day when I shared my story for the very first time at the Australia for UNHCR Mother's Day event in Parliament House in Sydney, there was a wonderful lady called Ros Horin in the audience, listening intently. Ros was a long-time supporter of the UNHCR and also a renowned theatre and film director. Little did I know when I met her that day what a huge part Ros would play in my life. Ros's award-winning play *Through the Wire* was all about the refugee experience in Australian detention centres, and after my speech Ros and her daughter came up to meet me, and both of them had tears in their eyes.

Ros tells me today that when she first met me I was really timid and shy. She thought I was about sixteen years old, not a woman in her twenties, and she sensed a raw vulnerability in me. A few days later she asked if I would be willing to talk to her: 'I'm trying to come up with ideas about how

I can reach out to refugees. *Through the Wire* was about men, but now I'd like to talk to refugee women who have gone through violence.' Ros was planning to create a piece of theatre that would give an Australian audience some insight into the traumatic back stories of refugee women.

At that time she had no intention of casting refugees in the roles; she simply wanted to gather stories as background. Even so, I realised that talking to her would be a big thing for me. In my speech, I had talked about the war and, though I had referred to my captivity, I hadn't gone into any detail. I hadn't told anyone the full story and I had no intention of doing so – and certainly not in a public arena.

But there was something about Ros that made me trust her immediately, and when we met up a couple of months later I knew this woman was going to be a vitally important part of my new life. I felt close to her right away. She's such a bubbly and in-your-personal-space person that you just go with the flow, and soon I found myself opening my heart to her. I didn't hesitate.

After we'd met once or twice, she asked, 'Do you mind if I record you?'

I would meet Ros at the office of her husband, Joe Skrzynski, down at Circular Quay, and even though it felt quite intense I started to talk about what happened, describing things I had never put into words before. It was still hard finding the words and having the courage to say them out loud. When I said 'rape', for instance, it would be really quietly under my breath. You could barely hear the word coming out of my mouth. And there were still many things I could not say at all – even to myself.

Generally, I don't think of my abduction at all when I'm not talking about it. But if I watch a movie and there's a scene that sparks a memory, it makes me gasp and think, 'That happened to me!' The movie needn't even be about Sierra Leone; in fact, it hardly ever is. The first time I thought of my exchange after I was freed was when I watched a James Bond movie, *Die Another Day*, with Pierce Brosnan. They had kidnapped him and when they were doing the exchange with him and another agent I saw myself physically in that spot on the road where my own exchange had taken place. Similarly, I never consciously think about the time Coal Boot raped me – it is buried deep in my subconscious – but sometimes memories are sparked into life. For example, there is a scene in the movie *Monster* where Charlize Theron's character is raped in a car with a stick. Watching this scene in the cinema, I jumped off my seat and left the theatre. I didn't cry, but I immediately felt that my heart had been ripped out of my body. What I've learned with memories is that they come when you least expect them. When my memories are triggered, it's always by something that has nothing to do with Sierra Leone.

As Ros tells it today, the details of my time with Daramy and Coal Boot poured out of me. It was a relief, I think, to finally let go of it, but I believe it was the special bond I developed with Ros that made me feel able to talk. We became really close. Ros would take me out for coffee and to the theatre, and she let me into her life.

Maureen Collins had told Ros that I worked in fashion and Ros introduced me to her daughter Nina, who was a fashion designer then and is now an interior designer.

I started doing some work for Nina making necklaces and bracelets and helping to sell them. It was a lot of fun and I gained so much experience working with her. I spent a lot of time at Ros's house and was included in all sorts of family occasions, including Christmas dinner. As with the Dwyers, I felt as if I was treated like a member of the family. Janelle and Michael Dwyer were my spiritual mum and dad, and Ros and Joe became my second family, who loved me and supported me in any way they could.

Ros wanted to do a series of theatre workshops with a group of four refugee women with a view to investigating our stories. I was the second potential candidate Ros spoke to for her project, and at the start I don't think she knew where it was going, she was just feeling her way. Over the next twelve months, Ros met other African refugees who had suffered sexual violence. She worked in conjunction with STARTTS, which is the NSW Service for the Treatment and Rehabilitation of Torture and Trauma Survivors. She hadn't anticipated having four African women – she was initially thinking she would have a mix of refugees from different countries – but it just ended up that we were all African. Ros tells me today that she was struck by the fact that none of us had ever talked about our stories, not even to those closest to us, and she hoped she could help with that by having us talk to each other.

Gradually I met the three other women Ros was talking to for the project and we started to work together. The first was Yoradanos Haile-Michael – Yordy – who is from Eritrea. Ros had met Yordy before she met me and she thought that, since we had similar stories, we would automatically be friends. She

Grandmother, mother and newborn daughter – my wild butterfly Sarafina – share a special moment, just minutes after birth.

Proud father Antoine with me and Sarafina a few days after she was born.

Antoine takes Sarafina to physiotherapy for the shoulder injury she sustained in childbirth.

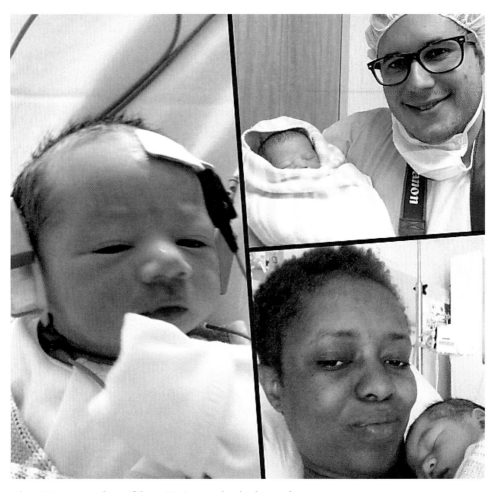

Above: We meet our beautiful son Matisse on the day he was born.

Below left: Our Matisse, who loves to play. *Below right*: Bathtime for my cheeky Biger babes.

elebrating Sarafina's first birthday at the home of my spiritual parents Janelle and Michael Dwyer ar left), and with my wonderful mother- and sister-in-law, Marine and Eva Biger.

ur first perfect family portrait. Our delicious Matisse is only a few days old here.

"A MUST SEE! AN EMOTIONAL AND UPLIFTING EXPERIENCE."
GILLIAN ARMSTRONG

"IMPORTANT AND INSPIRING!"
GEORGE MILLER

OFFICIAL SELECTION
MELBOURNE
INTERNATIONAL FILM FESTIVAL
2016

OFFICIAL SELECTION
SYDNEY
FILM FESTIVAL
2016

THE BAULKHAM HILLS AFRICAN LADIES TROUPE

REFLEX PRODUCTIONS PRESENTS "THE BAULKAM HILLS AFRICAN LADIES TROUPE"
AMINATA CONTEH-BIGER YORDANOS HAILE- MICHAEL ROSEMARY KARIUKI-FYFE YARRIE BANGURA AMINATA DOUMBIA GUY GROSS
JUSTINE KERRIGAN ANDREW ARESTIDES ASE MARGIE BRYANT TRISTRAM MIALL JOSEPH SKRZYNSKI ROS HORIN

Check the Classification

WWW.AFRICANLADIESTROUPE.COM

erforming in *The Baulkham Hills
frican Ladies Troupe* was one of the most
warding and empowering experiences of
y life.

Opposite: The fabulous poster for our
eatre show.

ove: With Ros Horin, the wonderful
eator and director.

ght: On stage.

London calling: Every trip to London is always packed with family time – so much love.
Above: A great night at *Tina Turner the Musical* with Fatmata, Mabinty and their children.
Bottom left: The twins Mabinty (left) and Fatmata. *Bottom right*: Mama and me in her home.

I am so proud of and excited by the work of the Aminata Maternal Foundation.

Above: Penny Gerstle (left) and I catch up with the inspirational Dame Ann Gloag in London. The Aminata Maternal Foundation partners with Ann's Freedom From Fistula charity to help fund the Aberdeen Women's Centre.

Right: The kids and I spread the word for the AMF Mother's Day walk.

Below: The AMF Cheer Squad team that works so hard to bring my vision to life.

On my 2016 visit to the Aberdeen Women's Centre in Freetown. Spending time with these brave young women is a very special memory for me.

Staff and patients at the Aberdeen Women's Centre. We serve the poorest of the poor for free at the centre.

JULIET RIEDEN

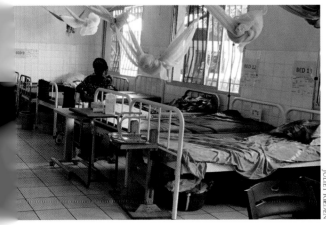

JULIET RIEDEN

Top: The AWC maternity ward is on the ground floor. Above are the rooms where we stay during our visits.

Middle: Ladies queueing for maternity check-ups at the AWC.

Left: A ward at the AWC.

Left: The Dream Team Girls present me with a wonderful plaque at the Freetown hostel for vulnerable mothers, a pilot scheme funded by the Aminata Maternal Foundation.

Below: With the Dream Team Girls at their weekly craft classes at the AWC. They have been knitting baby clothes for their newborns and also to sell.

> *Opposite*: Some of the many beautiful babies born at the AWC.

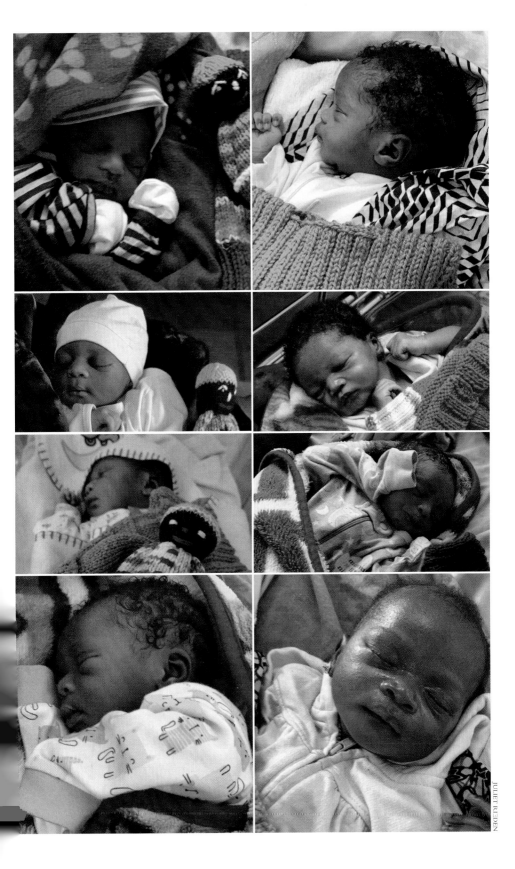

My 2019 visit to Sierra Leone filled me with pride, hope and excitement.

JULIET RIEDEN

JULIET RIEDEN

JULIET RIEDEN

life in modern Freetown. *Top*: The First Lady of Sierra Leone launches her 'Hands Off Our Girls' initiative. *Middle*: Sellers and buyers gather on a beach for a daily market where fish, fruit and all sorts of things are sold. *Bottom*: The shocking Kroo Bay slum is one of the poorest places in the world.

JULIET RIEDEN

JULIET RIEDEN

Above: On the rooftop of my home in Kissy.

Far left: Reunited with Nga Kadiatu who helped raise me and my siblings. We are at her home in Kissy.

Left: Showing Sierra Leone to my ghostwriter Juliet Rieden.

The hotel Papa built in Wellington, Sierra Leone, as it is now. I have a dream to make this hotel into a st free hospital for women and children.

Visiting Papa's grave in Kissy, always a painful trip for me.

This is my family in my new homeland – a place of safety, which is a wonderful feeling.

thought we would be able to talk to each other about our experiences and that it might help us somehow, and I think she was a bit disappointed when we didn't become bosom buddies. But mostly when African women meet each other they don't share their stories; it's not how our culture operates. We don't like to put our burdens on others and we are by nature quite private. It is our business, not anybody else's.

We met in a cafe outside Vaucluse House, a heritage property in Sydney's eastern suburbs. I liked Yordy and could sense her pain, but I was in a place Yordy wasn't. She was relaxed but not to the extent that she was going to open up. I had already told Ros my story and I had met her family and we had spent time together, so I felt close to her. Also, I was more used to talking about myself from my public speaking. But Yordy was very guarded when we spoke, which meant I was too. We were both resistant to sharing. I think Ros was really surprised to see us both clam up, but looking back I can't help but feel it was very optimistic of Ros to think we would just meet and discuss the intimate details of our lives and our journeys to this place just like that. It took a long time before we reached that point with each other.

We worked together for five years and slowly, slowly our stories tumbled out. It was a long and often painful journey, but in that time we did all share and Ros was right: the empathy between us as victims of sexual abuse was powerful.

We would meet regularly in a community centre studio in Parramatta, west of Sydney. Ros would run workshops and we would tell our stories. Early on, Ros introduced drums and singing and dancing, so we weren't just talking about our traumatic pasts, we were also embracing the joy of Africa and our culture. Aisha, a brilliant dancer from Guinea-Conakry, joined us and taught us how to move our bodies and then use the drums to create dances. She would sing in Susu, beautiful evocative songs. A choreographer, Lucia, also came along and started to shape our dance moves. Then, finally, Ros added some professional actors to our group and we started to look at our stories as small pieces of theatre that were all about us. It was a fascinating process, but also a tough one.

Ros didn't have any background in trauma, as such, and how best to deal with it. And for us, what was trauma? We had no idea. We would just carry on from day to day and then it would come up and hit us in the face when we least expected it. As we talked more and more memories would flood back, and putting them out there made things I had buried deep inside real again. After a while, Ros consulted a specialist counsellor because she was concerned that she might be exacerbating our trauma. But she was told that the process we were going through was exactly the sort of thing that would happen in counselling. This put her mind at ease, but nevertheless she decided to bring a counsellor on board for us to talk to. Unlike my previous experience with counselling, this lady was really helpful and I still see her today.

However difficult it became, there was also a lot of joy in participating in the project, and there was never any question that I would pull out. My word is very important to me, so when I said yes to Ros, I meant yes. I was in it for the long haul, come what may, and I became really dedicated to the show. On the very few occasions I was late, Ros would get super worried that there was something wrong with me because I was *never* late!

After our workshops, Ros would go home and synthesise everything she had seen and heard into a script. The nature of trauma is that it comes out in fragments, and Ros's task was to pull those fragments together into some sort of narrative. Then she would come back to us with the script to ensure she had got it right. It was a beautiful collaborative process, which I think is why it worked so well.

Right from the beginning we told Ros that we wanted the show to be about laughter, about joy, with dancing and music. Without that we would not have done it. We wanted our culture to be part of it, and although, yes, horrific things had happened in Africa, it should feel universal, because these things happen everywhere.

As we went on, Ros started to see the potential in us as actual actors in the piece, and we began rehearsing scenes with us playing ourselves. When it came to the kidnap scenes, Ros used this conceit of me handing over my role to one of the professional actors and I would observe her on stage. Or in another scene I played a lawyer who was interrogating the actor playing me. It was very clever and something Ros devised to protect me and the others from having to replay our trauma. Of course I was never in court; this was a fictional situation that Ros created in order to give me a sense of justice for what had happened to me – a justice I never experienced in real life.

I didn't feel as if I was an actor because this was my story and I was very confident about telling it. But what was interesting was that for the first time I was not ashamed. I don't know how the other women felt. I will not speak for them. But like all rape victims, I had carried a sense of shame, and in this moment I finally felt free from that. The shame is all about people knowing that you had been raped, that something had been taken away from you, and the fear that nobody would want you now. I carried that shame for a long time and it played a big part in me not telling my story to my community.

With the play, it felt as if my story became real. All these years, since I had arrived in Australia in 2000, I had locked my story away. I would tell people, 'I'm a refugee,' and no more. I was always proud to be a refugee and wanted people to know that, but it wasn't until I started talking at the UNHCR events and now in this play that I finally felt as if I had been released from my captivity. I realised that I had felt imprisoned in my body for those nine years when I felt I couldn't talk about what had happened. Doing the play became much bigger than merely my own healing, though; it was for all those other women out there who were unable to talk about their trauma. I had found a purpose – *my* purpose. This was what I had been looking for.

In the end, the play was called *The Baulkham Hills African Ladies Troupe*; Baulkham Hills is a residential suburb north-west of Sydney with a significant refugee population. At one point, though, as our workshops developed and we all achieved a powerful stage presence, Ros said she thought she might call the play *Bahteh Guineh*, which means 'powerful woman' in the Susu language and was what my grandfather used to call me – and that's definitely how the play made me feel.

CHAPTER EIGHTEEN

My wild butterfly

I was part way through my work with the play when Antoine and I got back together. Antoine knew I was doing the play but not the full detail, and when he came to Australia for another visit and we started to become really serious about each other I realised it was time he learned what I had been through. Ros had been filming the process of developing the play for a behind-the-scenes film documentary she was making, and some of the filming was happening at that time. She had given us a full script for the play so we could go over our lines, and I left the script on the table at home. It was intentional. Antoine is very inquisitive and I knew he would pick it up. I wanted him to read it. I knew that I could never share my life with a man who didn't know my whole story.

Antoine's reaction to the script made me realise that he was the soulmate I had been waiting for. He was shocked, of course, because he had known me for a while now and he said he thought, 'Is that the same person? She's really gone through that?' But when he looked at me straight after he'd read the script, I knew it didn't change anything for him. He looked at me in the same way he has looked at me from the first day he met me, and for me that was wonderful. I didn't want my story, my past, to make a difference. I didn't want him loving me more or being unable to love me in the same way because of it. I didn't want him thinking he had to protect me or save me or find the men who had hurt me.

Antoine was . . . my Antoine. He was proud of me and he said so, but more importantly he had the same respect and the same feelings that had made him fall in love with me in the first place. His regard for me didn't change at all – he didn't love me any more or any less. Antoine's love is for *me*, and what happened to me makes no difference to that at all. It's pure and real and true.

After he finished reading, he said, 'I want to have kids with you, but if you don't want to have children that is fine too.' Me falling pregnant when I was kidnapped and losing the baby was not in the script, but when we talked that day Antoine asked me if I'd had a baby and I told him what had happened when I was a captive. He told me, 'Even if we don't have a child, I want to be with you forever.' I will never forget the beauty of that moment.

After staying with me for a couple of weeks, Antoine went to Paris for work, before returning to Réunion, where I was going to meet him. While he was in Paris we talked all the time over the phone. It was during one of those calls that he said, 'I want to marry you. I cannot be without you.'

It's funny, because it wasn't romantic, more a statement of fact. I said, 'Oh, okay,' and we carried on planning our holiday together. In my mind, we were engaged.

He wanted me to have a perfect holiday. It felt like a honeymoon only we weren't married yet. He had charged his sister, Eva, and her boyfriend with making the arrangements on Réunion. Eva had joined Antoine in Réunion a year after he moved there. He was and still is very close to her and she knew all about me.

I arrived in Réunion on a Tuesday. Antoine picked me up at the airport in his company car and took me straight to Eva's apartment. She had made us a lovely meal. Then we drove ten minutes down the road to Antoine's apartment.

Over the next few days Antoine took me all around the island – to the markets, to see his friends, to the beach. Mostly he wanted me to experience the local food, although my favourite place to go was Paul's patisserie, which is actually a French bakery chain. I became addicted to *canelés*, pastries filled with rum and vanilla with a soft custard centre and a dark caramelised crust which originated in Bordeaux. Today Antoine's mum always brings me *canelés* when we see her. On our third night Antoine took me to a brilliant zouk club in Réunion. Zouk is a sensual dance, based on the lambada, which involves your whole body. But even though it's quite an intimate dance, it isn't sexual; you can dance with a man you have just met in the club and it means nothing, just that you are both feeling the beat. I love to dance and we had a great night. This was a holiday the like of which I had never experienced before. He was determined to make our stay unforgettable.

The night after the zouk club, I was feeling really lazy and had been snoozing in bed, but Antoine wanted us to go out. He threw some swimwear and a bottle of wine into a bag and tried to coax me into joining him. I said, 'No, I don't want to.' But he insisted. Reluctantly I pulled on some of his clothes – his pants and shirt – so I looked like a real tomboy as we left in the car. He parked at a hotel, saying we could use their beach. But once we were inside they welcomed us and took us to a stunning room that Antoine had secretly booked. I was shocked but delighted. The hotel was really luxurious and set right on the beach, with a swimming pool and rooms that looked out to the ocean. I had never stayed anywhere like it before.

In the early evening, Antoine said, 'Let's go for a walk.' Antoine is terrible at keeping secrets, and I could tell by his eyes that he was up to something. He couldn't stop chuckling and seemed really pleased with himself. As we wandered through the streets, he was smiling at everybody, and I remember saying to him, 'What is wrong with you?'

We approached the beach just as the sun was starting to set. I saw people standing and looking at this mass of candles shimmering down on the sand. 'That looks beautiful,' I said. 'Let's go and take a look.'

As we got closer, I spotted what all the people were looking at. There were hundreds of empty water bottles cut in half and painted purple and pink. They had been arranged in the shape of a huge heart and inside each one was a candle. It was so pretty. Inside the heart was a picnic blanket. There was smoked salmon and champagne and a big rose, and all around this were Chinese lanterns. It was quite a sight. I thought it must have been set up for a movie shoot and I turned around to ask Antoine which movie it might be for, only to see that he was down on one knee.

Everyone was watching as he proposed. It was so romantic.

When Antoine and I first met in 2007, I had told him that if I was truly in love with someone and they proposed to me, all I needed was a Coca-Cola bottle cap ring. I didn't need diamonds or material things to prove our love was real. We used to make rings from the caps of Coca-Cola bottles in Sierra Leone. Antoine had remembered this, and as the final perfect gesture he pulled out a ring from his pocket. He had made the very Coca-Cola ring I had described.

It was magic, and I immediately said: 'Yes.'

★

When I returned from Réunion I started to feel sick and my legs were hurting really badly. It was agonising, as if they had been cut with a knife and then salt and pepper had been rubbed in the wounds. It was so bad that I couldn't sleep. I was crying with pain and thinking, 'I'm going to lose my legs!'

My cousins Fatmata and Isatu came around to my apartment to help. They were concerned to see me in so much pain, but because I had just been in Réunion with Antoine, Fatmata said cheekily, 'Maybe you're pregnant.' I said, 'No, that can't be.' I'd had two ovarian cysts in the past few years, the first in 2004 and the second just before Antoine and I got back together in 2011; I'd had the second operation only a couple of months before I went to Réunion. What with the cysts and everything that had happened during the war, I knew I wouldn't be able to fall pregnant; this had to be something else.

I went to the doctor, fearing the worst. He said, 'Let's do a pregnancy test.'

I laughed. 'I'm not pregnant,' I insisted, but he said we should do the test anyway.

It was positive.

I took a second test.

Yep. Pregnant. My legs were just fine and, bizarrely, they stopped hurting as soon as I found out.

It was a big shock to me. Falling pregnant was the last thing on my mind and I didn't know what to think. I wasn't scared, just surprised. But sometimes the best things come out of nowhere. I had always wanted to be a mother; it was something I had dreamed of as a little girl. But after what I had been through, I thought it was very unlikely it would ever happen for me. In my mind, I had surrendered to that idea, and I assumed that I would have to consider adoption to realise my dream of being a mother. One thing I knew for sure, though, was that when I became a mother I would find my purpose in life – and as it turned out it was my beautiful Sarafina's birth that led me to my life's work.

★

When I told Antoine I was pregnant, he was so happy. He said, 'I'm coming over.' We were talking on Skype and he was beyond excited. I thought he was going to jump out of the computer screen. But in that moment I didn't want to see him, and I begged him not to come. I just wanted to be by myself, to absorb the joy, to take my time to prepare for my next stage in life and grab hold of my emotions. But I couldn't stop him. Antoine was delirious, euphoric.

We had bought our wedding rings on holiday, and Antoine was already wearing his. When I said, 'But we're not married yet,' he said, 'It doesn't matter what people say – I can wear my ring if I want.' I didn't think a young man would be that excited about getting married but Antoine was bubbling over with pride. It was really beautiful to see. Even now, he loves being married and he loves our little family. I don't know if it's because of his parents' divorce, but family is so important to him.

We decided we should get married before the baby was born. I wasn't worried about being pregnant on my wedding day. Ever since I was a child I had always wanted to get married when I was pregnant. I never wanted a big wedding with bridesmaids and all that fuss. I wanted something simple, and if I was pregnant then it would be doing everything together, which made sense to me.

Antoine had already told his parents about our engagement and now we needed to tell my mum – and not just about the wedding, but about the baby, too. Tigidankay had met Antoine back in 2007, when he was first in Australia, but this would be the first time I had told my mum and Fatmata and Mabinty about him. I was over thirty by now, and I think Eleas thought I was never going to marry and certainly never going to have kids. That moment on the phone when I told her about Antoine and my pregnancy was the happiest day of her life, she said, apart from the day I was born. She was beyond excited.

Ros was concerned, though. She didn't realise that Antoine and I had known each other previously. I had never talked to her about him and she feared he was someone I'd met on the internet because I had told her we were talking on Facebook. She was extremely protective and it took some persuading from me to put her mind at rest.

Ros wasn't the only one looking out for me. My family asked to meet Antoine's family. I knew this was coming, because in my culture it's very important that the husband's and bride's families get to know each other, so the bride's family can approve the union. This sounds a little old-fashioned in Western culture, but I wanted to do the right thing for everyone. So, a traditional pre-wedding ceremony was held at my sister Fatmata's house in London. It was a Muslim ceremony, even though we are both Christian, but we didn't care. This was about respecting our families, and that meant a lot to both of us. We didn't need to be present for the ceremony, but someone from Antoine's family did.

Antoine called his mum Marine in Paris and said, 'You have to go to London in two days' time for this African Muslim pre-wedding ceremony.' She was so cool. She agreed at once.

Everyone was in African clothes, even Marine, who wore clothes my mum had picked out for her. They were the full Mandingo bazin dresses, bursting with colour and intricate embroidery. My younger sister, Mariama, dressed up like me and acted on my behalf and Marine was there representing Antoine. We watched it all over Skype. There was an imam who offered blessings and prayers, and my sister had a table laid out with a calabash, which is a big bowl made from a hollowed-out gourd. This is traditional in Sierra Leonean weddings. Family and friends put money and gifts into the calabash and then they wrap it in white cloth and pray over it. It was all accompanied by lots of African music and dancing. Antoine's mum was asked if she agreed to the wedding – she said yes – and then everyone sang. My mum and Marine connected right away, and I could see both of them were really happy. This first part of the preparations for our wedding had gone very well.

★

When I was three months pregnant, I had a really big scare. Antoine had gone out because I wanted to be by myself, as I often did at that time, so I was at home alone when I felt this sharp pain. I'd never experienced a pain like that in my life. It was so excruciating I couldn't move. I was on the floor. I remember calling the ambulance and then calling Antoine. He jumped on a train straight away and met me in the emergency department in the hospital.

I called my sister and her husband, and they came too. My sister was crying, Antoine was crying, I was crying and nobody could tell me what was happening. Having my baby was everything to me now, the most important thing in my life. It was a miracle that I had fallen pregnant and the idea that I might lose my child was terrifying.

The doctors said we would have to terminate the pregnancy because they didn't know what was happening, why I was in so much pain, and they couldn't perform an operation to find out without harming the baby. They said they would leave it for one hour and then take me to the operating theatre.

Before leaving my apartment with the ambulance officers, I had automatically grabbed my Bible, which I take with me everywhere. When the doctors left the room, I said to Antoine, 'Can you pass me my Bible?' He did as I asked and then – I know it sounds crazy – I put the Bible on my belly and said a prayer. I said, 'I trust you, God, to look after me and look after the baby.' I remember holding Antoine's hand quietly after that, and I just felt really light. I said to him, 'Everything is going to be fine,' and I slept.

One of the doctors came in as I was sleeping with the Bible on my tummy still. 'What happened?' he asked.

When I woke up, the pain was gone.

I stayed in the hospital under observation for two days, after which they sent me home. I was fine and back to normal.

In hindsight, I think maybe the baby was sitting on a nerve or something, but I do believe in the power of prayer, because whenever I have asked for something, my God has always answered me. I might not understand His answer immediately – sometimes I've had to work for it and wait – but it always comes eventually, even when I was kidnapped.

Once I was back at home, it was as if nothing had happened. I felt well and went back to work at David Lawrence and worked right up until two weeks before my due date.

When I told Ros that I wanted to get married before the baby was born, she immediately said she would host the wedding reception for us. Her family had recently moved into a beautiful new apartment in Elizabeth Bay overlooking Sydney Harbour and my wedding was the first big party they would hold there. It was so kind of her. I wanted a stand-up cocktail event because I didn't want to look at people sitting at tables and wonder if they were happy or not.

Our families flew in from London and France. There was Antoine's dad, sister and mum and some of his friends, and some of my family and friends. And for me there was a wonderful surprise. I had been talking to the twins on the phone, saying how much I really wished my dad could have been there. I would have loved him to meet Antoine because I know he would have adored him – they are so alike in many ways, which is probably why I fell for Antoine. I was so sad about it that I was crying to my sisters, which wasn't like me, but what with the baby it was an emotional time. So, without telling me, Mabinty decided to come over. She arrived on my doorstep two days before the wedding. I heard the doorbell, opened the door and there she was. It was incredible – I was really happy. The twins look so much like my dad, it was like a piece of him was there with me on our special day after all.

The ceremony was held on 11 February 2012 at my church in Penshurst. It was beautiful. I didn't have any bridesmaids, and Antoine didn't have a best man. It was all very simple. Michael Dwyer walked me down the aisle to Celine Dion's 'Pour Que Tu M'aimes Encore'. I had found a wedding dress by Sydney designer Collette Dinnigan in her store in Woollahra; it was the cheapest one there and it was perfect. It was cream, very long and elegant, with diamanté detail around the neckline. It was roomy, too, because I needed space for the baby. I was holding a bouquet of vintage ivory roses and my friend Renae had made a veil of tulle edged with French lace and studded with Swarovski crystals. Antoine was standing with the pastor at the top of the aisle. He looked really handsome in a blue suit with a rose from my bouquet in his buttonhole. I am not a fairytale person, but it felt perfect for me. Everyone whom I wanted to be there was, and as I had dreamed I was six and a half months pregnant. It felt right – as if finally the universe, my universe, was in tune.

After the ceremony Antoine and I went to Sydney's Royal Botanic Gardens to have photos taken. It is one of Antoine's favourite places in Sydney and he wanted our special day commemorated there. My friend Lameck, who I met at Australia for UNHCR, drove us there in his sleek black Chrysler car. While we were having our photos taken, the rest of the wedding guests made their way to Elizabeth Bay. We were all meeting at a beautiful little park there overlooking the harbour, and after our photos in the Botanic Gardens we arrived to greet our guests and have more photos taken before we all walked down the steps to Ros and Joe's house. The reception was held on the terrace, which her daughter Nina had decorated with fairy lights and flowers. The doors of the living room folded right back to reveal the luxuriant Moroccan furniture and colourful artwork in their home.

Sydney had turned on a lovely summer day with rich golden rays of sun and then a dash of rain for luck. At one point there were even fireworks on the harbour – they weren't for us, but I was happy to see them nevertheless. We ate paella and danced the night away to the beat of African drums. Everyone was dancing – even Michael and all the men.

I had invited all the people who had helped me in Australia and meant so much to me. I even tracked down my teacher, Mrs Harper, whom I hadn't seen since I finished high school in 2003. The day I called her she was moving house; if I had rung a day later I would have missed her. She came with her husband, and it felt so right to have her at my wedding, this lady who had ensured that I would see my dad before he died. I wanted her to see that I was okay, that I was doing well. I also wanted the people who had been there from the very beginning for me, like my good friend Robin, who has since died. Among other things, Robin taught me how to swim. Of course the Dwyer family was also there, and Ros and her family.

Antoine and I were the last ones to leave – we just couldn't stop dancing – and I know everybody had a good time. It was the most magical day. I loved every minute of it.

★

Wedding aside, though, I was a bit of a nightmare with Antoine. I can admit that now. I really didn't want him around through my pregnancy. My hormones were all over the place and it was poor Antoine who bore the brunt of my moods. We were still trying to sort out his visa, which was very complicated, and he didn't have work here in Sydney. He'd had a really good job in Réunion, but as soon as he heard about the baby he just quit work and flew over to be with me. Antoine didn't care about practical things, he just followed his heart.

But the problem was I didn't want affection from him. I was tired and not feeling great and I just wanted to be alone. I had said as much to him on the phone: 'Do not come, please do not come.' I couldn't have made it any clearer.

He said, 'Okay, I won't come.'

I was working in David Lawrence and was fine just going to work then coming home to rest. That was my routine. Then one morning I heard somebody banging on the street door, then the sound of the doorbell. I thought it was someone playing a trick on me. I said into the intercom, 'Hello, who is this?'

Nothing.

Then the doorbell again, and finally a funny voice said, 'Aminata, I wanted to surprise you.' It wasn't anyone I recognised.

A neighbour opened the downstairs door and someone ran up the stairs and pounded on my door. This was getting creepy now. Who was it?

I opened the door and there was Antoine.

He wore that babyish smile and his big eyes were full of love, but I wasn't happy. I said, 'What are you doing here?' It was supposed to be a romantic moment, but it wasn't — at least, not for me. I feel sorry for Antoine now, because I was so cold and he just couldn't work out why. It was a really sad time for him; I was being so standoffish and difficult, and he didn't know what to do. I think the wedding was the only good day for him when I was pregnant. I could not wait for that baby to come out because I wanted to be normal again.

It was something I'd heard of before. Pregnant women can turn against certain people, often those they love most. I thought it was rubbish, but here it was happening to me. I really did not feel any affection for Antoine throughout my whole pregnancy and all he wanted to do was cuddle and kiss.

In the last month of my pregnancy Antoine had to go to New Caledonia because his visitor's visa had expired. He had lodged an application for Australian residency from Réunion after our wedding. As my husband he was eligible, and we thought it would just be a formality. But the papers had to go via South Africa, because that was the closest Australian embassy to Réunion, and when we investigated, we found out that no one had even looked at Antoine's application and now his visitor visa had run out. Now that I was near the end of my pregnancy I really wanted him around; I didn't want to have our baby without him by my side. I called my Member of Parliament at Rockdale and explained the situation, and she was really kind. She called the South African embassy in the morning and they organised Antoine's visa just like that and he was able to come straight to Sydney. My mum was also with us for the birth as well as my sister Tkay.

It was good to have so many people with me, because Sarafina's birth was really tough. She was ten days late and I was starting to get anxious. Eventually we went to the hospital, where they decided to induce the labour, and gave me an epidural. (Ros had advised me to have the epidural because it was wonderful and stopped all the pain.) I still didn't go into labour. Eventually Antoine went home with my mum, and then I was taken to the delivery theatre where the baby was supposed to be born. Still nothing. I called Antoine. I was starting to panic. Antoine, Mum and Tkay returned to the hospital and finally, after nine hours, I went into labour.

Because of the epidural I couldn't feel a thing. The nurses were telling me to push, push, push, but nothing was happening. Sarafina was a big baby – five kilos – and it was too late for a caesarean because her head was already crowning. I could see by his face that Antoine was getting worried. Nobody was talking.

Then this woman came in with two other doctors. It was clear when she introduced herself that she was very senior. I realised that the situation was serious. I was pushing, pushing. Antoine was turning red, and my mum was distraught. My sister was crying and everyone was saying: 'Push!' I said, 'Shut up, please!' And everybody just went quiet.

I remember the doctor saying she could see the baby's head but she needed to turn her or turn me, but I couldn't move. It was really desperate. Intense. By now there were seven doctors in the room, plus Antoine, my mum and my sister. Everyone knew that my life was at risk and our baby's also. My mum was praying, my sister was panicking. Antoine was holding my hands really tight. They had to get the baby out immediately in order to ensure my survival. I think in their hearts the doctors all thought Sarafina was going to be born dead, but they weren't telling us that, at least not in so many words.

And then the doctor just plunged in with her bare hands and pulled Sarafina out. I could see the concern on her face, the urgency; she was acting on instinct.

At first there was no sound from my newborn baby, but after a few minutes she began to cry and we all heaved a sigh of relief.

Antoine said straight away, 'It's Sarafina.' We had already

chosen her name. I was sure I was having a girl even though everyone predicted the opposite. Sarafina is from the Hebrew word *seraphim*, an order of angels who were the highest of the high and had six wings so they could soar closer to heaven. I loved that idea. Also, there is a beautiful South African movie called *Sarafina!*, with Whoopi Goldberg, and the character Sarafina was so strong. The movie was set during apartheid, and Sarafina was a leader; she was fighting but she was also caring. So I always said, when I give birth to my daughter I'm going to call her Sarafina. And my Sarafina is incredibly caring.

I was very tired, and losing a lot of blood, so they took Sarafina out to check if everything was okay with her and let me rest. They were trying to stitch me up and I remember fainting twice. When they brought Sarafina back to me, I noticed that her arm was just hanging floppy; in the violence of the delivery, her shoulder had been broken. It's a condition called 'shoulder dystocia'; it happens when a baby's head has been born but one of its shoulders becomes stuck behind the mother's pelvic bone, preventing the birth of the baby's body. I didn't fully understand what had happened; to me Sarafina was perfect – here was my angel, albeit with a broken wing. Antoine was more concerned. I have no doubt that had the doctor not done what she did Sarafina and I might not be here today, but my daughter's injury wasn't insignificant. It's something we have had to work on with exercises and physiotherapy, and she might need an operation when she is older, but it doesn't hold her back.

I call Sarafina my wild butterfly. She is gentle and very loving. She loves people and she cares how people feel about her. She doesn't like to do things wrong. She loves art and she draws a lot. I think what I love most about her is how much she cares about people. She doesn't forget about other people and is always concerned with how they are feeling. She's very affectionate and I can see she will grow up to be a true force for change.

★

After Sarafina was born on 9 June 2012 my feelings for Antoine returned to normal. Hallelujah! In Africa we believe that when the woman doesn't feel affection towards the man in pregnancy, the child will look like the husband. And it's true Sarafina does look like Antoine.

I was in hospital for three or four days after Sarafina was born, with an endless stream of people checking up on me. My doctor would come in with her colleagues and they would look at me and talk about things I didn't understand. I don't know if I was a case study, but I was getting the most incredible treatment.

I remember when I went home with Sarafina I was so satisfied, so content, and I've been like that ever since. Sarafina was a good baby. She would sleep in her cot during the day and her bassinet at night – she didn't need to be with us – and she was happy, just like Antoine. The two of them are like one big happy pill.

As I gazed at my beautiful baby girl, I kept on thinking about the doctors who had observed me and Sarafina after the birth, and I realised that their conversation was about how they could avoid my situation happening again. They wanted to understand what had gone wrong so another mother wouldn't have to suffer as I had.

I remember going into Sarafina's room one day as she was sleeping in her cot. She looked so serene and perfect. I had an overwhelming sense of the privilege of having her there. And then immediately after I felt this huge awakening of consciousness. It came in a wave that washed right through me. I realised that if I had been in Sierra Leone giving birth, I would have died and Sarafina would have died too. That is guaranteed. I wouldn't have had seven doctors gathered around my bed trying to work out what to do. How was it that we had so much here, when in places like Sierra Leone, my homeland, women died doing the most natural thing of all, having a baby? This is not a disease that we need to find a cure for; it is preventable. Why are Western mothers and babies worth more than African mothers and babies?

I was so happy, but in addition to my happiness something else had been growing inside me. I started watching videos on YouTube of mothers giving birth in Africa, horrible videos. It started as just curiosity and developed into frustration, and when I looked at the statistics for maternal mortality in Sierra Leone I discovered that one in eight women die, making it the most dangerous place in the world to have a baby at that time. I just couldn't understand it. There was no war now. This should not be happening. Giving birth is a gift and every mother deserves to experience the wonder of holding her newborn baby regardless of where they live.

At that moment, Sarafina was the most important person in my world, and like all parents I would sacrifice anything for her. That was how all mothers felt – but why should my child be worth more than any other mother's? Something had shifted for me. A seed had been planted in my heart, and slowly, over the next couple of years, that seed would germinate into what I now know is my life's work.

CHAPTER NINETEEN

We are women, hear us roar

I was pregnant again at the premiere of *The Baulkham Hills African Ladies Troupe* on 9 May 2013 at Riverside Theatre in Parramatta. We had been working so hard on it all the way through my first pregnancy and also after the birth, and now I was expecting another baby. It seems crazy that after the pain and trauma of Sarafina's birth I would fall pregnant again so quickly, but that was what happened. We didn't plan it, but we were really joyful.

This time we learned the gender of our baby before birth, so we knew we were expecting a boy. We hadn't asked to find out; the nurses just mentioned it without thinking during the ultrasound. But I was very at peace with it. I had always wanted to have a girl first and then, after Sarafina was born, I wanted a boy. Some Sierra Leonean abuse victims had told me that they didn't ever want to mother a son. They thought they would always be scared that their boy might grow up to treat women as the rebels had treated us, and they didn't want to bring another rapist into the world. But I didn't feel that at all – quite the opposite. I wanted to have a boy and a girl, and I wanted to have the opportunity to teach them both from my heart. I wanted to teach my son how to treat women with parity and respect, and I wanted to teach my daughter how to be strong. I always say to them, 'Be kind. Be kind to yourself and be kind to others.' This is not just about them treating other people with respect and empathy; they should treat themselves that way, too.

So . . . having got over the shock that I was pregnant again so quickly, I was unbelievably happy when I learned that my second baby was to be a boy, and Antoine of course was flying. It was really a joy. And today, my goodness, my little boy Matisse really is something.

★

As rehearsals for the play had progressed and the structure was bedded in, with the four of us becoming actors in our own stories, rehearsals became more and more intense. But I was never tired, the energy just flowed through me. When I came home at night Antoine could feel that energy and how important this was to me. Fortunately, with this pregnancy I didn't have the same reaction to Antoine – we were both pleased about that!

When Ros announced that she had secured shows in theatres in Sydney, and that we were actually going to be performing in a professional production on a big stage, I was excited. Rehearsing gave me an immense sense of purpose, and now we would have the opportunity to share our stories and our message with everyone. This show wasn't about us anymore; I believed we would be helping other women and girls who had gone through the same experiences as us, and that was my guiding light. I knew in my heart it was going to make a difference and I felt blessed to have the opportunity to be a part of that.

As we finessed the content, a few of us started having trouble with the more confronting parts of our stories. There were a couple of scenes in the play that I struggled with. My leg would start shaking uncontrollably, which was always a sign that I was in distress, and I would be unable to move. The smells started to come back to me: Daramy's pungent sweat, the odour of burning flesh and putrid dead bodies. It was as if I was back there again.

Ros was very sensitive when any of us found the play overwhelming; the last thing she wanted to do was trigger more trauma. So with the specialist trauma counsellor on hand, she would devise ways to get around those scenes, as I have described earlier. I might come out of my role and let an actor take over as I observed, or if necessary I would leave the stage all together. She had a number of different scenarios prepared should any of us pull out at the last minute. Yordy did actually leave us for a while because she found it too hard. She was talking about things she had never revealed before, dredging up memories and incidents she had worked hard to forget. But with the firm support of her children she came back to us and I'm really glad she did.

I was certainly nervous on the opening night and so were the other women. It was an even bigger deal for one of the other women, who had never told her sons what had happened to her. For four women who had kept their stories hidden for so long, this was a watershed moment. And for our families and friends, even though there was a lot of joy and humour in the show, it was a night of painful revelation. The play ran for an hour and forty minutes with no interval and the audience was mesmerised.

I had my new family with me. Sarafina was there in Antoine's arms and our son Matisse was there, too, in my tummy. After Sarafina's birth I had taken her along to rehearsals. She was far too young to understand the words but she loved the dancing and the music. Antoine was so supportive. He was crying all the way through the play, but they were tears of beautiful joy. Antoine has never seen me as a victim and that is why I love him so much and knew that he was somebody I needed to be with. I'm really blessed to have him.

The play went very well. I knew lots of people in the audience, but even though they were hearing my story in detail for the first time, it didn't worry me. It was time. I remember my friend Marion told me that at first she wasn't sure if she could handle seeing the play, but then she said if I had the strength to stand up and tell my story to the world, she would have the strength to support me. Afterwards Marion was so proud of me. She said she respected my courage because a lot of girls wouldn't be able to reveal what I had revealed. She said it helped them and it helped her, which was good to hear.

Michael Dwyer was also in the audience with his family, and I think it was a shock for him to hear what I had been through. He, too, was really proud. He told me how brave

I was. I had already talked to his wife Janelle about most of the events described in the play, but she obviously hadn't shared our private discussions with Michael. He tells me today, 'It was on that night when the horror of it all and the tragedy of it all became very clear to me.'

One very real danger at that time was that news of the play – and of me – might reach Daramy's ears and he might come looking for me. This was something that had been lurking in the background for a while. I didn't even think about Daramy until 2011, around the time when Antoine and I had got back together. You always know that when good things are happening, there's something bad coming back at you.

When my childhood friend Safie called me out of the blue from Freetown I knew something was up. She said, 'Daramy has been back to your house in Kissy and was asking around about which country you are living in.'

This was chilling, and initially I was really scared. Ros and her husband Joe had already started an investigation into Daramy; they were concerned he might put two and two together if he saw media coverage about the play or the accompanying documentary film, which would be released globally. They knew that the rebels didn't have criminal records, so Daramy could potentially gain asylum in Australia through the usual refugee channels. They were right. Many of those who were emigrating had been rebels or involved with the rebels, and the authorities could never tell. That was a really frightening time for me, but I refused to be intimidated by him again. This was my country, my life, and everything was starting to go right for me.

But Ros and Joe wouldn't let it go. They wanted to see if they could lodge something in the Australian refugee system that would raise a flag if Daramy or Coal Boot tried to apply. They sought advice from a friend of theirs who was one of the prosecutors during the Charles Taylor trial, which was ongoing at the time. Charles Taylor was a guerrilla leader turned Liberian president who was the real power behind the Sierra Leone civil war, having helped to finance the rebel forces and encouraged their depraved behaviour. He was convicted for crimes against humanity in 2003, and in 2012 he was being tried by the UN in The Hague for war crimes. My name had come up in connection with their friend's work on this trial, and Ros and Joe talked to him about my story, hoping that he might know the whereabouts of Daramy and Coal Boot. They discovered that Coal Boot was in prison in Sierra Leone. He was one of only three people who were prosecuted.

This was great news, but Daramy was still at large and there were no plans to hold him accountable for his crimes. There was nothing I could do but refuse to live in fear. Also, I had decided after my release to embrace a spirit of forgiveness. And who was I to say that Daramy shouldn't have a fresh start too? I decided to put it to the back of my mind and moved forwards with the play.

A few months after its debut in Parramatta, on 15 August 2013 *The Baulkham Hills African Ladies Troupe* opened at Sydney's renowned Belvoir Theatre for a month's run. The reviews were extraordinary and I was really enjoying being part of such a powerful performance. Being in the play not only boosted my confidence, it reconnected me with my homeland, with the beauty and the horror, which I think was important therapy for me at that time.

★

After the issues I'd had with Sarafina's birth, I was booked in for an elective caesarean two weeks before Matisse's due date. No one was taking any chances. He, too, was a big baby; even though he was born prematurely he was the size of a full-term baby, so it was definitely the right decision. I was awake throughout the whole procedure, chatting happily to the doctor, who was from India. It couldn't have been more different from Sarafina's birth. We chose the name Matisse for our son because we wanted a French name to honour Antoine's heritage, but also because it is a version of Matthew, one of Jesus's twelve disciples, and the name means 'gift'. When he was born, I knew in my heart that he was indeed a gift from God. His eyes were so full of wisdom and light. Antoine thinks he is stubborn like me, but I say, 'He knows who he is.'

Now that Matisse was born, our family was complete. I felt stronger than ever, and like I was finally free to be who I was meant to be. Now it was time for me to concentrate on helping mothers in Sierra Leone to receive the care that I'd had. It was time for me to give something back, to my country, to my people.

CHAPTER TWENTY

Finding our nest

Today Sarafina always says, 'The foundation is about me. My arm was broken so the foundation could happen.' While I don't want to underplay what happened to her, I do think it was a sign. If I hadn't faced that difficult birth, I would never have conceived of the Aminata Maternal Foundation.

Beginning a foundation is no small task, particularly because life as usual must go on around it. After Matisse was born on 25 November 2013, I took maternity leave from David Lawrence. Antoine went to work, and I stayed home with the kids. In the evenings, I was busy with *The Baulkham Hills African Ladies Troupe*. But I was also preoccupied with researching maternal healthcare conditions in Sierra Leone as I began the journey of setting up the foundation to help the women and girls in my country. As I write this, I realise how big my plan was, but that epiphany I'd had when I gave birth to Sarafina was very real to me and I was not afraid of taking action.

I had always wanted to do something in Sierra Leone; of course, being involved with Australia for UNHCR was one thing, but that was a huge organisation. Michael Dwyer and I would have meetings where I would suggest all sorts of ideas. For instance, I used to collect a lot of clothes and send them to people in Sierra Leone, but I spent so much money on the containers and I could never be sure the clothes got to the people who really needed them. It was a drop in the ocean and inefficient, and I knew it.

It hurt me that Sierra Leone had become so poor and that this basic human act of giving birth had become an issue of life and death for so many women. I love my homeland, I love my people, and we are no different from people in the West, no worse, no better, but they had so little. I had long wanted to do something really meaningful for Sierra Leone, but I didn't know what. Now I knew.

I started meeting individually with a lot of great people I had encountered through Australia for UNHCR. My cousin's husband, Morlai Kamara, came along with me to some of these meetings; Morlai has a lot of expertise in development in Sierra Leone. One of the people I met with was my wonderful friend Andrea Durbach, who is a professor at the University of New South Wales and at the time was the director of their Australian Human Rights Centre. Andrea introduced me to Anthony Zwi, who is a doctor and professor of global health and development at the University of New South Wales. Anthony has worked in the health sector in various countries, from Bangladesh to Cambodia and South Africa. I also spoke with Maureen Collins, the woman who persuaded me to tell my story at my first UNHCR event. Maureen and Anthony were both keen to help me. This is how I progressed with my vision – one meeting, one introduction, at a time.

In order to register a company, you need a minimum of three board members. The foundation's originating board members were me, Maureen and Anthony. We registered it on 28 November 2014. It was the first big step, and I felt the foundation was finally coming to life.

But I was also busy with *The Baulkham Hills African Ladies Troupe*. Ros was taking us to London in March 2015 to perform three shows as part of the Women of the World Festival at the Southbank Centre. This was huge. We were going to be performing before a truly global audience. I was back working at David Lawrence three days a week by then, but I had lots of holiday owing, because for years I hadn't taken any time off at all. This meant I was able to take leave when I was rehearsing and travelling to London with the play.

It was the first time I had left Sarafina and Matisse but as I waved goodbye to my family at the airport I was super excited.

I love London. Maybe it's because my dad spent so much time there, maybe because my family live there, maybe because there are so many African and Caribbean people – whatever it is, I feel totally safe and comfortable. And I was a completely different person from the bereft girl who had flown in alone last time. Then I had been in London to say goodbye to the father I adored. Doing the play gave me so much dignity for myself; I wasn't scared anymore, and being able to live without fear is priceless. The Women of the

World Festival is not just for theatre and performance art; it's an activist conference of ideas shared between women, and I was part of that. I felt proud and brave and truly free – like I was dancing in the streets. The South Bank is the home of performance art in London and the Purcell Room, where we were to perform, is an intimate theatre with comfortable banked seating for 295 people. This is a place for music recitals, poetry readings and intense debates. It felt totally appropriate for our personal and lyrical production.

My mum and the twins came to see me in the show. For the first time, they heard about what had happened to me. At my wedding, Mabinty had given a speech in which she started crying. She said that when I was kidnapped, they had all thought I was dead, and to see me alive and getting married was the best day for her. I felt nervous about them watching the play, but now I realise this was the only way I could share my experiences with my family. I knew it wasn't something we would talk about to each other ever, but it felt right that they should know, and this way I could reach out to them without having to have the conversation.

When I saw them after the show, I could see they were shocked by what had played out on the stage. It was extremely emotional for them and they were all crying. They were hugely proud of me, but it was way more than that: they were mourning. When I talked to the twins about it recently, Fatmata said that she couldn't believe I had gone through such a horrific experience and then not said anything about it. They were pleased that I was talking out now because they didn't want me to suffer internally, to stay afraid. Mabinty, too, found it hard to come to terms with – she'd had no idea I had been raped and it really played on her mind.

While seeing the play brought us closer, the twins knew I didn't want sympathy. Like me, my sisters felt the key to release was forgiveness. Mabinty said, 'If you don't forgive, it's like you're suffering more, you're trying to find a way to get revenge, you don't want to move on. So it's better you use that experience for something positive, like this play or the foundation. You use that story to help other people, try to be forgiving and try to move in a positive way. That was Dad's way– that's how he brought us up. He was always looking at the positives. If something bad happened, use that to make something good out of it.'

For my mum, it was extremely hard; she now knew what I had been through and it tore her apart. I think the play was the only way I could have told her. We didn't talk about it afterwards, and we still haven't discussed it in any detail. It is too hard for both of us. But I think it has brought us closer together. Unlike me and the twins, my mum cannot forgive Daramy for what he did to her daughter. As a mother myself, I completely understand that. But I do think she saw me in a different light that night. Now she could understand why I wanted to do something bigger with my life, and I think she was really proud that I could say these things out loud, even in front of my husband and now that I was a parent. I know many things would have gone through her head as she watched me, because I did something most African women would never do. This was why I knew I could never have married a Sierra Leonean or an African man. It would have been impossible for me to speak out, but I knew I had a voice to talk about things that have happened to me and I wanted to do it. I know that watching the play my mum had huge respect for me. Today she feels sad that I didn't grow up with her, but that is something that cannot be helped. I love her dearly and think she's the most incredible, kind person. She is equal to my dad; it's just that he was my everything. When I go to London now, I always stay with her.

The Baulkham Hills African Ladies Troupe's final Australian season was in the Sydney Opera House in March 2015. By this time, I was starting to find performing difficult. It had begun in London. I think it might have been because when I was there I had seen Frances, and she spoke about things that happened, or that Daramy had done, which I had forgotten about. For example, she mentioned that Daramy used to tie my ankles together so I couldn't run away. I'd had absolutely no memory of that until she said it. That's the thing about trauma: it can sideswipe you at any time. It was like my demons were prodded awake. By the time we started performing in Sydney, I was experiencing intense physical reactions as I tried to perform. My feet would start tapping, loudly and uncontrollably, during scenes. Two or three times I fainted on stage and couldn't finish the show; another actor replaced me. Even so, I never thought about not performing. This was always going to be the final season, though, and that felt right. And even with the difficulties towards the end, performing in *The Baulkham Hills African Ladies Troupe* was one of the most important and valuable experiences of my life.

★

With the success of the play and my ongoing work on starting the Aminata Maternal Foundation, there was a lot on the go, but I was full of hope and excited for the future. But then my bubble was burst in a terrifying way.

I had put on quite a bit of weight after having Sarafina and then Matisse so close together, and I wanted to start looking after myself and go back to feeling good about my body. I was working part-time at David Lawrence, so Sarafina and Matisse were going to child care. On my days at home, I started going for several walks a day; walking is my favourite form of exercise after dancing. There was a small park near our apartment where I would go. In the evenings, my routine was to put the kids to bed between 5.30 and 6 pm (fortunately they were both great sleepers when they were little), then when Antoine arrived home from work, I would head out for my evening exercise.

There were three elderly people living in the apartment block of six units I had been living in since 2001. We were in number six, on the top floor. There was a lady from Israel, a lady from somewhere in Eastern Europe and a gentleman from India. In such a small block, we all knew each other very well.

Unit four, which I had to walk past to go up to our unit, was where the Eastern European lady lived. I used to talk to her a lot. She'd had a battle with cancer and her daughter, who worked for Qantas, would come back and forth, as would her ex-husband, and I talked to them all. But while I knew quite a bit about them, they didn't know my story, only that I was refugee who was now a busy married mum of two.

Over the years, this lady had told me about her son who was in prison for rape. As a mother, of course, she didn't believe he'd done it, but as far as I was concerned, if you've been in prison in Australia for ten years for rape, you'd done the crime.

Towards the end of 2015 the Eastern European lady died, and halfway through 2016 her son was released from prison and came to live in her unit. The police made frequent visits to monitor him; they weren't always in uniform, but you could tell who they were because they carried guns. He was tagged with an ankle bracelet but tried to hide it under his socks. He stayed inside most of the time or close to the unit because I think he wasn't allowed to go far, having just come out of prison. He was rough-looking and when I went out, I'd see him staring at me out of the window. He grew familiar with my schedule and would be there every time I came and went. Then he began to stand outside his unit and make comments like, 'You don't need to go for a run – you look good the way you are,' as he looked me up and down. I didn't want him to know that I was scared, but I was petrified. I told Antoine and he agreed this man might be very dangerous and we should keep out of his way. It was winter and it was getting dark earlier, and when I came home from the gym I would always bump into him in the garage or on the stairs. It freaked me out.

I started having nightmares. I didn't want to tell anyone, because I didn't want my life to be dictated by this man and my past, but it was really affecting me. Then, one day, he tried to speak to Sarafina and my blood ran cold. My nightmares got much worse after that. Daramy had never appeared much in my nightmares before, but now he was in there along with this man. In the dream I was being raped . . . but it also involved my daughter. It was truly terrible.

The only solution was for housing authority to relocate us to somewhere secure as soon as possible. I didn't want to stay in social housing forever, but I knew that it would be a while before we had enough savings for our own place.

Antoine and I started to fill out the paperwork requesting we be moved. By this time, I had been made redundant from David Lawrence. The parent company that owned the fashion chain had descended into administration and they closed a fifth of their stores immediately. In the fallout, I lost my job, and because of the administration proceedings it was a long time before I received my redundancy payout. It was like part of my world had collapsed, but I tried to see the bright side; it meant the foundation could become my full-time focus.

I had asked for accommodation north of the Sydney Harbour Bridge. I knew it was available because there had been a program on TV about a glut of social housing there. In many ways I was sad to leave the western suburbs, where I had happily lived for nearly twenty years – I would never have thought of leaving if this thing hadn't happened. But living in the north made perfect sense for me, as my office for the foundation and my support network was there and it would put a good distance between me and this man. But when I was next contacted about my application for new housing, the postcode on my application had been changed. The area now specified was around Blacktown or Parramatta, in Sydney's west.

'Why have you changed it?' I asked.

After a lot of to-ing and fro-ing, the lady on the end of the phone said, 'Only people from the north can live in the north. Bankstown or Parramatta is where your people live.' I was so shocked to hear her say 'your people', but I don't think she even realised how her words made me feel – so insignificant, as if I didn't matter at all.

I remember I was driving home one time after picking Sarafina up from day care, an ordinary day, and I just burst into floods of tears – I was in so much pain. After everything that happened in Sierra Leone, I'd thought Australia, the country which had offered me refuge and a sense of safety, was the last place I would face such a thing. Where could I run to now?

I talked to a few other friends about my situation, just casually. I didn't want to alarm anyone or for them to think I was complaining. They were horrified to hear what I was going through and shocked that they'd had no idea. They said, 'But you look so happy and well whenever I see you.' I completely understood where they were coming from, but at the same time I was confused. Why should I look helpless just because I am in a helpless situation? Why can't I be dignified and still ask for help? That will never make sense to me.

I tried everything I could think of. I reached out to anyone I thought might be able to help: the local council, my local MP, influential people I'd met at places like Human Rights Watch. I wrote passionate letters to them, which I still have. When I look back at them today I realise how distraught I was. 'I am lying on my knees begging you and pleading . . . help me not to live in hell,' I wrote. Also my therapist wrote to the housing authority explaining my situation. She was very worried about me and thought a letter from her might help. Because of *The Baulkham Hills African Ladies Troupe*, my story had been made public, so we were able to prove I was telling the truth.

The housing authority called me and said they'd had no idea this man had moved into the building, which surprised me. I told them I didn't want the man to know I was scared of him, and I didn't want him to know my story. 'I don't want you to remove him,' I said, 'because he will know it's me who complained and he knows where we live, and then he will come after me. I just want to be removed, so he can have his peace and lead his life. I don't want this to be a trigger for him to reoffend.' They said that they understood and would get back to me. But it seemed like nothing was happening at all. I had no voice.

Speaking out and fighting for what you deserve isn't always easy. I believe there isn't a single refugee in this country who isn't grateful; grateful to be offered refuge, to be safe, for the opportunities available to them in this country. But as a refugee, you can feel like you should *always* be grateful, and never complain about anything, be it the language, the environment, even a badly brewed coffee or a rainy day: I must take everything on the chin and be happy about it. Still today if I dare to voice any criticism I can feel what I call 'the look' burrowing into my head. 'The look' is a disapproving glower that means I should be grateful for everything in this country, and I should never presume to pass judgement or express any displeasure.

But I know what I have done to make it this far. I know how I fought to survive every single second when I was kidnapped, despite wanting to die many times and even falling pregnant to my captor. Every day I am told, 'You are so lucky to have so and so help you or be with you.' And every time I hear this, I wonder how can it be called 'lucky'. Where was luck when I was being raped by the rebels? Where was luck when I was taken from my father's quivering hands? So, I tell myself every minute of every day: 'No, luck only exists through opportunities.' My life and my surroundings have nothing to do with luck. I believe in my own strength. I believe in the power of my own choices. I believe in the goodness of the people I have chosen to surround myself with, and the goodness of people generally. And I believe in God's love – it is the only thing I have always seen clearly, in my darkest and brightest hours.

It is in this sense that what I can only describe as a miracle – no, it wasn't luck – happened to me. I remember it was 28 August 2017 when Sister Carmel called me. I knew Sister Carmel well because I would give talks at Monte Sant' Angelo Mercy College, a secondary school for girls in North Sydney where she worked. She's the funkiest sister and I've always loved her. I had been at the school earlier that day for a meeting about another talk I would be giving to the students. We got chatting and I ended up telling her about the issues I was having. It was a very light-hearted conversation, and I remember I said, 'I'll be fine, Sister Carmel. If this is where God wants me to live for now, this is where I will live, and I will just bless that.'

A couple of hours later she called me and said, 'You know when you said that God is looking after you? Well, you were right. I talked to the other sisters and explained your situation, and we can offer you a home. The person who is living there at the moment will be moving out in two weeks. It's in Wollstonecraft.'

This was beyond my wildest hopes. Wollstonecraft was just perfect. I remember messaging Antoine: *What do you think of Wollstonecraft?* Antoine called me straight away and said, 'What have you done?' I explained to him what Sister Carmel had told me: that they had an apartment available at a rent we could afford.

At first I couldn't quite believe it was real. I thought I must have imagined it, and all weekend I felt sick. I couldn't sleep a wink. On Monday morning, I couldn't stand it any longer. I drove to see Sister Carmel at the school. She said, 'Is everything okay?' I said, 'I just want you to repeat what you told me on the phone on Friday, because I can't believe it.'

She said, 'Yes, I've found you a place to live.'

My eyes were shining and my heart was pumping. I replied, 'I don't know if you realise that you've just changed my whole life.'

Sister Carmel then took me in her car to see the apartment. It was beautiful, on the top floor of the building with light flooding in. It had its own garage and was surrounded by tropical gardens.

It was six weeks or so before we could move in, because the sisters made sure everything was brand-new. They bought new carpet and wardrobes, and had the walls repainted. When we walked in, I felt like it was a home I had bought for myself because they made me feel that way. This could be our home for as long as we wanted, Sister Carmel told me. We had found our safe haven.

★

Antoine and I had a lovely new home and two beautiful children. Now the foundation could become my full-time focus.

CHAPTER TWENTY-ONE

The Aminata Maternal
Foundation

The years it took me to set up the Aminata Maternal Foundation, while also working part-time, finding a new home, participating in *Baulkham Hills* and caring for Sarafina and Matisse, were a struggle, but also very empowering when I realised that I was building a rewarding life from scratch. I came to Australia with nothing, no money, no contacts, no family financial support and no Antoine or children. With determination it can be done. I knew no one would support an idea with nothing concrete behind it, so I didn't ask anyone for financial input, just their valuable advice. I used my personal credit card to underwrite all those early expenses. I didn't know if I would ever be able to pay it off, but I had to believe.

Writing this now has given me the opportunity to think back over the genesis of the Aminata Maternal Foundation, which was a true baptism of fire. The AMF came to life not because I wanted to set up a charity, but because I was horrified at the injustice of mothers and babies dying in childbirth around the world and especially in Sierra Leone. In Australia, on average six mothers die per 100,000 live births, but in Sierra Leone that number is 1360. What's more, Sierra Leone has one of the highest infant mortality rates in the world.

I believe that when you witness injustice in any form, you have two choices: you can walk away, or you can do something. For me there was no choice. Pa Conteh raised me with an acute sense of responsibility; walking away was never my option, and this situation was dire and urgent.

But I have to admit, I didn't know what I was getting myself into. Caring for another human being felt so natural to me and I thought everyone would be the same. Despite what had happened to me during my months of captivity, I never once wavered in my faith in humanity, and I still refuse to let anyone take that away from me. But it hasn't been easy.

Back when I began my journey to establish what has become the Aminata Maternal Foundation, I knew that there was one person I could share my dreams with who would listen and have faith in me, and that was my spiritual dad, Michael Dwyer. I remember I felt a light burning bright inside me when I started talking to Michael about maternal health in Sierra Leone. I told him that I wanted to build a hospital in Sierra Leone, so that the women and babies in my homeland could have the same quality of medical care I'd received in Australia. He was very encouraging and has always been unfailingly supportive of me, but I knew that even he didn't think I was serious. I sensed it right away and was surprised. I thought, 'If Michael, who loves me and believes in me, doubts this project, it's going to be an uphill battle.'

But I'm never afraid to ask for anything, and I fully accept that people are free to say 'no' or 'yes', although of course I prefer the latter. The only response I don't accept is, 'You can't,' or, 'It's impossible.' I have never understood why people assume they have the right to tell others what they can do with their life. So I didn't give in.

Initially, I didn't want my name on the foundation. Michael Dwyer tried to convince me otherwise. He said, 'Aminata, you have a story, and have been blessed with a gift that makes people want to know you.' It was his idea to call the charity 'the Aminata Maternal Foundation'. But I was still unsure. I didn't want people to think that I was asking for funds for myself. While the foundation had sprung from my personal story of almost losing my daughter Sarafina in childbirth, as well as my abduction, and I understand that I will always have to tell these two stories for people to be interested in what I am doing, I would love to be set free from that. But everyone around me agreed with Michael. So Vanessa Ryan, who was building my website, created two different presentations in an attempt to convince me. One was called 'The Sierra Leone Maternal Foundation', the other 'The Aminata Maternal Foundation'. I could see immediately that Michael was right. Many of the Western people I come across have a vision of Africa. It's about poverty, wild animals, war, corruption and danger. Everything but the animals was brought to us by the West, but that doesn't change prejudices. I could see it was better to use my name for the foundation so that people's first connection was with me. We had a name. Now we needed a full team.

One of the most important members of that team was, and still is, Penny Gerstle. I'd met with Penny before the foundation was registered. I'd come into contact with her through my work with Australia for UNHCR, and loved her energy. As a young girl, Penny had posters of Martin Luther King Jr and Mahatma Gandhi on her walls when all her girlfriends had rock stars. She has a deep passion for social justice, a master's in international law – for which she studied refugee and human rights law – and a second master's in international development and global health. She is an inspiring woman and, on top of this, Penny is a lot of fun – although I didn't find that out until later. I'd told Penny that I was looking into maternal health in Sierra Leone and asked if she would be interested in helping me to set up a foundation. At the time, I didn't know what we could achieve or how we could achieve it, but without missing a beat, Penny said, 'Sure, why not?'

I approached Penny again after we were registered. At that point, she was working for the Australian Human Rights Commission. I asked her to join the Board, and she enthusiastically said yes. It wasn't long before I asked her to step into the role of Chair of the Board. It took a little bit more persuading to get her to say yes this time, because she didn't want to let me down. But I knew Penny was the perfect person for the position, and I was right: she is an excellent leader. Our relationship and our friendship is first and foremost full of mutual respect and admiration. It was Penny who, after she became Chair, quietly paid off those early expenses I'd incurred and kept the receipts for, from her personal account. I was not expecting this, it was beyond generous and to this day Penny has not once made me feel I owe her anything. More importantly, we both find equal joy in building the foundation. I love looking at Penny when she talks about Sierra Leone and its people; there's a twinkle in her eye. I always joke that my eyes never light up like Penny's when we talk about my country.

Obviously it was important to have people on the ground in Sierra Leone. Michael was concerned I might decide to go to Sierra Leone myself to set things up there. It was a dangerous time; there had been an outbreak of Ebola, and Michael knew I would feel I was immune and take risks. So he contacted a woman he knew called Marjie Sutton in London, whose work involved Sierra Leone. She in turn talked to Jude Holden, who she thought could help with my foundation. Jude was based in London and worked for Ann Gloag – now Dame Ann Gloag – who established the Aberdeen Women's Centre, a maternity healthcare clinic in Sierra Leone which serves the poorest of the poor for free.

I'd met up with Jude when I was in London with *The Baulkham Hills African Ladies Troupe* and was thrilled when she said Ann was interested in my foundation and suggested we might work together. This was one of those days when I could see God working for me. Ann Gloag never doubted me or questioned my resolve. She's smart, inspiring and fiercely committed to improving maternal health care in Africa and she could see that I was too. She earned her wealth with the Stagecoach Group, a transport company which she set up in 1980 with her brother, and is one of the most significant philanthropists in the health and education space in Africa. Ann's Freedom From Fistula Foundation helps African women left damaged by childbirth. She funds hospitals in Kenya, Malawi and Madagascar, and in 2010 she opened the Aberdeen Women's Centre in Freetown.

I spoke to Ann via Skype and realised my vision for a foundation to support maternal health in Sierra Leone was not only much needed, but also viable. She and I nutted out a plan that would see my foundation partnering with the Aberdeen Women's Centre. This was beyond my wildest dreams. I had no idea things would progress so quickly.

I continued work on pulling the board and the team together. There was a lot to learn. The registration process was dense and difficult, and I had no clue what a not-for-profit organisation looked like. So, I reached out to friends I trusted and admired, people who had known me for years. I remember spending many beautiful hours with Ros's husband Joe Skrzynski at his kitchen table as he schooled me on setting up a foundation and a board of directors. I still treasure his hand-written diagrams and notes. I didn't have any expectations of financial or pro bono help, but at the very least I hoped for encouragement and informed direction, and many people were kind enough to give it to me.

But very quickly I realised there was a problem – not with my idea or my determination to make a difference, but with others' perception of me. First, it was about my qualifications. How could I dare to presume I had the education or academic background to help these women and babies? Then it was about my own position as a mother. Shouldn't

I be at home concentrating on my own young family rather than trying to fix the world's problems? The judgements were coming in waves and the underlying message was: Who gave you permission to dream this big?

I was also surprised and upset to find that the most difficult preconceptions I encountered often came from people who expressed interest in my vision. For example, I was at a meeting about the foundation when the person we were meeting with asked in front of everyone, 'Aminata, do you want us to speak slowly so that you can understand what we are saying?' I was dumbstruck, and I know everyone else there was shocked too, though no one spoke up. A few months later I was in the car with a colleague who had been present at that meeting, and she told me how upset she had been for me. She had wanted to slap this woman then and there, she told me. While it was comforting to have this support, I remember thinking to myself, 'Why didn't you speak up then?'

As another example, I remember having a meeting with one influential woman who we felt could help us. I felt right away that this lady would love to be involved. She was excited by what we were trying to do and understood how urgently help was needed and why from our position of privilege in Australia we had a duty to act. But there was a fundamental sticking point. She wasn't at all comfortable with me being both Founder and CEO of the foundation. Her body language spoke for her, and as she questioned us her assumptions became more and more apparent.

'Who is going to Sierra Leone with you?' she asked.

I said, 'For now it's just me.'

And then it came – smack – right in my face: 'But if you go to Sierra Leone by yourself, who will believe what you report here in Australia?'

I was so shocked that for several moments I was unable to speak. This implication that I need someone else – presumably a white person – to accompany me to Sierra Leone so that other Australians would believe me really sticks in my throat.

It is awful and difficult to face situations like this, and even harder to have a conversation about race and racism, which is a complicated and nuanced issue. I have learned the hard way that calling out behaviour like this can provoke angry, defensive responses. It can also materially affect your own prospects or get in the way of what you are trying to achieve. In many ways, speaking out against racism is a luxury: you need to be able to afford the potential backlash. The woman who questioned me going to Sierra Leone alone is an example. I had many dealings with her, because she was so interested in the cause. Every time, she would say something diminishing – every time, she would humiliate me – but I continued to meet with her because the foundation was more important. Eventually, though, it got so bad that I decided it wouldn't be appropriate for this woman to be involved with the foundation. I made a stand and said enough was enough; it was important for my dignity and self-esteem. We parted amicably.

It doesn't always work out that way. When you point out racist behaviour, people can be quick to assume that you are saying they are a racist person, or even that, for example, all Australians are racist. I want to be really clear about this:

in no way do I mean to call all Australians racist. I have had so many positive experiences and friendships here. But I do feel a responsibility – as a refugee, as a woman of colour, as a mother and now as the CEO of a charity – to show exactly how this sort of behaviour can make people like me feel. That's why I'm writing this now.

*

I have learned so much in my life, but creating the foundation came with endless lessons, many of them painful. From 2012 to 2015, all I did was organise meetings with whomever would give me their time. However busy I was, I never cancelled any meetings and I was never late. My father always said, 'When you respect people, you must always show respect for their time.' And he was right.

Those meetings were gruelling. Many times, I would come home crying to my darling Antoine. I couldn't understand why people were so discouraging. I remember asking one obstinate potential donor I went to see, 'Do you believe I want to do good?'

'Absolutely, yes,' he replied.

'Would you ever discourage your daughter if she was trying to do good in this world?'

'Of course not,' he said.

That was a revelatory moment for me. I promised myself never to allow anyone to tell me what my future should be and, most importantly, I vowed to stay true to who I am.

I decided to take another approach, to reach out to new people. People who didn't know me and could meet me with no preconceptions. I guess in the Western world it's called 'networking'. At first I got nowhere, as I had no idea where to start.

Then Mark Davidson from Work Inc, a co-working hub for small business, contacted me about speaking at his daughter's school. By this time I was regularly speaking in schools and the students responded well to my messages of empathy, empowerment and helping women in my country. They wanted to hear more and were fascinated to hear about Sierra Leone's civil war. Mark's company is a very cool boutique space tucked within the foundations of the Sydney Harbour Bridge in Lavender Bay on the north side of the harbour. Here, start-ups and entrepreneurs work side by side. It's a community of people sparking original ideas and, as I soon discovered, their energy is infectious.

Mark was giving me a lift after one of my talks and he asked me what I was up to. I told him casually about my vision of building a hospital in Sierra Leone. Right off the bat, he said to me, 'I am ready and willing to help.' This was great to hear, but I honestly didn't think anything of it. Then, a few minutes after he dropped me off, I received a text from him: *Ready and willing to help.*

Mark didn't know me, but he trusted my vision for the foundation. For the next few years, Mark attended all my meetings and I know that I can still call on him any time. He organised for the foundation website to be designed and built and he offered the foundation office space in his building.

Mark helped me to bring my vision to life, but he wasn't the only one. I can never forget the lady I call 'Random Betty' – her real name is Roslyn. She literally appeared out of the blue, floating on a cloud of love and support. This was when I was still working at the David Lawrence store in Westfield shopping centre in Miranda, in Sydney's south. We started talking. I told her about the foundation and then Roslyn did this astonishing thing: right there in front of me she wrote out a cheque for $1000. This was the first donation to the foundation. Of course, I couldn't take Roslyn's money then, because the foundation wasn't fully set up, but we met again a few months later when we were a registered charity and I accepted the donation. Roslyn has donated every year since without fail. She is my beautiful angel.

★

The board of the AMF had its inaugural meeting on 28 January 2016 at Ros Horin's home in Sydney. Ros is one of our directors, and over the next nine months we worked together to set up the foundation to function in accordance with good organisational and governance principles. With Penny as Chair of the Board, I was flying.

We launched the foundation at our offices in Middlemiss Street, Lavender Bay, on 15 September 2016. By this time, we had a website and were able to issue tax-deductible receipts through a partnering arrangement. We had begun fundraising and had identified our first project on the ground in the Aberdeen Women's Centre hospital in Sierra Leone helping vulnerable pregnant girls. It was exciting work for us, and dealing with difficulties along the way was a small price to pay to save these girls' lives and bring healthy babies into the world.

By early 2017, under the leadership of the talented and hard-working Jo Hyde, one of our patrons, we had formed our Cheer Squad, a dedicated team of women who were passionate about supporting the mothers and babies of Sierra Leone. This team, and others who have since joined, has proven to be instrumental in helping us raise awareness of Sierra Leone and its maternal health problems, and in raising funds to invest in strengthening its health system.

The Cheer Squad has organised events such as the annual AMF Cherishing Mothers Morning Tea and our annual Bluff and Swagger African Fashion Event. 'Bluff' and 'swagger' are terms used in Sierra Leone to describe the attitude that certain people adopt when dressing to the nines in defiance of poverty. Fashion is an important means of relieving the tedium of poverty, to allow people to stand out from the crowd. I always think of the dynamic IB Love, a talented young sprinter in the national athletics team who comes from the Kroo Bay slum in Freetown, regarded by many as the most disadvantaged place on earth. IB Love would walk out of his shack dressed in crisp white pants turned up to show his ankles, a hot pink and purple open-necked shirt, with a cocked hat and spotless shoes. He eventually swaggered his way to the Netherlands on an athletics scholarship. We showcased IB Love at our inaugural Bluff and Swagger lunch in photos and film recorded by his dear friend and AMF supporter Jo Dunlop.

Our aim was to register AMF with the Australian Charities and Not-for-profits Commission and to be registered with the Australian Taxation Office as a public benevolent institution. This turned out to be a relatively smooth process, with the two agencies working seamlessly. From 1 July 2017, the Aminata Maternal Foundation was a fully tax-deductible entity.

In May 2017 we took on a new AMF treasurer and company secretary, Kim Stewart-Smith, from accountancy firm Ernst and Young. Kim negotiated a three-year pro bono accounting service. This was a crucial development for us, as we now knew we had the best accounting talent helping us set up processes.

One area of weakness for the organisation was in the digital space. But the exceptional Kat Hartmann joined our board as Director of Communications in March 2018. Kat is the head of digital content and optimisation for Woolworths, and she overhauled our website to deliver a much better online presence. Finally, in 2019 we hired two new board members, Simon Vaughan and Yolanda Saiz, to act as dedicated fundraisers.

By the end of 2019 we had gathered more than $400,000 in donations and had big plans for the future. I am incredibly proud of and fulfilled by what the foundation has accomplished; I'm almost in awe of what we've managed to achieve. And I'm bursting with energy and excitement about what will come next.

CHAPTER TWENTY-TWO

Sierra Leone, my heart

I have been back to Sierra Leone twice now with the foundation, and it fills me with hope and purpose. These field trips are undertaken to further the work of the Aminata Maternal Foundation and ensure our funding is fulfilling our aims, but for me they are more than that, of course, because Sierra Leone is my heart and always will be.

It is a big journey to get to Freetown from Sydney, involving several flights. When you exit the plane onto the tarmac, straight away the earthy heat wraps itself around you. After collecting your bags, you take a bus to the ferry terminal. I love this short bus trip: ten minutes bumping and rolling through lush green hills along a red dusty road. The ferry terminal is a bright, open-air space leading onto a beach, which is the first thing you notice. The crystal clear water and the mountains on the far horizon take my breath away. On either side of the terminal, both the beach and the water are bursting with life: children playing on the sand, adults fishing from their boats, friends playing checkers on a board. Hawkers and mini-markets try to sell the new arrivals anything from sim-cards to CDs to books about how to learn Krio. Today, many of these people are missing hands and arms, but that's not what you notice. It's simply a joy to watch the dance of Sierra Leonean life unfold.

Depending on which ferry you get, it can be a rather frenzied trip to the city. Almost everyone who arrives by plane has to use these ferries to reach Freetown, so it is quite a squeeze, especially on the last ferry of the day. And when you disembark at the other end, Freetown is right *there*. The market, the houses, the general hubbub of life – it's all right outside the terminal, against the backdrop of the mountains. You're plunged into it straight away.

Sadly, what is most striking about Sierra Leone, especially coming from the West, is the poverty, which was never as bad when I lived there as it is now. Kroo Bay, which used to be a small fishing village, is now a sprawling slum, considered one of the worst in the world. Home to more than 20,000 people, this labyrinthine shanty town is constructed from sheets of corrugated iron, poles, swathes of cloth and refashioned plastic tubs. Pigs nose through the swampy sludge that is filled with rubbish and the stench of raw sewage and fish is hard to take. Little kids run around the alleyways between the houses and girls sit on the steps of their dwellings, wide-eyed. You can't ignore Kroo Bay; you have to pass by it every day. Supposedly the government is fixing it.

Sixty per cent of Sierra Leone's population of almost eight million now lives below the poverty line, and at the last count it was ranked as one of the poorest nations in the world,

180 out of 187 in the Human Development Index. While it's easy to be weighed down by the problems here, what I have found is that a little help can go far.

Many chapters ago, I mentioned I'm sometimes asked why Sierra Leone is so poor. But I believe there is another question to ask, because Sierra Leone is also rich in so many ways. Before colonisation, Freetown was established as a sort of utopia, a 'free' town, for emancipated slaves. Some, who had fought on the side of the British in the American War of Independence, were resettled in Freetown, while others were sent to Freetown when their slave boats were intercepted by the British after the 1807 banning of the slave trade. The nation's foundation is therefore rooted in values of freedom and liberty. And the newly freed slaves brought with them an ethos of hard work, resilience and hope for the future.

When I returned to Sierra Leone in 2019, I was so proud to see my people recovering from the disasters that have beset them already this century. There were noticeable signs of a return to those early foundations of Sierra Leone: to hard work, resilience and hope, and to those cherished values of freedom and liberty.

Tourism is growing in Freetown. New building projects abound and, despite the rigours of war and the corruption of past governments, optimism fills the air. At night, the beach area is lit up with fairy lights and restaurants in the four- and five-star hotels serve everything from sushi to pizza and fish fresh from the ocean. A lot of the people staying here work with the many charities, NGOs and UN organisations helping to rebuild Sierra Leone. My country is still rich in resources; the war didn't take those away from us.

I am heartened to see posters of the First Lady, the stunning Fatima Bio, everywhere, promoting her 'Hands Off Our Girls' campaign to protect girls from sexual abuse, early marriage and teenage pregnancy. Sexual violence is still a massive problem. President Julius Maada Bio has declared rape a national health emergency and his government seems to be serious about ending what the president rightly calls out as 'the culture of indifference and impunity surrounding rape and sexual violence'. Forced arranged marriages are part of the issue, and according to the latest national health survey 13 per cent of girls are married by their fifteenth birthday and 39 per cent before their eighteenth birthday. Just seeing African leaders airing these issues is a huge improvement, and decisive action from the top can only help the girls and women we serve at the Aberdeen Women's Centre.

I am always asked if I would ever move back to my country and I say boldly, 'No.' It's not because I don't want to live there; it's because in Sierra Leone I would be completely useless. I would sit and eat and exist. I don't feel as if my voice would be heard or I would be effective. I'm not a doctor, I'm not an academic, I'm not a politician or a teacher. What I am doing in Australia to share my countrywomen's stories, to raise awareness of their plight and raise funds for badly needed maternal health projects, is exactly what I want to be doing for the rest of my life. I can work to help the mothers and babies of Sierra Leone from Australia, and that fills me with joy. But even though I know I will never live in Sierra Leone again, I do feel at home there. I think a large part of that is because it's where I can feel my dad's spirit most strongly. He is a part of me, as he is of all his children, but in Freetown Pa Conteh is in the air, in the soil, in the buildings. He is also my inspiration.

But I am equally at home in Australia. One of my favourite quotes comes from Maya Angelou: 'You are only free when you realize you belong no place – you belong every place – no place at all. The price is high. The reward is great.' Since then I have said to myself: 'Home is wherever I am present.' I came to Australia to be safe, to have a peaceful life and try to move on from the chaos and everything that I'd gone through. And for all the challenges, I love being in Australia. I have wholeheartedly embraced and respect its history, culture, communities, opportunities and, most importantly, its people.

When I compare the standard of my life growing up in Sierra Leone and my life now in Australia, I see no difference at all. I don't feel as if my life has become better materially in Sydney than in my home in Kissy before the war. But it is very different culturally, and that can be a struggle, not just for me but for my family as well.

Sarafina came home from school recently and told Antoine that a person in her class had told her that she was 'dirty' and called her 'dark chocolate'. Another girl who was supposed to be her friend said her skin was 'ugly'. She didn't really understand that it was racist, but she was hurt. She knew it was wrong and she wanted an answer. Antoine told her how much she was loved, how her angel wings could fly her high above such mean jibes and that she should be confident in herself – and be kind. What else could we say? There is no explanation for behaviour like this. Sarafina's school had an excellent policy in place to address this kind of behaviour and, generally speaking, whenever this happens, the parents of the children are horrified, apologetic and perplexed by their child's words – and yet this idea that dark skin is less beautiful somehow still found its way to my child's ears. My hope is to shift the axis, to implement change in this place where my children were born. Sarafina and Matisse are Australian, but also part Sierra Leonean and part French too, and that is something they are proud of even though it is hard sometimes for bi-racial children to find their place. As a mother, part of my job is to teach my children about identity and acceptance. So when a child innocently says to Sarafina, 'But you can't be French, you have dark skin', Sarafina is able to hold on to her identity because I've taught her who she is. And I've taught her and Matisse to meet everyone with an open mind, because we are all different and uniquely important.

For my part, I have been surrounded by the most wonderful and kind-hearted people. Getting involved with the UN became a way for me to say thank you. The journey that followed as I became an Australia for UNHCR Special Representative and then worked with Ros on *The Baulkham Hills African Ladies Troupe* to share my story provided the stepping stone to where I am now. I hope that bringing more awareness of Sierra Leone to Australia will go some way towards erasing the unconscious biases and prejudices that exist in our society.

This is my true calling, creating the Aminata Maternal Foundation and helping Sierra Leone. I feel that every single day. When I see the babies born there, and I hold them and look into their eyes, I see the same thing as when I hold a baby in Australia. I think how exciting life is and wonder what it has in store for this newborn. I value them equally; I don't see them as poor children versus rich children. There's no pity or sorrow in what I'm doing. I just know I can use my voice to help and it comes from a humble place. There's certainly a lot to do.

★

The first of my field trips to Sierra Leone was in 2016. When I first decided to go, I presumed I would have to travel alone; Ebola was still a very real threat at the time. But when one of the directors asked at a board meeting if anyone would like to accompany me, Penny Gerstle and Maureen Collins immediately put up their hands. I will never forget what that moment meant to me. So the three of us planned a trip to Freetown to see the Aberdeen Women's Centre in action and ensure the money we were raising was going to the women who needed it. Then SBS TV got in contact. Ros had been pitching her *Baulkham Hills* documentary to the TV network, and when she was talking to them she mentioned the Aminata Maternal Foundation and said I was heading back to Freetown. They were very interested and asked if they could come with us to make a documentary about me and the foundation. Video journalist Amos Roberts accompanied us on our journey to Sierra Leone and the resulting documentary, *Daughter of Sierra Leone*, was a huge success – it even won a silver medal in the Health/Medical

Information category at the 2018 New York Festivals TV and Film Awards.

On that first trip, we went out with the hospital team to return a patient to her village. En route, I quietly asked the midwife, Bernadette, to let me know when we were driving through Grafton. This was the place where the exchange happened with the rebels. I didn't want to stop there or make a big deal of it, but I wanted to see this place where my life changed forever. I couldn't pinpoint exactly where it happened, but I knew the road as we travelled along it. It was fine, straight and calm, surrounded by green trees on either side. As we passed through I made a promise to myself that I should always acknowledge my courage, my bravery, my brilliance, my wisdom, my gift, my gratitude and, most of all, my ability to start life over again . . . For this is my truth. This is who I am.

I went back again to Freetown and the Aberdeen Women's Centre in 2019, and on this visit I saw the new hostel my foundation is helping to fund for at-risk young girls after they have had their babies. On both my visits, AMF Chair Penny Gerstle and I, along with others who were travelling with us, stayed at the Aberdeen Women's Centre hospital itself, where they have accommodation for staff and visitors. It's basic but comfortable, and there is endless food made especially for us by the hospital cook. The rooms are above the maternity ward and every night we heard mothers going into labour, followed by that delicious first cry from a newborn. I spent many nights in the maternity wards myself, witnessing the babies being born – they were 'popping out like popcorn', the midwife joked. I was in awe. I also attended caesarean sections in the theatre. Coming out of that, I was speechless at the professionalism and the quality of service. I feel humbled to be a part of it.

The Aberdeen Women's Centre is the second busiest maternity hospital in the country, despite its modest size, and 3000 babies are delivered here each year. There is an urgent need for expansion, so we can service the vast numbers of expectant mothers who flood through our doors. Many of the mums are teenagers – as young as twelve – and they come from the slums, the streets or the country villages where maternal health care is limited, to say the least. There are no epidurals here – pain management is two paracetamol and a back rub from one of the midwives – but there is a beauty to the births. It's in the way the nurses talk to the frightened mothers, their gentleness and encouraging words. I was completely safe during my labours in Australia, and I think that's what we do well in the West – you know the doctors will do anything to save your child – but the nurturing emotion of these African births is something special.

The Aberdeen Women's Centre specialises not just in birth but in fistula operations. Obstetric fistula is a huge problem in Africa, both because women are unable to get to hospitals and because they can't afford the treatment. It is a complication arising from an obstructed labour, when the tissues between a woman's vagina and her bladder or rectum are damaged from the continuous pressure from the baby's head stuck in the birth canal. This results in a hole through which the woman continuously leaks urine or faeces, or sometimes both. Women who suffer the condition are often cast out from their communities, seen as dirty because of the smell which they cannot control. They are filled with shame, their dignity in tatters. But fixing fistula for the most part is a relatively easy operation and at the Aberdeen Women's Centre we have a whole ward devoted to fistula patients. We are the only hospital in Sierra Leone that performs the operation.

Zainab was brought to the Aberdeen Women's Centre for fistula repair surgery by Aberdeen Women's Centre outreach nurses from her remote village in Moyamba District. She had been suffering with fistula for a couple of years. Zainab told us that when she went into labour her family was unable to take her to hospital and couldn't afford an ambulance. It took her village three days to raise the money for the ambulance, but it had no petrol. Ultimately they found someone with a motorbike to go to the nearest petrol station then return to the village to refuel the ambulance before it could collect Zainab. By then, her baby had died and a fistula had formed. Zainab was malnourished, dehydrated and suffered from infected wounds. Tears flowed softly over her face as she told us that even her own children would not touch the food she struggled to prepare.

Zainab had successful fistula surgery at Aberdeen Women's Centre and returned home with her dignity restored. She was welcomed with open arms by her village, who held a feast with dancing and singing. Hundreds of Zainabs come to our hospital and we are almost always able to help, which is so satisfying.

Every day pregnant women crowd the courtyard outside, lining up for their antenatal checks, while new mothers queue for medical check-ups at which their children are weighed and receive malarial care and inoculations. Contraceptive advice lines the walls; family planning where possible is a key message.

Those who make it to the hospital are the lucky ones. Penny and I met the baby daughter of Fatimata, who didn't make it. Fatimata was probably sixteen years old – birthdays are not particularly important in Sierra Leone, so ages are estimated. She and her boyfriend were surprised to learn that they were to become parents, and when the time came for Fatimata to have her baby she attended the local health clinic a short distance from her village. The only equipment they had was a broken bed and a saucepan with some forceps and saline inside. It was a difficult labour, and about seven hours after the birth, the attendant noticed that Fatimata was struggling. Within an hour she had died.

Post-mortems are not routine in Sierra Leone, so the actual cause of death is unknown. It was speculated that she had malaria (hyper-endemic in Sierra Leone) and therefore she was more susceptible to anaemia. Her heart would probably have had to work so hard during the rigours of birth to carry enough oxygen around her body that she suffered a heart attack within hours of giving birth.

Her baby girl was otherwise healthy, but when we met her six days later, she had been fed nothing but crushed biscuits and water.

★

One of our special initiatives for pregnant girls under the age of eighteen is the Dream Team program. Twice a week the girls gather at the Aberdeen Women's Centre and spend three hours together under the guidance of inspiring teachers. They learn about what will happen to their bodies, how to look after their children, take birthing classes and are given some basic schooling, empowerment coaching and a good lunch. Some of these girls are rape victims (often the perpetrator is a family member), while others have fallen pregnant due to lack of contraception. None of them is prepared for motherhood when they first come to the centre.

Going to school was recently made mandatory in Sierra Leone, which is a huge step forwards, but pregnant girls are not allowed in school, so these girls' education has been cut short and often their family has also abandoned them.

The Dream Team program sees an estimated 400 teenagers, aged eleven to eighteen, each year. They receive pre- and postnatal care, a safe birth with access to surgical intervention, a feeding program (many are chronically malnourished and unfit for birthing), assistance to re-enter education, family planning and counselling support to reintegrate back into their communities and families, and vocational training where appropriate.

During the Ebola outbreak of 2014–2016, many schools were closed and villages and towns were put into lockdown. Due to the resulting boredom, there was a spike in teenage pregnancies. Such young girls are often too small in the pelvis to deliver their babies, and the only safe option is a caesarean section. The program costs AUD$100,000 a year, and the AWC performs more than 70 C-sections for the Dream Team each year, costing AUD$600 per operation.

The Aberdeen Women's Centre also does a lot of outreach work in the rural villages, bringing pregnant women to the hospital so their babies can be delivered safely.

It is really inspiring to think the money the Aminata Maternal Foundation raises supports this place, and the most uplifting part of our latest visit was to see the new accommodation hostel that the foundation is funding. The most vulnerable mothers are handpicked for support after they have had their babies, and we take care of them in the hostel for a period up to six months. For many it is the first time they have stayed in a proper house with stone walls and a proper bathroom and kitchen. Here they live in safety and comfort with their babies. They are taught housekeeping, home economics and mothering skills, and they are trained for hotel and domestic work, which the housemother hopes to secure for them once they leave the hostel. Those who want to are encouraged to go back to school to finish their education. All the new mothers come from the poorest parts of Freetown and are victims of abuse and neglect or have no family, but here they are wanted and nurtured and the results are astonishing.

I had seen the hostel building in photographs, but it was much bigger and smarter than I expected. The girls had prepared lunch for us and were beautiful hostesses, even singing us a song. To see the glow in their eyes was something I will never forget. The Dream Team girls I had met back in the hospital seemed lost and frightened; they wore the bewilderment of pregnancy like a heavy cloak around their shoulders. I hardly recognised those lost girls in these joyful teenagers dancing and laughing in front of me.

Their newfound confidence and sheer sense of fun was infectious. They were cheeky, happy, full of energy and potential. Now they had goals. They told me they wanted to be teachers, doctors, businesswomen – even president. These new mothers could now strive for a life beyond the circumstances into which they were born, and I knew they would make it. I felt so proud of them and also deeply satisfied that it was the Aminata Maternal Foundation that had made this happen. My Sarafina's six wings were beating fast here.

The housemother of our hostel, another Aminata, is an extraordinary woman in her own right. Aminata grew up in one of Freetown's many slums. At 31 she had already reached the life expectancy for Freetown's poorer areas – but that would certainly not be her fate.

Aminata was a top student. She had to fight hard to be allowed to go to school, but because of her good grades, her father allowed it. When Aminata was fifteen, her mother died, and she had to take over the maternal role in her family. School was out of the question. Now that she was a 'mother', she also needed to be married. Feeding her would then become someone else's responsibility. A 'suitable' husband in his forties was found. By sixteen she was married, pregnant, malnourished and living in grinding poverty with no prospect of escape . . . except for her spark.

Now she is fluent in Mandarin and has two university degrees, including a master's in hospitality and tourism from a Beijing university. She's financially independent and, unlike an estimated 65 per cent of graduates in Sierra Leone, she has a well-paid full-time job that she loves. How? It's a long story, but the bit most illustrative of her determination is the story of her scholarship to Beijing – the only international scholarship on offer that year.

Against her husband's wishes, Aminata managed to go back to school after having her baby. She finished at the top of her class and earned a place in a local university, where she studied home economics. Once again, she topped the class. In her mid–twenties, Aminata saw a poster advertising a master's scholarship to study in Beijing. She knew she had every qualification and would make a fine candidate. She made it down to the last two candidates and was confident she would win the place; she knew the other candidate and was surprised he was even considered.

When Aminata learned she had not been selected, she marched straight to the Ministry of Education, armed with her university results, and demanded to see the minister.

'Do you have an appointment?'

'No, and I don't need one, I have my results!'

'You need an appointment.'

'No I'll wait till he'll see me.'

And so Aminata took up her position outside the Minister of Education's office. She sat for days . . . Eventually, her old university lecturer came to see the minister, and he had an appointment. He had always been impressed by Aminata, so he put in a good word for her. The minister agreed to see her and she was offered a scholarship.

Aminata now teaches new skills to other young women from the poorest families. Under her tutelage they learn to have confidence, to work hard, to be independent and to contribute to society. Together with the Aberdeen Women's Centre and the Aminata Maternal Foundation, Aminata is running our pilot program in the hostel, and from what we saw she is achieving everything she has set out to do.

Aminata's story is just one example of the talent and potential we saw everywhere in Sierra Leone, and meeting women like Aminata I don't feel sad for my people because I know they're capable; they have just never benefitted from the kind of democratic political structure that we take for granted in the West.

★

I know my dad would be proud of the work I am doing with the foundation, and when I am in Sierra Leone it is like he is sitting on my shoulder, guiding me every step of the way.

I will always go to my childhood house and pay homage at Papa's grave. This is my home, and despite everything that happened it is in this house that I feel most safe.

On my last visit I was thrilled to meet Nga Kadiatu, who was my favourite cook throughout my childhood in the yellow house. I love it when I meet people who knew my dad and see they are still filled with respect and love for him, like me. After all everyone has been through during the war and since, that astounds me all the time.

Nga Kadiatu is in her nineties now, blind in one eye and just clinging on to life. I went to her house, where she was sitting on the floor of the verandah staring out at the cloudless sky and rich red earth of Freetown. As soon as I approached her, she stood up and reached out to hug me. We were both so happy, full to our fingers and toes with emotion. I know she would do anything for me and she told me she wanted to carry me on her back. Bent double with old age though she was, she would have tried if I'd let her.

Papa's grave is well looked after by our relative Abu Bakur, whose schooling my dad paid for. He also helps out with all our family business on the ground in Freetown. He sees this as his way of giving back to Pa Conteh.

On my last visit, as I gripped the metal plaque over my dad's grave and read his name, I found myself sobbing. I felt sad, but most of all I was filled with an overwhelming sense of how much Papa loved his children, and how much he wanted us to do good in the world.

I have a dream

Writing this book has not been easy, but it has been a healing process for me. I feel every day of my life has been about growing and finding my voice. This book has meant revisiting many dark times, awakening memories and forcing me to dig deep and confront situations, feelings, people and my whole story in a way I never had before. Part of my head will always be back in the mountains of Sierra Leone with the rebels. But I refuse to be their captive. From the moment I was released, I had a strong belief that I would do something meaningful with my life. So many women who have survived what I survived feel the shame of what happened to them, and that shame holds them back. But the values I learned from my father, from my relationship with God and people I look up to – people like Maya Angelou, Toni Morrison, Oprah, Muhammad Ali and Sidney Poitier – inspire me to move forward with optimism. Joy has mixed with sadness as I have looked back, but going forward there is peace and I am filled with gratitude for that and have a new sense of inner strength and purpose.

I don't like to use the word 'impossible', but ever since my abduction, my life has felt impossible. I think that's why gratitude has become my practice. Every single day I look at my children Sarafina and Matisse, I touch my husband Antoine, the walls of my Sydney home, the Australian flowers and trees, and I say to myself: 'Is this real? Am I going to wake up and discover I'm really not here?'

The practice of forgiveness, too, has set me free. I remember even after I was released from those months of torture, I knew my path to liberation could only come through forgiveness. I don't understand what was going through Daramy's mind when he hurt me. It was so cruel. I don't know what it meant to him, how he justified it in his head. But my first thought as I walked away from the rebels towards the government soldiers leading a ragtag trail of terrified children in that surreal exchange, was that I had been given a second chance. A shaft of light was shining on me and I knew I must follow that light and use it wisely.

At the time, I couldn't even take in what Daramy and his gang of rebels had done to me, and in some ways I am glad that I was able to shut it out, because it would have taken over my body – and anger would not have helped me. Instead, I was still able to enjoy life, which some people have found surprising, but it's the only way I know how to be. 'What happened to me was unjust and inhuman,' I told myself, 'but I am able to see the beauty of God's hands on me and there's real joy in that. I'm alive and I can see Papa's face again.' What I know now, truly, is that forgiveness is the ultimate gift you can give to yourself.

★

My sisters say that they see much of my father in me and I do feel he is in my heart, willing me to go on. With this in mind, there is a way in which I wish to honour Papa.

You see, for some time now I have harboured a *new* dream deep inside. I haven't shared it with anyone, because I didn't want to hear that it couldn't or shouldn't be done. But on my last trip to Sierra Leone I realised that maybe, just maybe, my dream could be realised.

The hotel my father was building in Wellington was sold to some local businessmen, but it is still standing – though this huge, solid structure is empty, which is a crime in itself. My cousin Abu Bakur whispered to me that we could buy the building back, and it planted a seed in me. Now when I look at that place where so many families took refuge during the war, I see instead a hospital, a place of healing. A maternity hospital which would also train midwives and obstetricians. A free hospital with Western standards for all the women and babies of Sierra Leone.

I took a photo when I was there. The sun was just setting, and to the right of the hotel there was the most beautiful soft light winking at me. I knew that it was him, it was Papa, with that cheeky smile of his, and I felt something touch my soul. Pa Conteh was telling me to have my dream and make it come true.

The Aminata
Maternal
Foundation

Afterword

Sierra Leone is among the world's poorest countries, having been ravaged by eleven years of civil war, the Ebola epidemic, then devastating floods and landslides.

Sierra Leone also has some of the highest death rates in the world for both mothers and babies, it being about 200 times more dangerous to have a baby in Sierra Leone than in Australia. One in eight women will die and more than twenty per cent of children will not live to their fifth birthday.

I have written this book and established the Aminata Maternal Foundation to improve these outrageous statistics. I long for change for my Sierra Leonean sisters and, in seeking the most efficient and effective way to achieve that change, the AMF has partnered with the exceptional Aberdeen Women's Centre (AWC), a private hospital in Freetown. AWC delivers over 3000 babies a year. That's 3000 mothers and their 3000 babies guided safely through childbirth, with access to surgical intervention. And all free of charge – unheard of in most parts of the country. AWC also treats more than 20,000 children a year, providing primary health care and immunisations.

Proudly, my foundation, with the help of a generous Australian donor, is now also playing a role in addressing the desperate lack of midwives in Sierra Leone. Needing some 3500 midwives, the country has less than 400.

★

I invite you, my readers to join us on this powerful journey.

If you chose to support the Aminata Maternal Foundation, your donation will make a significant difference. $75 enables the AWC to ensure a safe normal delivery. $35 enables 5 children to visit one of our GPs.

I would love you to consider making a **regular monthly donation**. Such continuity of funding gives us sustainability. Please go to our website, to see what your donation can achieve:

www.aminatamaternalfoundation.org

Of course, should anyone be able to help me build my much dreamt of hospital, I would love to hear from you.

Personally, I pledge a percentage of my royalties to the work of the foundation.

Deepest gratitude
Aminata Conteh-Biger

Acknowledgements

I have always visualised my life as a tree. At the moment I was placed on this planet, a seed was planted at the same time. You see, for a tree to flourish it must be taken care of – nourished. As my darling Papa would say, 'We get out of the world what we put into the world.' I have always lived my life by this lesson, no matter what the situations might be. My tree has flourished because of the incredible human beings that I have been blessed to call my friends and family. Their generous love for me has paved the way to this incredible life I am so grateful for. I know from the depth of my heart that I would not be where I am today if it wasn't for them.

Above all, I joyfully thank my Heavenly Father, who I call God. Please continue to keep me humble and guide me with your wisdom, grace and love. For with you, I am all that I'm supposed to be.

My papa, Yayah Kelfala Conteh, who taught me discipline and the recipes of life: your unconditional love and devotion for your children was magnificent. Your generosity to all humanity was the most beautiful thing. Thank you.

My mama, Eleas Diané: thank you for being my prayer warrior and for your unwavering love. Watching you love and take care of those around you has always enriched my soul.

To my grandpa, Alhaji Kelfala Conteh (Baimba): I will never ever forget you. I know that I have an angel on my shoulder wherever I am. I am not happy about how you departed this world; it breaks my heart into pieces. But I know that you will be proud of who I am becoming. Your premonition about my life is living inside me, brighter every day.

My beloved husband, Antoine (*Ma Puce*): thank goodness that I was able to cast my magic formulas of the African marabouts (*les formules magiques des marabouts d'Afrique*) on you when we first met and then over four years until you returned back to me, hehe. I am so blessed and full of gratitude that I get to see your beautiful eyes smile every single day. My Papa would have loved you. You dare me to look at my history. Thank you for the memories, and for loving and liberating me. I cannot wait to experience the world with you.

To the loves of my life, Sarafina and Matisse: you are my reason for daring to be true and to dance with life. Whenever a challenge arises, your two faces rise next to it. What a privilege to have carried you each for nine months and been entrusted with such gifts. It is the greatest blessing that I could ever ask God for. Thank you for choosing me and your papa to be your parents.

My Conteh family: Alieu, I would not have survived my kidnapping without your unconditional love. I know it hurt you to see me hurt, but you never showed me your pain, which gave me strength. I love you and all my beautiful, confident sisters – Mabinty, Fatmata, Tigidankay, Aminata and Mariama – and brothers – Ibrahim and Mohammad – with the extended love of our dearest Papa: I am so incredibly blessed to belong with you all and be part of the fabric of the Conteh family.

★

What would life be like without all my friends and family here in Australia, who have continually shaped my life and always shown up for me? Your friendship has strengthened and brightened my life in so many ways.

Janelle and Michael and the entire Dwyer family: I know now that coming to Australia was part of God's plan for my life. You are my family in every way possible. Our love for each other is a firm foundation of my own family. Thank you so much for all your love. My heart is so full of gratitude and love for each of you.

Naomi Steer: you welcomed me into the Australia for UNHCR family with open arms. I admire how hard you continually work for refugees for twenty years as their National Director. And as a woman, mother and wife, it was so important for me to see a woman as brilliant as you are be a leader as well as all of the above. Thank you for giving me the opportunity to tell my story and to be a Special Representative for Australia for UNHCR. This has been my greatest privilege; I have learned and grown in many ways.

Maureen Collins: I always say to people, 'I recognised that I had a story and a voice when I met my dearest friend, sister and mentor Maureen.' You are the true definition of what a mentor and teacher is and my first real Australian friend. It doesn't matter how crazy my dreams are, I am never ever scared to tell you, because you will always encourage me to follow them.

Ros Horin and Joe Skrzynski: how blessed I am to be part of your family. Ros, you have shown me that family doesn't have to be only blood-related. Working with you on *The Baulkham Hills African Ladies Troupe*, you cried with us, laughed, danced and became angry for our injustices. I am overwhelmed by your generosity and passion for your family and the people that you love dearly. You always stand up for me and worry about me as if I am one of your daughters. I really look up to you and Joe in every aspect of life.

Penny Gerstle (*Mon Amie*): oh, how I love and respect you. You are the kindest, smartest, most intelligent and brilliant human being I have ever met. I don't ever want to imagine my life and the Aminata Maternal Foundation without your spirit. I am living my happiest, best life with you as part of it. In my heart, you are equally as much a Sierra Leonean as I am. This is 100 per cent *our* journey. There is no you and me; there is only us. Don't ever let go of my hands, and I will always hold on to yours.

Sister Carmel McDonough: you and the Sisters of Mercy make me believe that miracles will always happen. In the lowest time of my life here in Australia, you and the Sisters of Mercy gave me and my family hope when I felt the most hopelessness. Without your miraculous gift I would not have written my book – that I know for sure. You offered my family a safe haven.

Jo Hyde: what a journey we have had together these last few years. From the moment we met, we became soul sisters. We came from two different parts of the world but we have so much in common, especially our deepest love for our late fathers. Being around you has changed my world. You and Sophie McCarthy firmly insisted that I must write my story. Well, it's here and I can never thank you both enough.

Marion Massaquoi: you are really truly my best friend for life. Seeing you with your precious Ariana has filled my heart with joy for you.

Pastor Anne and Pastor John Luliano, you are two exceptional examples of what a spiritual leader is. I am so grateful to belong to the Life Source Church family. Thank you both so much for your warmth, love and encouragement.

Nicole Abadee: there is absolutely no way that I could ever write this book if it wasn't for you. You believed in this book from day one and breathed life into *Rising Heart*. I adore you so much. My goodness, what an incredibly beautiful and brilliant friend you are to me and my family. Your smile always makes me feel so happy. Thank you for making all this possible.

Catherine Drayton, my literary agent from Inkwell Management in New York: thank you for representing me so professionally and generously. My whole journey with you has been such a wonderful experience.

Ingrid Ohlsson: I knew at my very first meeting at Pan Macmillan with you and Georgia Douglas that my story had found her home. My heart is full and content with how I have told my story, and I owe it to you and your excellent team. You have listened to me and allowed me to stretch deep into my true self. I see how much you care for me personally and how much you believe in my story. Georgia Douglas, you have been so patient and professional: thanks for your wisdom and your thoughtfulness to make sure *Rising Heart* is at its best, but most of all for always making sure that I am happy with it all.

Juliet Rieden: I could not have a more extraordinary ghostwriter than you. I honestly believe that we chose each other. For me, my ghostwriter was going to be the most important person in this whole process; I needed someone who would give me permission to be vulnerable, strong, kind, fearless, brave, joyful, angry, sad and more. You have been beyond perfect. I love spending time with both you and Katie. I knew that I was going to be in the best and safest hands from the moment I met you. You coming to Sierra Leone with me is a memory that I will keep with me forever. *Rising Heart* would not be the same without you, my dearest friend.

The Aminata Maternal Foundation board directors and teams: I truly believe that we have the most exceptional, humble and dedicated board of directors in any organisation. With Penny Gerstle as our Chair, one could not ask for anything more. Katherine Hartmann, Ros Horin, Yolanda Saiz, Kim Stewart-Smith, Simon Vaughan, Anthony Zwi: I am deeply appreciative to every one of you. To the remarkable, intelligent women on our Cheer Squad – Grace Atkinson, Louise Birt, Erin Booker, Fiona Collard, Anna Curran, Sharlene Dadd, Belinda Dowsett, Cathy Hodgkinson, Jo Hyde, Linda Morrice, Jenny Pridham, Rachel Reynolds, Kate Swinney, Kyle Thurkettle, Kim Veitch and Electra Wiggs – I cannot begin to thank you enough. And our tireless volunteers that make the foundation look and be its best: Erica Sufani, Mónica Silva Astorga, Fabiana Eisenmann, Elena Di Palma and Sophie Roden, I thank you all from the depths of my heart.

I am overwhelmed with gratitude for the heart and generosity of all the private ancillary funds who have continually believed and invested in the Aminata Maternal Foundation. Thank you all so much: Ros Horin and Joe Skrzynski and the Sky foundation, Katrina and Russell Leslie and the Leslie Foundation, Electra AMF, Peter Wiggs and the Wiggs Foundation, Penny and Gary Gerstle and the Hand Up Foundation, the Ernst & Young Foundation and the Norton Rose Fulbright Foundation.

Dame Ann Gloag: my admiration and respect for you is beyond words. You are my personal hero. You have demonstrated to me what believing in someone truly means.

Mark Davidson: your kindness and willingness to support me from the very beginning was something I needed to start my journey.

Libby Allaway: your beautiful sweet compassion is something every woman needs in sisterhood. You thrive and you uplift everyone around you. Your joy for life is contagious and I love being around it.

Mary Read: when I came to you, I was trying to sort out my life. I didn't know where to start but you listened to me and guided me to your most trusted friends. I know that I can come to you anytime.

Andrea Durbach: I remember so clearly the first meeting that you put together at the UNSW campus. Your courage and fighting spirit for humanity is marvellous to know and be part of. I love you dearly and my respect for you is beyond words.

Imroze: you made it possible for me to attend all my meetings during the early stage of building the foundation. I always knew that I could count on you to look after Sarafina and Matisse while I rushed to endless appointments, and you never once made me feel otherwise. Ayaan, thanks for sharing your mama with my family.

Anthony Zwi: thanks for always looking out for me, right from the very beginning.

Morlai Kamara: I needed someone who was knowledgeable and loved our country: I saw your hope for Sierra Leone in your eyes.

Ruth Layton: thank you for your support and for reviewing all the legal documentation with such care and attention.

★

Finally, to my Sierra Leone: I have never been more proud to call myself a Sierra Leonean as I am today. Our beloved country has gone through so much; every time I visit home I feel the beauty, resilience, strength, struggle, pain, determination and courage of my dear Sierra Leone. But above all I feel hope. I feel it despite the hardships that we still endure. Because it's never too late. Let's build our future together.

Aminata Conteh-Biger

★

First and foremost, I want to thank Aminata Conteh-Biger for putting her faith in me, allowing me to tell her story and having the confidence and strength to not hold back, however tough that proved to be. Aminata's courage and determination to face the trauma of her past and use it to help others takes my breath away. It was an honour to travel with Aminata to Sierra Leone and London to retrace her past, to meet her family and to witness the amazing work going on at the Aberdeen Women's Centre in Freetown, and for me it has been a life-changing experience.

It was a privilege to spend time with Aminata's family – Antoine, Sarafina and Matisse – and I want to thank you all for your help and support through what has been a tumultuous journey. Antoine, thank you also for being so open and honest with me in sharing your own story. Already I feel a part of the Conteh-Biger clan.

Thanks also to Penny Gerstle who welcomed me into the Aminata Maternal Foundation, along with all the Foundation's board members and friends, and who guided me through Freetown life on our unforgettable trip. Penny's unbridled delight as we all witnessed a night of babies being born on the maternity ward and caesareans the following day revealed her passion to help women in Sierra Leone – the poorest of the poor – give birth safely.

I am in awe of everyone working at the Aberdeen Women's Centre, and thank you Ivy and Dame Ann Gloag for giving me the opportunity to witness your groundbreaking work changing the lives of women and girls in one of the most dangerous places to give birth in the world. To the beautiful Dream Team girls whose futures lie ahead of you, thank you for welcoming me and sharing your pain and your hopes for a better future. I know you will make the world a better place.

Meeting and talking to Aminata's mother Eleas and her sisters Mabinty and Fatmata in London was a joy. The stories you all shared with me proved vital in the layering of Aminata's story and I want to thank you for letting the truth shine through and being so candid and unfailingly helpful.

To others who shared their life stories and connections with Aminata – Derek, Marion, Fatmatta, Michael and Janelle Dwyer, Ros Horin – I really appreciate your time, support and honesty.

Thank you Ingrid Ohlsson at Pan Macmillan for giving me the opportunity to write this book and for your endless support and encouragement throughout the journey. Thanks to Georgia Douglas, Candice Wyman and the whole Pan Macmillan family.

On a personal note I would like to thank my partner Katie for keeping the coffee flowing as Aminata and I worked for long hours in our study at home, for supporting us both and for your unparalleled advice and proofreading eye.

Juliet Rieden